ISLES OF THE NORTH

This
be
dat
—

ISLES OF THE NORTH

A VOYAGE TO
THE REALMS OF THE NORSE

IAN MITCHELL

BIRLINN

This abridged edition first published in 2012 by
Birlinn Limited
West Newington House
10 Newington Road
Edinburgh EH9 1QS

www.birlinn.co.uk

ISBN 978 1 84158 944 2

British Library Cataloguing-in-Publication Data
A catalogue record for this book is available from the British Library

Typeset by Hewer Text UK Ltd, Edinburgh
Printed and bound in the UK by Clays Ltd, St Ives plc

This book is dedicated to the memory of my mother,
who came from the North and whose generosity
made possible the purchase of *Foggy Dew*

CONTENTS

INTRODUCTION TO
THE SECOND EDITION

It is nearly ten years since I embarked on the voyage described in this book. The publication of a second edition offers the opportunity of a follow-up view, which might give an illuminating time perspective to what I discovered in 2002. I contacted people in many of the places I visited on my trip and concluded that the story of all of them could be told through the story of one of them because developments everywhere are so similar in underlying form. They have two elements: continuing population decline and intensified bureaucratic interference. The question is whether these two trends are connected.

The first island I visited on the trip was Mingulay, abandoned in 1912 in part because the government, in the form of the Congested Districts Board, would not provide proper berthing facilities for vessels on the island, which made trade growth impossible. Today, the state sees its role less as a selective facilitator of rural enterprise than a general controller of it, usually in the interests of nature conservation. The result has been that, since 2002, Scottish Natural Heritage – or SNH, a body the reader will learn a lot more about in the pages that follow – has seen fit to designate an area of seabed off the east (and therefore sheltered) coast of Mingulay as a marine Special Area of Conservation (or SAC) in order to conserve a reef which represents an estimated 0.03% of the total United Kingdom resource of that type of habitat. Protecting this would cost the equivalent of between 4 and 6 full-time jobs on the neighbouring island of Barra, depending on how severe the protection regime was, according to research commissioned by the Scottish government and adopted by the Western Isles Council, or Comhairle nan Eilean Siar, in its official letter of objection to SNH. 'Although small in scale, this represents a

significant level of activity, particularly in the context of a fragile local
economy,' the Council commented (21 February 2011).

The issue here is one of proportionality. Just as there is no absolute
right to freedom of speech, contract or association, so the protection of
nature is always in a mature society balanced against competing public
interests. All governments are happy to sanction developments which
damage nature – farming for instance – so long as they bring substantial
economic benefits. It is a question of balance. Four jobs on Barra, which
has a population of just over a thousand, are equivalent to 4,000 jobs
in Birmingham, which has a population closer to a million. A factory
employing that many people in the Midlands would not likely be threatened with closure because of, say, concern for the corncrake, or worries
about a certain type of sub-soil. And quite rightly so. Islanders do not
complain about the protection of Birmingham, only about the bullying
of places like Barra. The Council's letter of objection goes on to make
this point clearly:

> In discussing this issue, the Members of the Comhairle were very much
> aware of the fact that it is now 100 years since Mingulay was aban-
> doned. Depopulation remains a critical issue in the Outer Hebrides,
> with some of the forward projections for the loss of human popula-
> tion being the starkest in Scotland. Our members contrasted the level
> of effort going into preserving small areas of reef with the perceived
> lack of concern in regard to the loss of the human population.
>
> The introduction of this environmental designation will lead to a loss of
> democratic control of development in the area at a time when the islands
> require a range of measures to promote sustainable economic develop-
> ment, improve economic performance and address population decline.
>
> There is clear evidence over the past period that unrestrained envi-
> ronmental designations lead to negative socio-economic impacts.
> It is the view of the Comhairle that the Outer Hebrides is already
> over-designated.

This was exactly the point put to me ten years ago. Government was
seen to be ready to sacrifice human communities on the altar of environmental 'concern'. I put that word in quotes since I do not believe that the
concern is genuine. The stories told below of the seals on Barra, the corncrakes on Egilsay and the raingeese on Yell all show that considerations

beyond the interests of the wildlife are the primary drivers of the protection process. In the case of government departments, it is the inappropriately literal interpretation of European Directives. In the case of wildlife charities it is usually due to a desire to attract funding, either from members of the public by means of grandstanding demonstrations of pharisaic virtue, or from government by means of science which is often shallow and amateurish, and which is frequently used misleadingly – occasionally almost fraudulently. These are seriously allegations and I have dealt with them seriously and at length in my other book on this subject, *Isles of the West*. Therefore let me confine myself here to the problem of government departments and the European Union which, in 2002, I wanted to throw into practical relief by continuing my voyage to Norway.

The problem is a genuine, practical one since the two instruments which principally control environmental management in the United Kingdom, the European Habitats and Birds Directives, emanate from Brussels. These are drafted in conventional European terms, which means they are intended to operate effectively as legislative codes, not detailed statutory enactments of the sort which Whitehall (and I include its branch in Scotland) is accustomed to producing. The difference is crucial.

The modern British legislative approach developed around eighteenth-century notions of liberty, which – common law crimes excepted – were based on the idea that everything was permitted which was not explicitly forbidden. Therefore laws had to be very detailed; and as society became progressively more complex, those laws became progressively more detailed. Today we have arrived at the situation, which the late Lord Bingham of Cornhill complained about shortly before his death, of 'legislative hyperactivity'. By this he meant the production of laws at such a rate that lawyers and judges themselves find it hard to keep up with them, much less the general public that is supposed to obey those laws.[1]

---

1 See Lord Bingham, 'The Rule of Law', *Cambridge Law Journal* (2007), p. 66, at 69: 'Given the legislative hyperactivity which appears to have become a permanent feature of our governance – in 2004, some 3,500 pages of primary legislation; in 2003 nearly 9,000 pages of statutory instruments – the sheer volume of current legislation raises serious problems of accessibility, despite the internet.' His point was that over-prescriptive government, by making it in practice impossible to know what the citizen's rights and duties are in many situations, is a long-term threat to the rule of law.

In Europe, since Napoleon promulgated the *Code Civil*, the tradition has been to lay down general principles covering everything, and leave detailed interpretation to the magistrates, taking into consideration the circumstances of the time and place. Though more restrictive in a simpler legislative environment, it is arguably a better system in the highly complex society which we live in today. Whether that is true or not, the fact is that the worst of all possible worlds is one in which broad principles are laid down in supra-national law, but in such general terms that a vast army of legal draughtspeople in common-law jurisdictions have to specify in minute detail every possible eventuality so that the government can allow its citizens the right to do whatever is not forbidden by law while at the same time satisfying the European Union bureaucrats that nothing is being done contrary to the general principles established in – for example, since it covers the Mingulay reefs – the Habitats Directive. This is what has been called 'gold-plating' European legislation. It is part of the cause – though not the only part – of Lord Bingham's 'legislative hyperactivity'.[2]

The question arises: why do British bureaucrats not oppose, if need be by passive resistance, European demands? Their answer is that they risk fines and terrible punishments. But this is an inadequate response, given the scale of the problem. Last summer I visited Estonia and talked at length to the ex-Prime Minister, Mart Laar, who was in power both when the country left the Soviet Union and when it entered the European Union. Given his very pronounced free-market principles, I asked Mr Laar why he wanted to jump from one massive bureaucracy into another. He explained the strategic reasons why a small country like his, especially given its geographical position, needed to feel the security of being part of a powerful body like the EU. (Estonia joined NATO at the same time.) 'But even so,' I said, 'we have the most horrific stories of bureaucratic interference by

---

2 Scotland, it should be noted, is especially disadvantaged by this situation, having a partly civilian legal system applying a body of law which is nonetheless not codified. Yet within Scots law there is ample scope for the broad, 'code-like' approach which is taken, for example, in breach of the peace law. This is completely different from the similarly-named law in England. It is very simple and therefore more flexible and effective. The continued imposition of the complicated English draughting tradition on Scots law, which Devolution has done little to change, ignores the Scots preference for principle over prescription.

the EU in Scottish affairs, especially rural affairs. Do you really think that is a price worth paying?'

His answer, though shocking, was directly relevant to the Mingulay reefs. It can be paraphrased thus: Estonia – a country with the population of greater Glasgow – simply tells the EU, quietly and politely, which Directives it will obey and which not. It is forever negotiating opt-outs, quite lawfully. Less lawfully, if it feels a vital interest is threatened and Brussels won't back down, it simply refuses to obey. In Scotland, I replied, we are told by the Executive that the country risks huge fines and infraction proceedings unless every Directive is applied with minute precision. He simply laughed. 'Who ever pays fines? The Spanish? The Italians? Get real: this is international politics, not some sort of club. How exactly is the EU going to force Estonia, much less the British government, to pay fines if it is determined not to? It simply is not going to happen'. 'So why,' I asked, 'does he think our government make such a noise about the threat of fines?' He gave me a look which said roughly: because they are weak; because they are working for the other side; and because they value their jobs more than their country's freedom.

Finally, he said explicitly, 'What you have to remember is that the most left-wing party in Eastern Europe is to the right of the most right-wing party in Western Europe. We have had nearly half a century of having socialism forced upon us, often very brutally. We know the realities of rule by bureaucracy. We are simply never going to accept it. The EU knows that, but they are empire-builders too, like all bureaucrats, and they want us in their orbit. We know that, and they know that we know that. So we bargain, and in the end we get on very well together. Ultimately, it's not a big problem for us, or them. Your government is your problem. That's the meaning of democracy.'

Ian Mitchell
Khimki
Moscow
March 2012

INTRODUCTION TO
THE FIRST EDITION

THREE FACTORS COALESCED TO bring this book about. The first two are obvious: the continuing success of my previous book, *Isles of the West*, which has just gone into its third edition, suggested a follow-up might be popular, while a simple love of sailing provoked the question: where next? The third, more complex, factor helped to answer the second question by suggesting a visit to Scotland's nearest non-British neighbour: Norway.

Since first publishing *Isles of the West* in 1999, I have come to realise that the problem I described in it, the 'museumification' of the Hebrides, is almost as high on the agenda of the Scottish Executive as it is with the conservationist groups which have a financial interest in promoting a static society that they can dominate as it quietly, but gracefully, dies. Official Scotland is frighteningly ignorant of rural Scotland, both human and natural, so is inclined to listen to self-interested lobbyists as if they are disinterested observers without axes to grind. That is the root of much of the misgovernment in the Hebrides. Is this inevitable? Given that civil servants work in towns, and the most influential of them in the capital, maybe they will always think of rural areas in clichéd terms and treat them as if they are incapable of managing their own affairs. But perhaps an old country with a new parliament is capable of rising above this second-rate approach. I certainly hoped (and hope) so. The only way to find out was to visit a neighbouring country which has a reputation for thorough-going, egalitarian democracy, yet with an admirable record of pragmatic management of its ecological, human and economic resources. Could there be lessons for Scotland at the price of a trip across the North Sea? I decided to try to find out.

A project like this, though simple in concept, involves a great deal of organisation and expense. First, I needed a larger boat than *Sylvia B*, which I had sailed in *Isles of the West*, but which in any event I had already sold. Part of the reason for the larger boat was that, secondly, I needed crew. I do not like sailing single-handed overnight on busy seas: the first rule of seamanship is to keep a good lookout at all times, even when the skipper is asleep. Finally, there were the unavoidable expenses of being so far from home for so long. The result was that I had to call on a wide range of people for assistance, Scottish publishers' advances being what they are. I received substantial help from Sandy Mactaggart of Islay, Mark Pattinson of Couldoran, Lord Barber of Tewkesbury, Sir William Lithgow of Ormsary and, pre-eminently, Lord Pearson of Rannoch. Others who gave welcome practical support include Oddrun Midtkandal, Sven-Erik Myrtveit, Brit Osgerd, Michael Russell, Jamie McGrigor, the late Giles Gordon, Lord Vinson of Roddam Dene, the Earl Peel, Ardbeg Distillery, Lagavulin Distillery, Martin Lawrence, Roland Worthington-Eyre and, of course, Michael Gilkes, who preferred to sell his old boat to me rather than give it the 'Viking funeral' which he threatened whenever problems of the transaction seemed overwhelming. I am grateful to all of them, as well as to everyone who gave of their time to talk to me on my travels and make life comfortable and/or amusing in other ways. I also appreciate the attractive combination of seriousness and informality at Birlinn.

Finally, three people deserve special mention. First, Brian MacKenna, who joined as crew at the last minute and who did so much to make the voyage go pleasantly, particularly on the catering side; secondly, Robert Cunyngham-Brown who, together with Catherine Haworth, made the North Haa on Yell Sound home from home for Brian and me for ten days' deeply appreciated 'r & r'; and lastly Kirsty Macleod, without whose help my research into the darker sides of Scottish island maladministration would not have progressed nearly so far. By her inde-fatigable pursuit of the truth behind the spin, and her implacable refusal to accept second best for rural Scotland, Kirsty has done more than any single individual I can think of to move the national debate forward from the self-serving clichés of the conservationists who had the stage entirely to themselves only ten years ago.

NOTE TO THE
ABRIDGED EDITION

THIS, THE SECOND EDITION of *Isles of the North*, has been reduced in size in order to be published as a trade paperback. Essentially, it has been cut back to carry only the material relevant to Scotland, with a few aspects of Norway which illuminate important points made about Scotland. No changes or cuts have been made to the material about Scotland. Readers wishing to read the material about Norway as published in the first edition can find copies for sale, second-hand, at www.amazon.co.uk

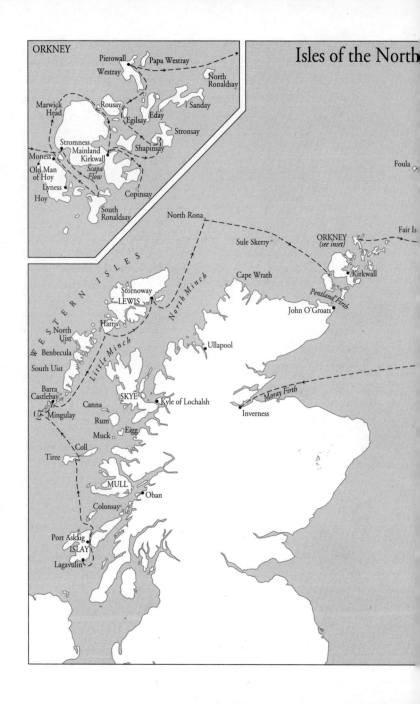

Isles of the North

ORKNEY

Pierowall · Papa Westray
Westray
North Ronaldsay
Marwick Head · Rousay · Egilsay · Eday · Sanday
Stromness · Mainland · Stronsay
Moness · Kirkwall · Shapinsay
Old Man of Hoy · *Scapa Flow*
Lyness · Copinsay
Hoy · South Ronaldsay

Foula

Fair Is

North Rona

Sule Skerry

ORKNEY
(see inset)

Kirkwall

Cape Wrath

Pentland Firth

John O'Groats

W E S T E R N   I S L E S

Stornoway
LEWIS
North Minch

Harris

Ullapool

North Uist

Little Minch

Benbecula

South Uist

Barra
Castlebay

SKYE · Kyle of Lochalsh

Mingulay

Canna

Moray Firth

Rum

Inverness

Muck · Eigg

Coll

Tiree

MULL · Oban

Colonsay

Port Askaig
ISLAY
Lagavulin

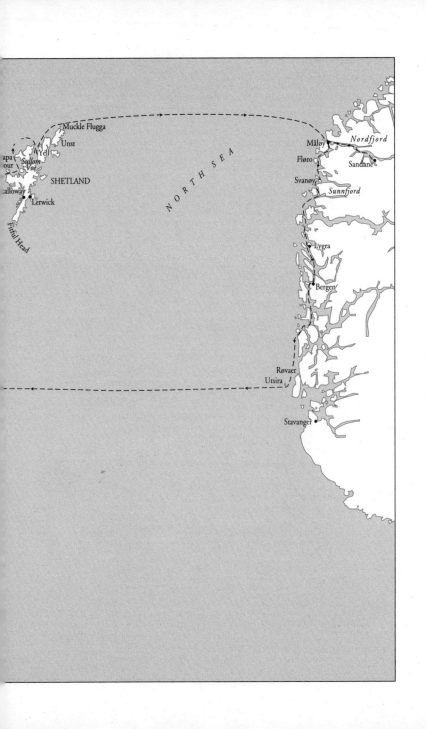

NORTH SEA

Muckle Flugga
Unst
Yell
Sullom Voe
SHETLAND
Lerwick
Fitful Head

Måløy
Nordfjord
Fløro
Sandane
Svanøy
Sunnfjord

Lygra

Bergen

Røvaer
Utsira

Stavanger

PROLOGUE: A BEDROOM IN BREMANGER

LESS THAN A FOOT from the end of the luxuriously quilted double bed in the large log house by the side of the fjord lies a bank of ferns nestling under a moss-covered granite rock. On three sides the bed is surrounded by thick grass, dappled with late summer sunlight and the deep, cool shade of the silver birch trees scattered all around. Beyond the bed the ground rises, beautifully unkept, to a rowan tree whose scarlet berries sway noiselessly in the afternoon breeze. Beyond, the skyline is unbroken by any sign of human habitation. The only sound is the quiet ticking of the clock beside the bed.

Above the walls of double-glazing, the roof is planted with grass, rendering it almost completely invisible from the public road a mile away which runs across the otherwise bleak stoniness of the remote island of Bremanger off the west coast of Norway, on a latitude some way north of Shetland.

The designer, builder and owner of the house is in the kitchen, making afternoon coffee for his partner, the post lady. When I ask if he minds my taking a photograph of this remarkable room, he marches through with a grin on his face. 'If you give money, we will perform for you.'

After coffee, we wander a short distance down hill to another grass-roofed wooden building by the water's edge. This one has no windows. But it has four wide doors on the front because it contains a two-seater, single-engined seaplane which can be rolled straight through them and down the short concrete slipway into the water for take-off. The back wall is covered with neatly arranged tools and spares; the west wall with life jackets and leather flying caps.

Beside the hangar is a house for guests. It has a verandah on two sides and a dock in front. Moored alongside is what I am told is the fourth in a series of powerboats which this remarkable man has built. He sails them across to Shetland, on one occasion accompanied by 120 other similar craft from the Florø–Bremanger–Måløy area. The latter town is a large fisheries centre fifteen miles away which is twinned with Lerwick. But the contacts between the two communities run deeper than modern marketing schemes and parties at the Lerwick Boating Club. Men from Bremanger were amongst the most prominent in the extremely danger-ous traffic in arms, agents and refugees between Britain and occupied Norway during the Second World War. They used the only vessels to hand: the small, inshore fishing boats built on this coast. They were local fishermen and proud of it, with no naval or other marine pretensions. But their courage was matchless.

In his classic account of this campaign, *The Shetland Bus*, David Howarth has described these men and their equal contempt for civilian convention, military discipline, officers of the Royal Norwegian Navy or danger. Four miles from the glass-walled bedroom is the tiny fishing village of Grotle, then home of Bård Grotle, one of the most success-ful of the skippers. Howarth writes that this man, who voyaged to the Arctic and back, braving storms and enemy attack alike with buccaneer-ing insouciance, looked like a pirate, even when attired in modern civil-ian clothes.

He never dressed without some flash of colour, usually a red spot-ted handkerchief round his neck, like a gipsy's; and after uniforms were issued to the men he showed his scorn of naval formality by never wear-ing all his uniform together. Sometimes he would have naval trousers and an army battledress blouse, and sometimes civilian trousers and a naval jacket; and always, however correct or incorrect his suit, he wore a decrepit and filthy trilby hat, from which long golden locks of hair escaped and blew about his face like the hair of a friendly sheepdog . . . One day when I asked him whether he slept in it, he said, 'Of course. Then when I get up I'm all ready for breakfast.'

Bård was physically a splendid figure, tall and strong, with a classi-cal nose and the blue eyes and fair complexion which tradition gives to Norse pirates . . . [He] was a man who could not take a serious view of himself or anyone else. There was always the recollection or anticipation of a joke in the twinkle of his eyes . . . Successful though he was as a skipper, he was rather a trial to us. We could never rely on him to start a trip within a couple of days of the time he said he would be ready, and he set a bad example by his dirty old clothes, his unshaven face, his habit of staying in bed till dinner time and his lack of interest in anything but the essentials of sailing his ship. He was the skipper and nothing more. He would sail, at his own convenience, to anywhere between Bergen and Lofoten, and to hell with the Germans.[1]

If Bremanger was the furthest island from home amongst those I visited in the voyage described in this book, the closest inhabited one was Barra, at the southern end of the outer Hebridean chain. Made famous by Compton Mackenzie in *Whisky Galore*, Barra produced its own quota of maritime heroes in the Second World War. Like most of the western isles of Scotland, it furnished a disproportionate number of men for the Merchant Navy, the arm of service which, along with Bomber Command, suffered the highest rate of casualties. They were the unsung heroes of the Battle of the Atlantic, yet they, too, retained their sense of humour. Compton Mackenzie himself has described it in these words:

> Barra is an extraordinarily happy place. Laughter is the keynote. There is always a good story going the rounds. Gaelic is a great language for wit, and with three-quarters of the population speaking both Gaelic and English, the native Gaelic wit salts the English. And it is not empty laughter. Barra has passed through fierce ordeals during the last three centuries in the way of persecution, evictions and famine . . . [Consequently] the laughter has experience behind it. It is a mellow fruit which has ripened after a frosty spring.[2]

But the personal freedom on which the cultures of both Barra and Bremanger were founded has not survived with equal vigour in the two communities. On Barra, no-one would be permitted to build a house in which the bedroom has glass walls on three sides. The Western Isles Council, on instruction from London, via Edinburgh, prohibits the erection of dwellings with windows wider than they are high. Tradition now has the force of law, stifling the development of the culture of Barra and thereby slowly killing it.

---

1 *The Shetland Bus*, David Howarth, Lerwick 1998 (London 1951), pp. 80–1.
2 *My Life and Times Octave VII*, Compton Mackenzie, London 1968, p. 190.

Traditional windows had a vertical emphasis . . . Modern window styles have a horizontal emphasis which tends to create too much void in what should be a solid dominated facade . . . The critical point [for new designs] is to maintain a vertical emphasis to the windows.[3]

The comparison is instructive because the two islands have a lot of similarities: they have poor ground, so that historically most of the population has earned its living either from the sea or by temporary emigration. Of course, there has been a lot of permanent emigration too. Both islands suffer from the common contemporary diseases of uncertain economic times and excessive bureaucracy. But this bureaucracy works differently in the two places. An example of this is language. The vernacular of the west coast of Norway, Nynorsk, ('new Norwegian') has official status and equivalent funding to Bokmål ('book langauge'), the language of government and commerce. By contrast, the vernacular of the north-west of Scotland, Gaelic, is starved of funds and status by the Anglophone government in Edinburgh.

Barra protects its housing tradition by bureaucratic means, while Norway protects its linguistic tradition by the same means. Is there a difference? Yes, and it is fundamental. On Barra you are *compelled* to build according to tradition; on Bremanger you are *offered* the option of Nynorsk or Bokmål. Any individual may speak either language; every parent may decide in which language his or her children are educated; every community can decide the principal language of the schools in its area. The final authority for such decisions in the case of Bremanger is the local Kommune, or municipality. The final authority in the case of Barra is the Scottish Executive in Edinburgh.

Another similarity between the two islands is that both are connected to smaller neighbouring ones by recently built causeways: Frøya in Bremanger's case; Vatersay in Barra's. A visit to each is edifying. Whereas Frøya is full of smart houses, both new and old, many of them large and elegant, Vatersay is a desert with a few old croft houses of the meanest, plainest and most unimaginative design, plus a small new settlement with less than a dozen cramped and dreary houses, some little more than Forestry Commission-style chalets.

Frøya has a restaurant offering fresh seafood in huge vats which the

---

3 *New House Design Guide,* Comhairle nan Eilean Siar, Stornoway, undated, p. 92.

diner can select for immediate consumption in a beautifully appointed room furnished with elegantly presented marine relics: the bar, for example is made from one of the open, clinker-built boats which used to be the main inter-fjord transport until thirty years ago when roads and causeways started to be constructed on a big scale. Vatersay, by contrast, has no restaurant, indeed it has no public facility of any sort, except a single phone box situated in the windswept open space surrounding the new settlement. The nearest thing to a restaurant on Barra is the two hotels in Castlebay which provide meals. Bremanger, by contrast, has hotels, cafés and a 'Rockklubb'.

Vatersay has no facilities for visiting yachts, despite being situated in a strategic location in one of the most attractive cruising grounds in Europe – even Barra has only a ferry and fishing boat pier, with no pontoons or even sheltered moorings for yachtsmen. Frøya has a fifty-berth marina complete with showers and laundry facilities right next to the restaurant. It also has a much larger fishing quay with a fish factory which processes up to 50,000 tons of herring and mackerel per annum, plus bunkering facilities for commercial craft and a substantial engineering facility. There is an air of commercial hum to the place, despite its architectural grace. The result is that though Vatersay and Frøya are about the same size, the former has a population of about 120, the latter has one of nearly 700.

Finally, it might be observed that whereas Bremanger and Frøya have high-speed catamaran ferries running almost hourly to the large town of Florø ten miles to the south, making it easy for residents and schoolchildren to commute, and a similarly frequent service on a vehicle ferry to Måløy in the north, Barra has only in the last year acquired a vehicle ferry which connects to the rest of the island chain, even though Eriskay, its port of call, is just five miles away. Before that it was impossible even to get a daily newspaper on the island. This new service is infrequent, but that has not prevented the government in Edinburgh from trying to scale back the island's only fast connection to the outside world, the air service to Glasgow. The reason given is that the existence of the ferry to Eriskay means that the air link is no longer a 'lifeline' service. This has had the predictable consequence that the only independent business which has come to Barra in recent years, an optical equipment trading company run by a Ukrainian married to a Barra woman, has recently announced that it is going to have to move away to the mainland.

Scotland and Norway both have small but well-educated populations. Both have abundant natural wealth in the form of oil and fish. Both have strong manufacturing and trading traditions, and distinguished histories of sea-faring. Scotland, in addition, has a world standard record of scientific innovation and philosophical thought, yet it is the Norwegian island, Bremanger, which is today wealthy and free, while the Scottish island, Barra, is poor and culturally cramped. Why can rural Norway change and develop, when modern Scotland is so backward and constricted? That, in a nutshell, was the question I set out to answer on the trip described in this book.

Whatever its problems, though, Barra is not dull. The people have a sense of subversive fun which is, naturally, more highly developed in a place so badly run than it is in orderly Norway. I remember an example of the Barra wit which still makes me chuckle. It came about because I needed fuel for the boat. I asked a friend if it was possible to buy marine diesel on the island.

'Yes,' he said. 'At the butcher's shop.'

'The *butcher* sells diesel?'

'Oh yes, and he sells the papers too.'

'Really?'

'Yes. There was a rather disdainful tourist here recently who asked him if he could buy a newspaper on this island. The butcher said to him, "Do you want today's paper or yesterday's?" "Today's, of course." "Well, come back tomorrow then!" '

I

ISLAY TO RONA

AN EXPERIENCED SAILOR CASTING a critical eye over the yacht *Foggy Dew* as she lay alongside the pier at Port Askaig on the Isle of Islay on 1 July 2002, the day of her departure for Orkney, Shetland and Norway, would surely have pronounced her unfit for sea. She is a handsome plywood boat built forty years ago for spare-time cruising and racing by a Brighton eye surgeon whom I knew because he had a holiday home on Islay. Due to a catalogue of accidents, misunderstandings and mistakes, I was about to put to sea in this boat long before she was ready for the journey contemplated. But I had a plan which could not be delayed except by a full year, which I was reluctant to do. I had a crewman, a friend from Glasgow called Brian MacKenna, who had almost no experience of the sea but had agreed to stand in as chief cook and bilge washer at the last minute after another friend with professional sea-going experience had had to pull out due to an unexpected health scare. Brian and I had worked on the boat for two weeks and thought we were as ready as we were ever likely to be.

Foggy Dew was designed by one of the most gifted amateur yacht designers in twentieth-century Britain: Guy Thompson. She had won innumerable cups in her early racing days, and had travelled far and wide in subsequent cruising years. More recently, she had become a store-house for the marine gadgetry which her owner collected. A complete inventory would have needed a small book, but it would have included five torches, six fire extinguishers (two of which contained poisonous phosgene), four basins, three buckets, two portable stills, seventeen fenders, three bilge pumps (only one working), three logs (likewise), seven gas fog horns and an oral one, fifteen cushions, twenty-five drinking glasses, two vacuum cleaners, an inclinometer, a ventometer, four first aid kits (one of them containing an 'anti-tensive for cases of emotional instability or irrationality' which was marked 'Poison S4: on prescription only'), eight additional syringes, a pouch of surgical instruments, a tube marked 'solid eau de cologne', eleven sails, a canvas-bagged 1960s life raft which looked as if it would detonate rather than inflate, two radio receivers – one doubling as a now unusable radio-direction finder – two bolt cutters, three machetes, three 'Dad's Army' life jackets in disintegrating canvas shoulder bags, a stop-watch that ran backwards and a navigational plotter which had been salvaged from a World War II Wellington bomber and bought at a car boot sale.

And that list omits the infinity of ropes, ties, bungees, burgees, lamps, lanterns, toothbrush holders, corks, playing card packs, books on fishing, waterproof pencils, toothpicks, damp-proof matches, underwater illumination devices, ancient tooth-marked snorkels, pieces of wood and ply which 'one day you might find jolly useful' and about ten cubic feet of miscellaneous tools and spares, only some of which worked. Whatever I may have thought of the condition of most of the equipment, I could make no criticism of its quantity and variety. The surveyor who inspected *Foggy Dew* before I bought her said, 'There's enough gear aboard this boat to start a shop.'

The transaction nearly came to grief over the matter of flags. The owner was a stickler for etiquette in this respect. As a member of the Royal Cruising Club, he was allowed to wear the blue ensign. But, he said that I, not being a member of a yacht club with a Royal warrant, would have to wear the red. I replied that I'd always worn the saltire, and had no plans to change.

'Are you serious?' he said one evening while we were taking a dram together aboard.

'Yes. Why not?'

'Because it is against the law. This is a registered British ship and you have to wear the British flag.'[1]

---

1 The Merchant Shipping Act (1894) lays down the rules for flags and ensigns and provides for a fine of £500 at the current scale for offences, even by pleasure yachts. This law, very unusually, may be enforced not just by policemen but by Customs Officers and officers in H.M. Forces. Not only that, under the Scotland Act, flags are a reserved matter, which may only be dealt with by the Westminster parliament. However, Douglas Thompson, who campaigns for the liberty to use the Scottish red ensign which was the flag of the Scottish merchant marine before 1707, recently sailed round the world on his boat, *Tomcat of Kip*, and subsequently wrote to me saying, 'I flew the Scottish Red Ensign in seventeen countries. A lot of people recognised what it was; a lot of people asked me what it was. But nobody in authority raised any objection to it.' (19 November 2002)

'I'm sure the Norwegians are not going to worry unduly if we arrive in Bergen with a Scottish flag flying rather than a British one,' I said.

'They won't know where you're from,' he countered.

I thought I would leave it at that so did not reply.

He sat in silence for perhaps ten seconds then drained his glass and set it down heavily on the saloon table. 'I am not going to have this boat going around with the Saltire on the stern,' he said in genuinely angry tones. 'I'm just not going to have it. If you're going to take that attitude then the deal is off. I'll return the money you have paid so far, OK?'

There were lighter moments, including what Sir Arthur Conan Doyle might have called 'The Mystery of the Exploding Exhaust Pipe'. Picture the scene: a balmy early evening at the end of May. Standing on the pontoons at the Ardfern boatyard in mid-Argyll hardly a sound is to be heard except the piping of the oystercatchers wheeling round their nests on Eilean Inchaig out on Loch Craignish. Though the yard workers have gone home, there is one man still at work, a portly looking gentleman above retiring age, who is fussing round the cockpit and main hatch of a powder-blue yacht. His Royal Cruising Club sweater is rather eccentrically accompanied by black brogues and a capacious pair of pink dungarees. His hands are oily, his dark hair tousled and his thick-rimmed spectacles awry. He is not in the best of moods.

Part of the reason for his annoyance is the idiocy and incompetence of the person to whom he is selling his boat. The vendor has more or less ordered the purchaser off on grounds of ignorance of subjects like the operating principles of the Tilly lamp, with special reference to the ways of avoiding under-heating the mantle upon firing and thereby producing a noxious plume of black smoke.

The purchaser is quite happy standing on the pontoon, enjoying the peaceful evening scene, while the vendor works below, trying to get the engine started for the first time in two years. After a bit, the tousled hair appears briefly in the main hatch. Tools are laid down on deck and a rag is used to wipe hands and face. The sense is of a job well done.

The head disappears again. Presently a mechanical wheezing sound emanates from the boat, followed by a few isolated thumps, then the sound of the engine roaring into life. A few of the oystercatchers flutter apprehensively but the throttle is soon pushed back and they return to their previous activities. The vendor looks at the engine for a moment, chuckles triumphantly and calls up to the purchaser, 'That doesn't sound too bad!'

'No,' replies the purchaser cautiously, 'it doesn't.'

The vendor starts putting tools away, but after a minute or so, by slow degrees and without any human intervention, the engine begins to slow down. The vendor looks puzzled, and puts his head down into the engine bay. The revs continue to drop, apparently of their own accord. A few seconds later three things happen simultaneously: the engine stops, a bang like unmuffled shotgun report rings out across the silent loch, scattering the oystercatchers, and a plume of black smoke emerges from the main hatch of the boat, quickly followed by the coughing figure of the vendor, now in an even less agreeable mood.

'What the *fuck* was that?' he says to the purchaser, looking as wide-eyed as someone with an oily mist over their spectacles can ever look.

The black smoke drifts slowly away like the cordite from a howitzer. A joke about Tilly lamps seems ill-advised.

A quick examination reveals the fact that the silencer, a rubber device which sits near the end of the exhaust pipe and doubles as a one-way valve preventing water running back up the pipe into the engine, has come adrift from the fitting in the transom. This is refitted, and the engine restarted. With the same result: slow deceleration, another bang, another plume of smoke and another flight of frightened oystercatchers. After a further couple of experiments, when exactly the same thing happens, it is clear that the bang results from the silencer inflating and suddenly deflating at the moment it forces itself away from the fitting in the transom.

Clearly there is a blockage. So we – now I am recruited to help, my ignorance forgiven in the stress of adversity – check every possible point of blockage. I poke things into pipes; he confirms that they come out the other side. We find no blockage of any sort. So we restart the engine which runs for a minute, slows down and gives off another bang and plume of smoke.

We spend another half hour at this, with the owner getting progressively angrier since the delay is threatening a dinner engagement we have with another yachtsman. Then, in a flash of intuition, he comes up with the reason: since the engine was last run, the transom has been replaced and the exhaust fitting renewed. Too long a fitting would appear to have been used. When the engine is started the cone inside the silencer which prevents the backwash of seawater expands slightly, fitting snugly into the tube through the transom. That blocks the pipe, so the pressure builds up to the point where it smothers the engine and the whole fitting comes adrift with an explosive decompression.

It was a simple matter to refit the silencer an inch further back, whereupon the engine started and ran perfectly. So it was with a Holmesian sense of triumph that the owner walks hurriedly up to his digs above the yard to straighten his Royal Cruising Club jersey and put on a clean pair of pink dungarees for dinner.

On our voyage back to Islay for the handover, we noticed a slight, occasional loss of power in the engine which we put down to fuel surging in the steep chop in the Sound of Jura. After the handover, Brian arrived and electrical problems started to manifest themselves. Brian did most of the work trying to solve them, while I finalised the wider arrangements for the voyage. The general condition of the equipment was so bad that I was faced with a decision: either leave in an unready boat or call the whole trip off for this year. Perhaps foolishly, I decided that we would go and just deal with our problems as they confronted us. I thought the hull was sound and the rig reliable, which after all are the main things at sea.

On 28 June we sailed from Lagavulin round to Port Askaig on the Sound of Islay without undue difficulty, but two weeks behind our scheduled departure date. If we were going to get to Norway and back before the equinoctial gales hit the North Sea, there was no time to lose.

So it was that at 6 a.m. on the morning of Monday 1 July, we cast off from the Port Askaig pier and motored out into the Sound, heading north on a calm sea. The last of the flood tide carried us quickly up past the Caol Isla and Bunnahabhain distilleries and out towards the huge Rhuval lighthouse which sits in isolated splendour at the northern tip of Islay. By then some wind had come up along with spits of rain, with the look of more of both to come. We put our tea mugs away, pulled on our waterproofs, cut the motor and raised sail. Now we were off.

By the time we had Oronsay abeam the sea had risen to the point where the skerries south-west of the south end of the island were heaving lumps of white sea up above the tops of the swells. The wind was slightly south of west and strong enough to keep *Foggy Dew* powering along close-hauled. Once past Oronsay, we could bear away a bit as we headed north-west for Tiree. At nine o'clock, I see from my log, Brian was sick, the first and last time on this voyage. Considering he had never made a sea passage on a sailing boat in his life, this was a very commendable performance. I felt queasy for a while too, which I almost never do unless I am nervous about some aspect of the boat. But with every passing mile I became more relaxed about *Foggy Dew*, which was sailing beautifully.

Just before ten o'clock we raised the Dubh Artach light on the port bow, and a fine sight it made, eight miles away on its rock in the middle of the windswept waste. It is one of the most striking of the Stevenson lighthouses. When it was built in the early 1870s construction was regularly halted by storms, even in the summer months. On one occasion the stone mason's quarters were flooded by breaking seas. Yet those quarters stood 60 feet above the high water mark. No wonder the frail youth, Robert Louis Stevenson, who visited the site as a student with his father Tom, the main contractor, opted soon afterwards for a life of letters.

By noon the clouds had thinned, though they had not lifted much. From time to time we would see dramatic shafts of sunlight tracking across the sea, which now began to sparkle and glow under the increasingly translucent grey. Iona, seven miles away to the north-east, began to look more blue than black.

Though the swell was heavy, it was not long before we were sailing in bright sunshine, with jackets off, while the distant smudge of Ben Hynish on Tiree rose slowly above the horizon, dead ahead. For a moment I thought of carrying right on to Barra, the first stop on the itinerary. The wind was steady and fair and the weather was turning gloriously fine. Always on this trip there was the thought that we had left two weeks later than planned and so should make up time whenever possible. But then I calculated that it would be nearly midnight before we would arrive in Barra, which seemed a bit long for my crewman's first day at sea. Plus, the wind very often dies at dusk, which would have meant an even longer night's sailing.

In fact the wind started to die well before dusk. It had already turned light as we reached into Gott Bay, the very exposed anchorage on Tiree, at a quarter to four. After anchoring, I repaired a torn sail batten and Brian swabbed out the bilges which were, ominously, far from empty. The water had a thick slick of diesel on it. Failing to find any obvious reason for the presence of either the water or the diesel, we concluded that they must be consequences of the last-minute work we had done on

Islay, and went ashore for a wander round the harbour and a pleasant hour or so in the bar of the Scarinish Hotel.

Next morning, we had the anchor up by 7.30. We motored in bright sunshine and a ghostly southerly round to Gunna Sound, which separates Tiree from Coll to the north-east. After racing through the narrow channel on the flood we found a very light north-westerly and so were able to raise sail and lay a course for Mingulay, which we had decided the previous evening in the bar to add to the itinerary. If we were heading for inhabited islands in Norway, it might be interesting to see a now uninhabited Scottish island.

The wind held steady while Brian made breakfast, which we ate on deck in what was by now very warm sunshine. After he had got everything cleared away and stowed, the wind started to pick up until we were scudding along at over 5 knots under a clear blue sky. A long swell was rolling in from the Atlantic, the remains of the previous day's big seas. When added to the short swell building up from the north-west where the wind was now coming from, this gave the boat a lively motion. I lashed the helm, made myself a seat from the rolled-up dinghy by the transom and sat reading while *Foggy Dew* steered herself for Mingulay.

At 1.30 I called Brian, who had been asleep down below, to come up on deck and see the traditional sign of good luck, dolphins. Three of them were playing about the boat, leaping, diving, twisting away then shooting back underneath. Puffins provided entertainment too as they frantically paddle-flapped trying to get airborne.

It was well into the afternoon before the wind changed in any way, when it freshened and turned cooler. By then we were close in under the hills of Mingulay and starting to look for the beach on the east side which Martin Lawrence in his *Yachtsman's Pilot to the Western Isles* says offers 'occasional anchorage, [though] in even the most apparently calm weather there is often enough swell to capsize a dinghy'. The only other anchorage is a rocky cove on the south side. It looked less suitable in this weather and also a lot further from the township whose remains I wanted to see.

We tacked up and down the beach under mainsail only. I steered while Brian called out the depths. At 4.15 p.m., shortly before low water, we cast anchor in 10 feet close to the north end of a wide expanse of beautifully sandy beach. The wind was blowing almost directly off-shore and the conditions were settled. While Brian made what he called a 'mush tea' – very tasty with plenty of Tabasco on it – I inflated the dinghy, organised my cameras and made ready to go ashore.

Mingulay is a fascinating island, partly because of what is there now and partly because of its history. It was abandoned in 1912 after the population moved to Vatersay, the island opposite Castlebay on Barra, where the soil is more fertile and the amenities of civilisation, such as they existed in the Edwardian Hebrides, were more accessible. The abandonment of Mingulay was accompanied by none of the publicity which happened when St Kilda was evacuated just eighteen years later. Mingulay and Hirta, the main island on St Kilda, were similar in both population and area. The quality of the soils and the nature of the island economies were comparable, though the St Kildans supplemented the produce of the land by catching sea birds while the people of Mingulay fished. Mingulay was closer to the main arteries of national life than St Kilda, though a glance at a chart is misleading since the strength of the tides round the Barra isles makes the journey very hazardous between Mingulay and Casltebay in the small, unhandy sailing boats which were all that was available in the late nineteenth century. On one occasion the Castlebay priest was said to have been stormbound on the island for seven weeks.

However, the greatest and most interesting difference between the evacuations of Mingulay and St Kilda was in the public response to them. The latter had long been a subject of public fascination. Since the 1870s, writers had been travelling there and returning to publish books describing the customs and curiosities of the St Kildans. Few people expressed any great interest in the people of Mingulay, either when they lived on their island or when they left it.

It was not until 1938, a quarter of a century after the move to Vatersay, that Sir Hugh Roberton, conductor of the Glasgow Orpheus Choir, composed the Mingulay Boat Song, celebrating wives who waited for returning fishermen 'by the pier head'. It is ironic that Sir Hugh's great choir was founded in 1906, the year the first people left Mingulay, one of the main reasons for doing so being the difficulty of landing and loading goods because the island never had a pier.

Whereas the St Kildans' economy was undermined by the falling price of the commodities they produced, principally feathers and fulmar oil, the economy of Mingulay was undermined by lack of amenity at the interface between land and sea. The islander needed a sheltered harbour or, at the very least, a usable pier and slipway. The men of Mingulay were 'hardy fishermen, well known for their skill', as one official observer put it. But without port facilities their catch was at the mercy of the swell which, as Martin Lawrence noted, is rarely absent from the bay.

In 1901 the Congested Districts Board, which had been founded four years earlier to assist overcrowded communities in the crofting counties, installed a derrick on the south side of the bay, having concluded that the construction of either a pier or a slip was not feasible. But the derrick did not provide the solution hoped for, partly as it was unsuitably located and partly because it did not, in any case, solve the problem of what to do with the boats once they had been unloaded. The islanders soon realised that, however benign the Board's intentions, its intervention left the islanders no better off.

So it was that in July 1906 three cottars from Mingulay joined a much larger number of others from Barra to raid the island of Vatersay where there was good ground and only a single farming tenant. The owner, Lady Gordon Cathcart, also owned most of South Uist and all the islands down to Berneray, including Mingulay. She lived in Berkshire. The raiders built wooden huts and planted potatoes. Six months later a much larger number moved from Mingulay to Vatersay, all of them soon to face eviction by Her Ladyship. The raiders knew that what they were doing was illegal, but as the estate had turned down every suggestion for amelioration of the crofters' position, they were desperate. Others had done the same on the neighbouring island of Sandray.

Though the raiders were brought to court in Edinburgh and jailed, they were all released early after a public outcry at the injustice of their convictions. In 1909 the Congested Districts Board acquired Vatersay and created fifty-eight crofts there, settling most of the population of Mingulay amongst many others from Barra. The last resident left Mingulay in 1912 completely unremarked, in contrast to the cacophony accompanying the final departure of the St Kildans from their island eighteen years later.

The main cacophonist on that occasion was Alasdair Alpin MacGregor, who had been sent by *The Times* to cover the evacuation and who subsequently wrote a book about his experiences called *A Last Voyage to St Kilda*.[2] It is arguably the most bizarre example of Scottish insulogra-

2 London, 1931. See also, by contrast, *Mingulay: an Island and its People*, Ben Buxton, Edinburgh 1995. For more about Alasdair Alpin MacGregor, see *Isles of the West*, pp. 159–161.

phy, if I may coin a word. MacGregor ranged far beyond the immediate issue of the evacuation, encompassing everything from the pretentious accents of Kelvinside and the inadvisability of tipping railway porters to the barbarities of vivisection, the problems of being a vegetarian on a 'carnivorous' island, the beauties of Glasgow's soft water, the 'sanctimonious hypocrisy' of the Scottish Sabbath, recent improvements to the Edinburgh tram system, the unsurpassed quality of the paintings of Mr Lockhart Bogle and the death of his own beloved dog, Torquil the Timid, to whom the book is dedicated – and that is all before our guide, conductor and friend has left Finnieston Quay in the SS *Hebrides* bound for what he calls 'the Edge of the World'. Indeed we are half way through the book before MacGregor starts describing St Kilda, and it is not until page 213 (out of 303) that he actually lands on the island which is the subject of his story. Nothing so 'creative' was written about Mingulay until Sir Hugh Robertson composed his song.

MacGregor reflected general opinion in his concern for the St Kildans. Times had changed since Mingulay was abandoned. After the carnage of the First World War, the past came into fashion in the form of ethnology. People like Margaret Fay Shaw (later Campbell of Canna) came from America and Werner Kissling from Germany to study the obsolescent lifestyle of the Western Isles which was thought to embody an admirable simplicity and closeness to nature.[3] Sympathetic concern by individual researchers was accompanied by the new phenomenon of bureaucratic conservation. St Kilda was acquired by the National Trust for Scotland in 1935. Since then a local by-law has laid down that 'no-one will be permitted to leave the Village Bay singly, and no-one will be permitted to climb any of the cliffs without first obtaining the Trusts's authorised representative's permission'.[4] Today it is a World Heritage Site, recognised by the United Nations, and therefore almost completely rule-bound.[5]

---

3 See *Folksongs and Folklore of South Uist*, Margaret Fay Shaw, Edinburgh 1999 (1977) and *A Poem of Remote Lives: the Enigma of Werner Kissling*, Michael Russell, Edinburgh 1997.

4 Even more draconian is by-law number 17: 'The National Trust for Scotland, the Trust's authorised Representative, or any officer of the Trust, may refuse entry to the Reserve to any person without cause assigned. Such a person if he be on the island will leave forthwith by the first available civilian transport or Ministry of Defence transport if available.'

5 This status was achieved in 1986, when the rules prevented a site being both a natural World Heritage Site and a cultural one. The rules have since been

After the evacuation, Mingulay was tenanted by a Barra sheep farmer who dismantled the derrick to make sure none of the former inhabitants returned. In 1919 he bought the island from Lady Gordon Cathcart. Two other farmers owned the island and its immediate neighbours before it was acquired by the Barra Head Isles Sheepstock Company, a syndicate of Barra crofters, who ran it quietly but successfully for forty years until sheep prices collapsed in the late 1990s. They put Mingulay, Pabbay and Berneray on the market for £1 million, but found no buyers. With no current economic value, the question was, what price heritage? Eventually the National Trust for Scotland was professionally advised that they should pay no more than £450,000 for the islands, which the Barra crofters accepted in April 2000.

Part of the purchase price was contributed by the Chris Brasher Trust. Mr Brasher himself was quoted in the press as saying, 'On my last visit to these unsullied beaches, I was telling the one-year-old son of the skipper of our boat that when he grew up he might see holiday hotels littering this paradise.'[6] Developers have long been the bogeymen for those who enjoy the amenities of a developed environment themselves – Brasher lived in Richmond, Surrey – but who wish to prevent areas of the countryside which they like but do not own from being used in a way that they disapprove of. A century ago a Mr Norman Heathcote wrote a book about the island which ended by asking, 'What will happen to St Kilda

---

changed. Accordingly Objective 7 Prescription 7.1 of the National Trust for Scotland's Management Plan for St Kilda 1996–2001 states that the Trust 'with support from Historic Scotland will request that the Secretary of State for Scotland nominate St Kilda as a World Heritage Site for its cultural significance'. The award of both designations 'would reflect the truly global significance of this property'. (p. 73) An example of how the Trust is considering preserving this heritage is given in paragraph 7.2.2.2, where the turf on the roofs of the cleits is to be replaced with 'biodegradable geotextiles'. (p. 74) But a difficult question has arisen now that it has been shown by Professor Meharg of Aberdeen University that the soil of St Kilda has been polluted by the heavy metals and toxins which leeched into it from the remains of the tens of thousands of puffins and other seabirds which were killed each year. Is it the Trust's 'cultural' duty to continue the islanders' toxification of the soil or its 'natural' duty to clean it up?

6 *The Herald*, 14 April 2000. Chris Brasher was the Olympic runner who helped found the London Marathon and the John Muir Trust. He was a noted sports journalist and latterly Chairman of Reebok UK Ltd. He died in March 2003.

in the future? Will it remain the lonely island home of a primitive people and continue to afford a charming refuge for those who wish to escape from the rush of life? . . . Or will it be invaded by the purveyor of health and amusement and shall we see a hydropathic establishment erected on the slopes of Connacher and an esplanade round the shores of Village Bay?[7]

Immediately the ownership of Mingulay was transferred from Barra to Edinburgh, the new proprietors rushed to claim that the Barra people as a whole would now be involved in its management. Trevor Croft, the Trust's then Chief Executive, said, 'We will be working closely with the people of Barra and Vatersay . . .' Andrew Batchell, the Trust's then Director of Countryside, said the Trust would 'work closely with the people of Barra and Vatersay to develop a management plan for the islands'.[8]

But that is not quite what has happened. According to Jessie MacNeil of Voluntary Action Barra and Vatersay, the National Trust's perform-ance has been below expectations. 'It's extremely disappointing because they did carry out, in the first year that they took over, extensive local consultation, but from what I can see they've put none of that into practice.' The main issue is the location of the office from which the Barrahead islands will be managed. The Trust gave a commitment in the round of meetings soon after they took over that management would be from Barra. Castlebay is the natural point of departure from the islands so it is logical to base the position there. However, the National Trust subsequently announced that it would manage all its Western Isles prop-erties (including St Kilda) from Benbecula. The councillor for Barra on the Western Isles Council summed up the feelings of his constituents in a letter which ended: 'I regret to say that I have no doubt that this community will see these proposals as an act of treachery and a betrayal of trust.'[9]

It was overcast and chilly when Brian and I rowed ashore. Even in these calm conditions, there was a light swell which made landing on the beach impossible. So we pulled to the rocks at the north end and

---

7 *St Kilda*, Norman Heathcote, London 1900, p. 201.

8 Respectively *The Scotsman* and *The Herald*, 14 April 2000. Both Croft and Batchell left the Trust after a serious financial crisis. As of this writing, no management plan has been produced.

9 Letter from Donald Manford to Alexander Bennett, NTS, 3 March 2003.

scrambled ashore there. We dragged the dinghy out of the water onto a grassy ledge where the scent of violets was strong. Looking up, I saw an array of puffins idly following our movements. I took some photographs of them, after which we set off to explore the island, followed by terns which swooped and glided overhead.

The first thing we noticed were footsteps in the sand. We were not alone. Soon we found three Dutch people, two men and a woman, sitting under a canvas shelter, next to a couple of kayaks, drinking a bottle of Irish whiskey. They told us they had paddled all the way from Uig on Skye.

We wandered the few yards up to the ruined village, still highly visible amidst the encroaching sand and vegetation. However, the most remarkable aspect of the built environment was not the houses but the little road which leads south from the village round to where the derrick was installed in 1901. Amidst a profusion of irises and buttercups, it winds over the hill, with stones holding up the edges. A carefully wrought drystone bridge takes it over a little stream. It had withstood storms and floods for a century almost completely undamaged. Brian was surprised to see something so cleverly constructed in a place so close to the 'Edge of the World'. He pointed out that the Kingston Bridge in Glasgow needed major repairs after less than thirty years of life.

We followed the path round to the loading place. The cleft was no more than 10 feet wide. Even in a calm sea there was a surge and wash which would have damaged any boat without substantial fendering. Not only that, the sides of the cleft and the path down to the derrick were so steep that they must have been extremely dangerous in wet weather, for livestock especially. No wonder the islanders considered this did not solve their freight movement problems.

Then we trekked up the hill, under another flight of terns, to have a look at Berneray, the smaller island to the south on which the Barrahead light stands. By then a cold sun had come out and cloud-shadows scudded across the heather. Even on a quiet day like this, it was obvious that winter on the islands must be wild. A military plane which crashed on Berneray during World War II hit the ground close to the lighthouse during an especially severe storm. The lighthouse keepers heard neither the impact nor the subsequent explosion of the fuel tanks and armaments. It was long after the end of the war before a climber happened to discover the wreckage and decomposed bodies of the crew.

By the time Brian and I got back to the dinghy, we both felt ready for a little supper. We knew we had brie and oatcakes aboard, plus two bottles of Lagavulin which the distillery had kindly given us before departure. Brian had the bright idea that we ought to take our dram with the island water which we had tasted in the burn near the drystone bridge. While I tried to get more photographs of the puffins, using the flash this time, he walked back to the Dutch camp, begged an empty plastic bottle, tramped up to the stream where he rinsed and filled it. In the gathering darkness, at about midnight, we had our nightcap on board diluted by soft, peaty Mingulay water. It tasted absolutely delicious.

Next morning the sun was shining and I felt so full of the joys of travelling that I plunged overside for a swim before breakfast. The water was so cold that I did not repeat the experiment until we got to the glacier-fed fjords of Norway, where it was much warmer. Martin Lawrence recommends sailing round the west coast of Mingulay to see the cliffs. With the wind now in the north and quite boisterous, this seemed an entertaining thing to do. The tide was flooding, which meant we would have it against us going west through the sound of Berneray. But we would then be under the lea of Mingulay, so that should not be a problem. For the rest of the short hop of 18 miles or so into Castlebay it would be wind against tide and pretty choppy.

On his third day at sea, Brian was starting to look at home on the boat. We motor-sailed down round Geirum Mór, the stac at the south-west end of Mingulay, and into a sea that had the contours of an empty egg tray. The birds milling around the cliffs of the west end of Berneray looked like specks of dust in a shaft of sunlight. The damp in the air made the green on the tops of the cliffs appear almost luminous. Every tiny ledge of the near-vertical faces of the cliffs glistened. Brian remarked that it looked as if 'the top of the mountain has melted'. Everywhere that was not either green or vertical seemed to be white with bird droppings.

Martin Lawrence was right – this was a sight not to be missed. But we had a very wet sail. If *Foggy Dew* has a fault at sea it is that she easily buries her head in a short, steep sea. Also there was a lot of spray flying across the deck while we had the wind almost on the beam. But none of that could conceivably explain the fact, which we noticed shortly before coming to anchor in Castlebay, that the cabin sole was awash. The bilges were full of water. Where on earth had it come from? While Brian pumped it out, I checked the boat and could find no leak. A total mystery. The only thing to do was to keep a regular watch and try to detect a leak, first while we were at anchor and then when at sea.

Due to a slight but persistent diesel leak, the bilges and the lower lockers had been given a fine coating of oily liquid. After lunch, Brian heroically set to with bucket and soap to clean everything, while I went ashore to meet Donald Manford, the councillor who had written to the National Trust about Mingulay. Donald is a bearded, solidly built Barraman whose varied career has involved the police force in Glasgow, which he left when asked to help cover-up a false accusation case, and the cockle trade on Barra. He used to send his cockles off the island in a de-commissioned ambulance since the main cost in the cockle trade was the high commercial vehicle charges from Castlebay to Oban. Ambulances travel free on the ferry, of course.

Donald is an independent-minded man representing a community of independent-minded people. But it is a community under threat. I first became aware of the problem three years ago when he asked me to help resist an attempt by Scottish Natural Heritage (SNH) to impose a seal sanctuary on the Sound of Barra, the stretch of water to the north of the island, between Barra and South Uist and including the *Whisky Galore* island of Eriskay.

Due primarily to the problems of the British fishing industry, Barra has considerable social and economic problems.[10] The obvious answer to economic difficulties is to allow more flexibility for development. SNH, however, seeks to restrict flexibility by imposing controls on two of the areas of sea around the island which can be fished in all seasons. As the fishing industry is by far the largest non-government employer on the island – the other two significant ones are agriculture and tourism – this is a matter of the highest importance. The particular designation concerned was something known as a Special Area of Conservation, or SAC.[11] The basic way of making this assessment for animal species is by counting them. If the site holds more that a 'qualifying percent-age' of the national population, usually 1 per cent, then the site may

10 It has 4.4 per cent of the Western Isles population, and just 3.5 per cent of the jobs. *Barra and Vatersay Local Plan*, Western Isles Council, Stornoway 1996, p. 17.

11 SACs are promulgated under the European Habitats Directive (1992) which relates to all habitats and species other than birds. They are protected by SPAs (Special Protection Areas), promulgated under the Birds Directive (1979).

be designated. This sounds scientific and objective, but in fact few sites have natural limits and can, like the 'seal areas' of Barra, be extended until they include 1 per cent, or any other proportion, of the national population.

The species of interest in the Sound of Barra is the common seal, approximately 33,000 of which breed around the British Isles. So if the Sound could be shown to 'host' more than 330 seals then it would qualify as an SAC. The Sea Mammal Research Unit in St Andrews does the counting, at four-yearly intervals. In 1992 the count revealed 752 common seals within the Sound of Barra; in 1996, 510. Both figures are comfortably above the 330 needed to cross the 1 per cent threshold. But the year 2000 count revealed only 140 animals in the area. On that basis, SNH should have abandoned the designation.[12] Instead they simply suppressed the 2000 figure and proceeded.

Worse still, SNH issued a press release headed 'Public Meetings Reassure Sound of Barra Concerns'. This was the opposite of the truth. Donald Manford has described the public meeting which SNH held in Castlebay, ostensibly to 'consult' local opinion, but in fact simply to inform the islanders of its intention to designate the Sound. 'There wasn't a single person there who was for the designation. I would describe the attitude as "quietly hostile". SNH put on this act that they were not aware that there was such hostility towards this designation, and it was probably that we didn't know and didn't understand and if they came over and met with people on Barra then they would allay these fears.'

This view was corroborated by Callum MacNeil, one of the fishermen likely to be affected, but also Chairman of the Barra Heritage and Cultural Centre. He said, 'What I was so taken aback by was that they were trying to portray the fact that people weren't worried. I think that is not only standing the facts on their head, but deliberately misleading. The mood of the meeting was one of frustration because the fishermen could not for the life of them understand why SNH wanted this designation when the place was alive with seals.[13]

The Chairs of both the Castlebay and Northbay Community Councils, the only two on the island, were equally adamant that SNH

12 The probable reason for the drop in numbers was the alteration to the tides and currents in the Sound due to the construction of the Eriskay causeway, which SNH had not objected to.

13 Author interview, 6 April 2001.

had deceived the people of Barra. 'It is positively untrue that we are untroubled by the designation,' Marybell Galbraith of Northbay wrote, 'The fishermen are absolutely incensed.'[14] Her memory of the public meeting is that, 'SNH did not listen to what we said. They were treating us with disdain. [The local officer] was very angry. I said we are not going to listen to unelected bodies telling us what to do, and that did not go down well. We appreciate the beautiful island we live in and we do not want it desecrated.'[15]

Canon Angus MacQueen, the priest of Northbay, the parish opposite the Sound, spoke for the majority when he wrote publicly, 'Hebrideans cared for and conserved all species without payment and before jobs were created for people who try to teach us how to look after our islands and their surrounding waters. Please let our fishing industry, which is worth millions to our economy, continue to thrive.'[16]

SNH's response was not to accept that it had misjudged the feeling on the island about the designation, but to attack the canon for speaking out. 'SNH were furious,' Canon Angus told me. 'I'm a complete upstart, and how dare I, who know nothing about anything, comment! But I agree. Yes, I know nothing about anything, but I have a feeling about the seals, about the sea, about ourselves, and I don't like seeing people taking us for a ride or telling us you can't do this or that. I knew that SNH were dangerous. They consulted who? They consulted two people on Barra, I think. Did they ask one fishermen? Did they ask the people at the fish factory? Did they ask any of us? We have not been consulted. We the people, the fishermen, the crofters, have not been consulted.'[17]

The whole episode was succinctly summarised by the laird, MacNeil of Barra, a retired American law professor who lives on the island and in Edinburgh and who has done a lot to 'democratise' the relationship between the estate of Barra and the people of the island. MacNeil wrote publicly as follows:

The 'scientific' basis for an SAC to protect seals is nothing short of laughable. Local consultation was a farce. Not only had SNH already

14 Letter to the author, 9 May 2001.
15 Author interview, 5 April 2001.
16 *The Herald*, 27 October 2000.
17 Author interview, 8 April 2001.

made up its mind long before, but it thereafter misrepresented local views.[18]

Watching SNH suppress science that did not suit it, then announcing publicly that the people of Barra were happy with a designation which they were bitterly opposed to, has changed Donald from being a supporter of both the principles of conservation and the practice of the conservationists to one who still supports the principles of conservation but is deeply suspicious of the practices of most conservationists, especially when they have, as SNH does, the power of government behind them. He now speaks and writes regularly about this aspect of his island's politics.

Donald lives on a croft at Eoligarry, at the north end of the island, not far from the house in which Compton Mackenzie lived during the years when he was gathering material for, amongst other books, *Whisky Galore*. A couple of hundred yards to the west of Mackenzie's house, Atlantic rollers break on a mile and a half long beach of pearly bright sand. A hundred yards in the opposite direction is the Tràigh Mhór (pronounced 'try vore ', meaning 'big beach'), the great cockle shore where Donald harvested his produce and which, twice every weekday, also acts as Barra's airport. A sign at the high water mark says 'Keep off the beach when the windsock is flying and the airport is active'.

The finger of land in between the two beaches is the Eoligarry machair, a flat, sandy links which explodes with wildflowers in the spring. To the north, the ground rises gently towards Ben Eoligarry Mòr, the 300-foot high hill which overlooks the township. Both areas are grazed by the crofters' sheep and cattle, in competition with a rapidly increasing population of rabbits. This has caused a further conflict with SNH. Donald told the story with typical Barra wit at a conference the year before we left on our trip:

The Barra Common Grazings encompass a flat area of machair ground. It is classified as a Site of Special Scientific Interest (SSSI) and together with the hill to the north covers an area of approximately 400 hectares. We have a perimeter fence to allow the cattle to graze and roam the flat land and hill unimpeded. This allows the cattle to

---

18 *Times Literary Supplement*, 31 August 2001.

find shelter depending on the direction of the wind and rain. But this area has a serious rabbit infestation problem. Under our wonderful new environmental managers, in the form of SNH, we were led to believe we would be allowed to control the rabbits sensibly. To us, the local crofters, who have for generations cared for the land, the obvious method was to initiate a gassing programme for the entire machair and the hill area, as the sandy terrain is ideal for rabbits. But not a bit of it.

We were instructed that assistance for eradication was only available for machair rabbits, not hill ones. I should explain that the area is made up of different designations. The south machair is both Environmentally Sensitive Area [ESA] and an SSSI, the in-bye an ESA but not an SSSI, and the hill an SSSI but not an ESA. Scientific reasons underpin these bureaucratic designations which the crofters do not understand. Crucially, neither do the rabbits.

We are supposed to deal with the rabbits on the machair but not the rabbits on the hill. But the same rabbits move up the side of the hill when the machair water table rises in winter and back down again as the water table falls in summer. These rascally rabbits refuse to respect the finer points of the clever SNH and Scottish Executive bureaucrats and their letter soup of designations.

So what were the local crofters required to do in order to receive the blessings of SNH? They were required to build a mile-long fence across the middle of nowhere on the ESA/SSSI boundary. As the rabbits had chosen to defy SNH designations, we had to build a £5,000 border, a frontier, a Barra Bunnies' Berlin Wall.

As with all frontiers, creatures develop a strategy to get round them and the wily bunnies were up to the task. They simply hopped onto the beach, round the end of the fence, and on to the ESA/SSSI on the machair, then hopped back onto their enclave on the hill SSSI whenever the gasman visited the ESA/SSSI. What purpose does the £5,000 fence serve? Well, the answer to that is simple. No useful one.

Let me turn to the cattle. They once roamed freely but now they were hindered by the fence. But they, like the rabbits, simply walked onto the beach and round the fence. That of course gave rise to problems with young calves who often found themselves on the opposite side of the fence to their mothers. Panic set in, the calves got distressed and in some cases were injured.

Now, after all these problems and difficulties, it would seem sensible to remove this ridiculous fence. But were we crofters allowed to do that? No, we were not. We were in a contract to be environmentally friendly. The fence had to stay for at least five years. It looks as if the Barra Bunny Berlin Wall will come down only when the contract ends, or when SNH or the Scottish Executive apply some common sense.

That has not happened yet. Last year we found it necessary to replace a few hundred metres of boundary fence to prevent cattle straying onto the beach. The beach on Barra also serves as an airport and it goes without saying that the mixture of cattle and aircraft can be a highly dangerous one.

The Scottish Executive advised us that our fence repair did not require prior approval and that we could just get on with it. So we did. On completion, the township paid 45 per cent of the cost and asked the Scottish Executive to pay the balance, as agreed. This they refused to do as there was no accompanying letter from SNH to sanction the fence replacement. We now find that we need SNH permission to replace our fence even though, under Crofters Commission regulations, we have a legal obligation to maintain our boundary. Delaying or preventing payment ensures that no more work takes place, further crippling an economy already accepted to be in crisis.

These kinds of bureaucratic games sap the energy and vitality of even the most doughty crofters who wish to stem and reverse the trend of depopulation and bring young people back to our communities. We have not only inherited the natural environment from our ancestors, it is also said we borrow it from our children. If we destroy it by capitulating the democratic environment to the SNH dictatorial environment we will not be able to return what we have borrowed. We must not leave our children that shameful legacy.[19]

As we drove north round the east side of the island towards Eoligarry, I asked Donald what the individual SNH officers were like.

'They are all right sometimes,' Donald said, 'as long as they can patronise you. The local officers make it bearable, so long as they get

---

19 People Too conference at Dewar's Conference Centre, Perth, 12 October 2001.

their own way. They come in trying to sound magnanimous, but they start imposing on you little by little. After a while the inevitable clash comes. Here, on Barra, it really came to a head with the seal sanctuary. The fence was never really an issue, it was just stupid. But the seal sanctuary was a designation too far. But even that was not the main issue. We didn't like it but what could we do? What really made the difference, was when they actually started saying we had agreed to it. I said, wait a minute, this is lies.'

'What did they say to that?'

'That was when it got patronising. It is really the Executive, they said, "We're trying to put your case, and anyway there'll be rewards in it for you." Then we started fighting it. Then there was a step change in the attitude of SNH to us. It came back to me that people were whispering round the Uists that I was a trouble-maker. I am now a crank, an extremist, though it did not really start until I made fun of them at my speech in Perth. I saw it as a bit of inane stupidity and I spoke about it. Boy, did they take exception to that! The local officer has never spoken to me since, not one-to-one, and no more money has come into this village. The level of discretion left to these people is seriously unhealthy. For example, I was employed as what is called a "crofting animator", to help get new schemes off the ground. I got two six-month stints. Then suddenly the third six-month stint wasn't happening. It continued in Uist, but not here. Then it was whispered to me at a meeting in Northbay, "Oh, the money's still there, Donald, if we could only overcome some of the difficulties we have with yourself." In other words: shut up and we'll pay you. I was to be starved until I could be slapped into line.'

In glorious sunshine we drove round the hill past Compton Mackenzie's enormous, barrack-style house. 'I presume a building like that would not now have a hope of getting planning permission,' I said.

Donald laughed. 'We have a big problem developing in the islands,' he said. 'Even if young people do get a piece of land – which is not easy – objections come in from SNH that the proposed house will destroy the view, that it is not in keeping with the current habitation. If the local community can accept that it is not a problem, what the bloody hell has an environmental organisation got to do with it? I am sure that the eagle or the sea eagle that is flying around isn't going to be upset by the view. Planning is a real problem. The people who are taking the decisions have bugger all to do with living here.'

Donald gave me a particularly absurd example of the obsession with stasis: the road on which we were driving. The Eoligarry machair where the rabbits have to be controlled in order to prevent erosion by the sand blowing away is about 18 inches above the level of the road. The road was built in the 1930s. Before then the carts and occasional motorised vehicles crossed the Tràigh Mhór when travelling to Eoligarry. The road was laid on top of the ground, but with all the blowing sand, captured by the grass, the ground has risen. Yet the entire reason behind the effort to 'conserve' the machair is to prevent it falling.

At Eoligarry, we visited the cemetery where Compton Mackenzie is buried. Donald told me about the problem of the ageing of the community, which does so much harm to the economic fabric of the society. Added to all the normal restrictions on, for example, window shape, there is the new one that no new building may be undertaken in Eoligarry during the summer in order that the corncrakes which use the pasture there are not disturbed. With a world autumn population of that species variously estimated at between 15 and 20 million birds, it might be thought excessive to prevent all building during the only time of the year when the weather is favourable, particularly as the reason the birds are there now is because they have not been put off by those activities in the past.

'And it is not just the natural environment which causes problems,' Donald told me. 'We've recently had a row on the other side of the island with the Church of Scotland Minister who wanted to put a wee extension on his church. It was objected to by many powerful organisations and people, small in number but large in influence, but who have nothing to do with this island. It was actually the people on the island, a Catholic island, that took the side of the protestant minister and said he should be allowed to extend his church if he wanted to. There were three individuals, who have nothing to do with this island, who said that the extension was not sensitive to the traditions of the island.'

My curiosity aroused, we set off to see the Reverend Iain Urquhart at the Manse over towards the west side of the island. His church is a fine, square, early nineteenth-century building which looks carefully maintained both outside and in. Behind the plain table on which the Bible sits, a red velvet wall-hanging, about the only decoration in the building other than pots of daffodils in the windows, proclaims in gold letters: 'The Lion of Judah has won the Victory'.

The Manse, a little further down the road, is a pre-conservationist, design from the 1970s, with windows wider than they are high, which makes it light and airy inside. Iain is a handsome man in his thirties, with an attractive, voluble, dark-haired wife and three lively-looking children.

'We called an open meeting for the congregation on Tuesday 6 March 2001 at 7.30 p.m. in the church,' said Iain after handing out tea and biscuits. 'We wanted to discuss the possibility of building an annexe to allow us to have a crèche and Sunday school facilities. The community could use it during the week for Alcoholics Anonymous, parent and toddler and other groups. There were two proposals. One was to build onto the west-facing wall and the other onto the south-facing wall where the door presently is. The proposals were put before the congregation and there was a unanimous vote that we build onto the front, onto the southern wall of the church. That was an open, democratic vote. Then round about the turn of the year I received a phone call saying that we couldn't proceed with the building of the annexe because the listing of our building was such that we would be kept back from doing so. I informed the person who phoned that it was a C-listed building, which meant that we could do it. He then informed me that he had been on the website of Historic Scotland and that we certainly couldn't build on to it as it was a higher grade of listing than I said.'

Iain spread his hands as he dwelt a brief, rhetorical pause. 'That very day,' he continued, 'I went onto the website and found that it had been a C-listed building since, I think, the early 1970s – certainly up to October 2001.' Another pulpit pause. 'The same phone caller got in touch again and said the reason you cannot touch it is because it is a Telford design.'

'Is that true?' I asked.

'Ten days later, he admitted that it wasn't a Telford design at all, but he said it may have been Telford-inspired, which is a slightly different situation, I think you would agree. Then there were letters and phone calls coming in my direction and a lot of statements to the effect that we couldn't proceed and that this individual had contacts within Historic Scotland and the Scottish Civic Trust. He said that we would not be able to proceed because our proposal did not take into account the building, the site and the setting and that it would be detrimental to the look. He also went to Edinburgh to the archives and did some research in our presbytery records and maintained that the building had been designed in the 1820s with a weaker mid-section in the west wall which was built thus because an extension was going to be built to the west, not the south, and if we were going to be in sympathy with this we must build onto the west, not the south, wall. For us it is vital to be able to build because we have no toilet at all. In the year 2001 you must have the proper facilities so we are putting in a disabled toilet, a kitchenette and a small hall. And Historic Scotland told us they were impressed by the fact that we were building in a manner which was so sympathetic to the present building. We are even using Ballachulish slate on the roof, which is no longer quarried, and so on.'

'So how did you react to all this pressure?' I asked.

'You must understand that I am very inexperienced in this sort of thing and when I heard names like Historic Scotland and the Civic Trust being thrown at me I just assumed it to be the truth, and I just saw a thing that I think is positive for the community evaporating. At that point a dear man who is dying from cancer phoned me and said he would put his weight behind the proposal, which he did.'

'Who was that?'

'It was Joe MacDougall, actually, Chairman of the Castlebay Community Council. Joe put his hand in his pocket to buy concrete for us. RJ Macleod's were building a pier down at Ardveenish and they had an excess of materials and Joe, from his hospital bed, phoned up and said, "Reserve me three tons; I'll pay for it." It was something in the region of £500 and he also asked a friend of his in the Catholic community if they would help us out in fund raising. It was just a case of people saying, "We're not getting pushed about any more." The person who was so opposed to our building said in one of the letters to me, "I do realise that your friends in the north" – meaning on the Western Isles Council in Stornoway – "will see this through planning without regard to aesthetic considerations." So he was trying to turn it into a Protestant versus Catholic thing. Now that disgusts me. It absolutely appals me. It was rubbish anyway as it was our Catholic Councillor, Donald here, who proposed it at the Planning Committee and who saw the thing through. When others heard through Joe the way the project was being attacked, they came to our help as well. It was the Catholic community in Barra actually that got behind me personally and gave me their support.'

'Is that unusual?'

'Not on Barra. I don't believe it is even vaguely unusual. Coming here without knowing anyone, I have really been taken aback by the kindness of the whole community. People dropping off meat, dropping off potatoes, you know all these kindnesses. I said to my mother how well I'd been treated and she said to me, "Iain, 'S iad na daoine againne", "Iain, they are our own people." She wasn't surprised at all. "Why are you making such a fuss about being well treated?" '

I asked Iain about his own background. He said it was not at all religious. 'I came from high energy dance music and heavy rock to old organs, some of which were 200 years old.'

'How did you come to Barra?' I asked.

'Somebody knew that I had a longing to be minister in Barra, and unbeknownst to me he dropped a word into the congregation that he knew somebody in Glasgow who had been praying and had a longing to be minister here, so they got in touch.'

'How do you like it?'

'After Glasgow, and Aberdeen as well, I love the pace here – far more sensible. I love the island and the people of Barra. I delight in the fact that my children can be brought up in a place like this with so many freedoms and such beautiful surroundings – hills, beaches, machair lands. It's just fantastic. And a heritage as well, I also like the fact that the people in Barra are so proud of the culture I love, the Gaelic culture, links with Ireland. They have an idea that they are a special people and I think they are. They know that Gaelic is precious and that it carries a culture as well, the music, the clarsach, the boran, many of the traditional instruments are played here, and I just think it is great. It gives me a sense of identity and standing and strength that I know who I am. I belong to a people, a lineage, a long line that goes back into history. I keep my language. My children speak Gaelic, I want them to be taught in the medium of Gaelic, I am translating books into Gaelic when I can, to help pay for the extension to the church. I love those things. It is not true to say that we are unthinking modernisers or that we should be the custodians of everything historic. It is a very, very bad picture that is given. I'm a Gael but I'm a Gael living in the twenty-first century. I want to protect our heritage. What I don't like is what I call conservation theology.'

'What do you mean by that?'

'Some people get very gung-ho in conserving stone and brick, and they completely jettison any sensitivity to people, and where they are at in their hearts, and being kind to them, and discussing things sensibly

and face-to-face, and having an open dialogue rather than letters being
fired at you in almost an accusing manner. I would prefer that people see
that, yes, we do have lovely buildings in Scotland and certainly some of
them are worth being kept up, but when you start to abuse people in the
efforts to maintain these buildings, I find that incongruous and I think
it shows a distinct lack of humanity and kindness and grace.'[20]

On our way back to Castlebay, we drove past Archie Maclean's slaughterhouse at Craigstone. 'This is interesting,' Donald said brightly, as he
swerved off the main road onto an even narrower one which led into the
only crofting community on Barra with a reasonable amount of arable
ground. Amongst the crofts we found a half-built shed and a tall, cheerfully untidy man who ambled out of the house and showed me around.

The particular interest of Archie's slaughterhouse is that he has run it
for years *without subsidies*.

'Not even for new buildings?' I asked, looking at the uncompleted shed.

'No,' Archie said. 'This building, which I want to put up to extend the
slaughter house, will cost £20,000 if I take the subsidies because I will
have to obey all sorts of rules set by the enterprise company, particularly
that everything has to be bought new and may not come second-hand.
I would get 50 per cent, which is £10,000. But if I do not take their
money and do not have to obey the enterprise company's rules, only
those of the factory inspectorate and so on, which do not forbid you to
use second-hand materials in a new building, I can build it for £10,000
so am no worse off. Then of course, I am under no obligation to anyone.'

'I thought that government was supposed to support recycling,' I said.
'You'd've thought that they would be trying to *encourage* using second-
hand steel in new buildings, not banning it.'

'Aye!' Archie laughed.

'This slaughterhouse is an embarrassment,' Donald said. 'It is a serious
embarrassment to the argument that revenue subsidies are essential. The
rest of them have had to close because the subsidies stopped under new
European Union regulations. The argument is that they can't exist without a subsidy. This one is thriving and what the other ones find difficult

---

20 The lack of kindness, humanity and grace resulted in the opposition to the
church extension being pursued so aggressively that Iain suffered a year later
from a nervous breakdown. One of the allegations against him was that he
had become too close to the Catholic community on the island. In late 2003,
he was forced to leave Barra. He now has a parish on Skye.

is that it doesn't want a subsidy, that it is actually profitable in its own right. That is causing serious embarrassment. Archie's in a very difficult situation because he's trying to keep them on board but he doesn't want the subsidy.'

'Who's they?'

'The Council, the Food Standards Agency, the Scottish Environmental Protection Agency [SEPA], all these agencies that make life unbearable. So he's treading a fine line. Not to get anything from them but not to insult them too much by taking nothing from them.'

'They being who? Not the Council?'

'No, but bureaucrats have a vested interest in being seen as providing people with assistance of an absolutely essential nature: life couldn't survive without them. But here business is thriving without a Development Officer coming in and spending time preparing plans to find ways to subsidise Archie.'

The only other large slaughterhouse in the Western Isles used to be a municipal abattoir which was closed in 1992, partly due to new hygiene requirements and partly because the arrangement was considered by the EU as an anti-competitive subsidy. Donald explained that Heather Isle Meats was given a revenue subsidy partly because it employed eight people who could not work all the year round, due to the seasonal nature of the business of any small, country abattoir. But that does not affect Archie, who, as a part-time crofter, has his cows and his sheep, so he only works at the slaughtering when there's slaughtering to be done. This enables him to be much lighter on his feet, financially, than cumbersome organisations which work on a more 'industrialised' basis.

'Up to last year £100,000 a year went to Heather Isle Meats,' Donald went on, 'a small amount of money went to one in Harris; one in Uist got £12,500 and the one here got £1,500. And the purpose of the £1,500 was to make it look like the Council were doing it all throughout the islands. Archie never asked for the subsidy. Someone came round and asked him why he wasn't claiming. Obviously he didn't want to offend a bureaucracy which could close him down at any time, so he accepted the smallest amount he could decently get away with.'

Archie wanted to show me his new cutting room and chill, but Donald was more interested in the politics.

'There are very powerful people in the Western Isles,' he went on, 'who, if Archie becomes too much of an embarrassment, will find a way to break him, in order to justify their own arguments for subsidies. Right now, there is public money going to buy Heather Isle Meats back from the receivers, perhaps to compete with this guy who is getting nothing. As things work now, you have to be dishonest to obey the rules. The system stinks.'

Early next morning, Brian hauled the anchor in and we motored out of Castlebay under grey skies in a southerly breeze. We were soon able to cut the engine and glide along silently and comparatively swiftly. Within an hour we had turned again and were heading north for Rodel in Harris with the sails goosewinged on a smooth sea. Due to the bar across the entrance to the pool at Rodel, we needed to be there around high tide, which was at 16.45.

Though we had a brief rain squall off the Muldoanich outside Castlebay, the clouds soon began to break up and shafts of sunlight illuminated variously the hills of South Uist to port or the distant cliffs of Skye on the starboard side. Occasionally the tops would recede into the mist, while we sailed on a sea which was dark here and silver-speckled there. Rhoda Campbell of the Barra Heritage and Cultural Centre had given me a bag full of cooked crab claws to which her husband, Callum MacNeill, had added a lobster he had caught the day before. Fortunately for me, Brian does not like seafood, so I settled myself down in the cockpit with mole-grips to crack the shells of the claws, a bottle of Hellmann's mayonnaise to dunk them in, a bit of salad, fresh bread and a can of decent lager – a memorable meal. The only thing more delicious than freshly cooked seafood is freshly cooked seafood eaten at sea.

We sailed into Rodel in patchy sunshine. After anchoring we checked the bilges. They were nearly empty. Whatever leak we had was not below the waterline, but there was still a film of diesel on the bilge water. We took the engine's cover off and started it up to see if we could see any obvious leak. As we did so, Brian was hit by a thin spray of water jetting out from one of the coolant drain holes in the after cylinder jacket. Eureka! That was why the bilges had been filling only when we were motoring. Three twists of a spanner cured that problem, but we gave up trying to find the source of the small, but still annoying, diesel leak.

We spent an interesting evening being shown around south-east Harris by John MacAulay, the well-known boatbuilder and scholar. He is possibly the only native Gaelic speaker to have studied Old Norse,

the language of the Viking sagas. He sees the two languages as similar.
Old Norse, John said, was a completely different language from modern
Norwegian.

'There are so many examples,' John said. 'Take "grass" for example.
The Gaelic for grass is *feur*, a general term for grass. *Fiar* is the Old Norse
word for "grass", pronounced in the same way. That was the amazing
thing when I started looking into it. Words that were absorbed into the
Gaelic langauge haven't changed. We pronounce them and speak them
in exactly the same way as the Old Norse did. And they borrowed some
words from Gaelic. One of them is the name for a sheiling: *airidh*. It was
in common use in Norway and in Iceland in the Middle Ages, though I
don't know if it has been transferred to the Norwegian language.'

According to John, this point has more than purely linguistic significance. His research has convinced him that the Gaelic-speaking people
of the Western Isles have a lot of Norse blood in them. He distinguishes
between two phases of Viking history, the first of the raids and the second
of settlement. The raiders were generally aristocratic warmongers from
the south of Norway and other parts of Scandinavia, whereas the settlers
came from the north, some of them being Lapps, or Sami as they are now
known. What happened was that in the Middle Ages there was a general
warming of the climate in northern Europe – this is established fact –
so that the previously poor land of the north of Norway started to yield
good crops. The covetous eyes of the Viking raider class fell upon this new
economic resource and the locals were 'cleared' in a way not dissimilar to
that whereby the crofters of the west Highlands of Scotland were cleared
to make way for sheep in the nineteenth century. It was those cleared
Norse who came to settle in the Hebrides and the Northern Isles.

'Why has this been ignored by historians?' I asked.

'I think most people just accepted that most Norse people were
Vikings. The Sami people and generally the folk of northern Norway
have been looked upon the same as many British people looked on
blacks. Until very recently, the Sami people were ignored.'

'Yet many of the folk who settled here would have been Sami people?'

'Not the majority. I am almost certain, though I haven't proved it yet,
that there would have been quite a high percentage of Sami people along
with the Norse people who settled here.'

'So part of the racial inheritance of the people of the Northern and
Western Isles is Lapps?'

'Yes. But what percentage, I don't know. One of the kings of Norway married a Lapp, the links were that close in those days.'[21]

Next morning we had to be up early to cross the bar before mid-tide. We only just made it. We anchored immediately outside the pool in Loch Rodel and Brian cooked up a huge Sunday breakfast which we ate on deck in bright, warm sunshine. The weather was definitely improving the further north we went. Islay and the central belt of Scotland had been having the worst summer for decades up to the time that we left. The radio told us that nothing had changed, but also that the higher latitudes had been having unusually good weather.

After an hour ashore wandering, we raised the sails then the anchor and ghosted out of Loch Rodel intending to take the flood tide all the way to Stornoway, where Brian and I hoped to be in time for a curry in the only Indian restaurant in the Outer Hebrides. Outside, there was a nice clip of wind from the south, which was ideal. Heading north-east we had the wind on the starboard quarter. *Foggy Dew* surged along at 6 knots under a warm sun only slightly obscured by thin cloud. As the afternoon wore on, the cloud thickened and we could see rain squalls over the mountains of north Harris, and then later over the fascinating-looking landscape of unpeopled crags and cliffs, with deeply indented sea lochs, which lie either side of Loch Erisort on Lewis. From time to time the Shiant Isles, which we left to starboard, disappeared into the mist. But the wind held steady and after we turned due north round Kebock Head we had it directly astern. I thought this would be the moment to try to raise the spinnaker for the first time. But I had not winched it half-way up the mast before the quick-release shackle on the halyard failed and the sail fluttered down onto the deck, with some of it streaming over the rail into the sea.

I quickly gathered it up and spread it out to dry in the warm breeze on the coachroof. But the bigger problem was that the shackle was out of reach. This was going to mean a trip up the mast in Stornoway.

I was distracted from these matters by the sight of minke whales arching out of the water in the approach to Stornoway. The presence of a large shoal of fish was confirmed by an immense flock of gannets,

21 John MacAulay has published two books related to this theme, *Birlinn: Longships of the Hebrides* and *Seal-Folk and Ocean Paddlers*, both published by The White Horse Press, Harris and Cambridge, in 1996 and 1998 respectively.

some flying, some sitting on the sea. They were the first whales Brian had seen.

Even though it was Sunday, we enjoyed an excellent curry in the Stornoway Balti House on South Beach Street, the only restaurant in town doing business on the Sabbath. Most of the pubs were shut too, though we noticed that a couple opened for a few hours. After church finished, we saw knots of smartly dressed people – men in dark suits and white shirts and women in flowery dresses and hats – standing around in the street talking undemonstratively. Within half an hour they had gone, leaving the town entirely empty.

Next morning we discovered we were moored alongside a voluble, retired Glaswegian, Jack Williamson, who was returning from St Kilda with his daughter on *Northern Wind*, a 36-foot Westerly. In brilliant sunshine we took coffee with them on deck while Jack told us of his irritation at the petty rules of the conservationists on the island. I mentioned my spinnaker halyard problem and he offered to lend me something called a 'jumar', which he said would be much easier than the bosun's chair for getting up the mast. It is a French contraption which grips ropes allowing you to step your way upwards using the other halyards. The bosun's chair is used simply as a rest. As I was getting clipped in Jack cheerfully told me the story of a Frenchman who had been killed while using a jumar, 'due to the failure of his equipment, they said'. Jack was not sure if it was the jumar that had failed. 'It might just have been that the rope broke,' he called up to me optimistically as I began my ascent.

After a full day working on the boat, replacing the spinnaker halyard as well as the shackle, repairing the water pump and charging the batteries, Brian and I got an early night so as to be ready for a 3 a.m. start. We were heading for north Rona and wanted to be more or less out of the Minch by high water, which was 7.12 in Stornoway on 9 July 2002.

Infuriatingly, it took us half an hour to get the engine going. We motored out in the half-light with the fishing fleet, butting into a moderate swell from the south. The forecast the previous evening had been 'easterly then cyclonic 4 to 5, occasionally 6, occasional rain'. The outcome was southerly 3 to 4, which veered south-westerly 2, then died completely. There was no rain at all, just brilliant sunshine. The sun rose at 4.45 on a bearing of 30 degrees, which showed just how far north we were. By 8 a.m. we had the Butt of Lewis lighthouse abeam about 7 miles distant. Then a bank of cloud built up circulating round the low which was out to the west of us. In the wide sky the sweep of the clouds was dramatic. With the morning sun in the east, a flight of gannets glowed strikingly in the pale light when seen against the dark mass of cloud above.

By 10 a.m. Lewis had dropped beneath the horizon. However, at 11.05 it was 'Land ahoy!' A little smudge was visible directly ahead. It soon grew in both size and clarity as the clouds dispersed and the sky cleared. As it did so, the sea changed colour from pewter to a rich, deep blue. The wind dropped, but there was still a lumpy, uncomfortable slop. To stop the slatting of the now empty mainsail we took it down and motored. I noticed with dismay that the batteries were not charging.

With further dismay I realised when I went below that we had no large-scale chart for north Rona. I thought I had covered everything, but had failed to notice that Martin Lawrence's *Sailing Directions* for the Western Isles stop at the Butt of Lewis, assuming Rona to be part of the Northern Isles, while the Admiralty *North Coast of Scotland Pilot*, which we also had aboard, considered Rona to be part of the Western Isles. Shucks.

'What'll we do?' Brian asked rather nervously.

'We'll just have to make like Captain Cook,' I said, 'and go very slowly.'

The small-scale chart showed the main dangers, so we throttled right back, switched on the depth sounder and started a slow anti-clockwise circumnavigation of the island, starting at the south-eastern end. By the time we had rounded the tip at the north, it was obvious that the west coast was no place to anchor. The east coast offered a possibility in a place which I had seen on the Ordnance Survey map was called Geodh' a' Stoth. *Geodha* is Gaelic for 'a creek between high rocks' and *stoth* means 'steam'. This is clearly a wild spot in stormy weather. At that stage I had not read the accounts of visits to Rona as I prefer, if possible, to visit places *before* I have read about them so that my impressions are not coloured by other people's observations. Had I done so, I would have known that that is where all landings are made though there is an even less sheltered place occasionally used by yachts on the south coast.

Wild though this spot must be in a northerly or an easterly, when *Foggy Dew* nosed her way in, it was blissfully calm. We made a cautious circuit of the little bay which revealed nothing untoward and, at three o'clock, cast anchor in 20 feet of water on a bottom of white sand partially covered with weed.

Brian prepared a delicious salad which we ate with bratwurst and lager on deck in what was now really hot sunshine. Afterwards I went below for a siesta, which was welcome after our early start. So it was not until six o'clock that we finally set foot on the island. We took a bottle with us and had an 'Ardbeg Moment' to celebrate arriving at our first genuine 'isle of the north'. The distillery, which is a mile from Lagavulin, had kindly given me a supply of their product by way of support for our little enterprise.

In a beautiful evening calm, with the sun slowly moving round to light up the sea round Sula Sgeir, the gannet island ten miles west of us, we started exploring. Rona is a National Nature Reserve managed by SNH because of the grey seals and the sea birds, principally kittiwakes, guillemots, razorbills and puffins. Though deserted in 1844, the island is known to have been lived on for centuries. The original dwellers are said to have taken their surnames from 'the colour of the sky, rainbow and clouds'. From the few acres of fertile ground they produced 'faire whyte bere [barley] meal made like flour'.

But they died out around 1690 when, according to Martin Martin, rats got ashore from a passing ship and ate all their grain. Sailors from another one shortly afterwards stole the island's bull so the cows stopped giving milk. The whole population of perhaps thirty persons perished. Presumably they had no boat either to fish from or escape in. The island was resettled by people who did have boats because a hundred years later all the menfolk drowned while out sealing. The rest of the population had to be evacuated. After that only shepherds lived on Rona until the last left in 1844.

So difficult an environment for the human species attracted people like the 'pioneering conservationist', Frank Fraser Darling, who brought his wife and young son here in 1938 and 1939, ostensibly to study the grey seals. Darling was less of a scientist than a self-publicist, which helped him when he became one of the chief protagonists of the bureau-cratisation of life in the Highlands and Islands of Scotland. In 1944, the first Secretary of State for Scotland who tried to develop the economy of the Highlands and Islands, Tom Johnston, appointed Darling Director of the West Highland Survey, a position in which he made a name for himself as a human ecologist. Today the SNH office from which Rona is managed, in Inverness, is called Fraser Darling House.[22] There is

---

22 See further *Isles of the West*, pp. 22–5, 186, 227–9.

displayed the stone which Darling removed from the altar of the chapel on Rona, believing it to have been brought thence from Iona, possibly by St Ronan himself. He justified his act by saying, 'I have had the stone in my care.'

Though the father of the conservation bureaucracy which now bedevils places like Barra, Darling started out quite differently, as an eccentric individualist in the popular semi-bohemian mode of the 1930s. He argued in the book he wrote when on Rona that private owners are the best custodians of land, a statement which runs counter to every principle of the regime in Fraser Darling House today:

> While land is in private ownership certain creatures are fostered, others repressed, but broadly speaking there is evident a sense of responsibility and many forms of life have a better chance of survival than in a country where there is not direct ownership of the ground nor nominal responsibility for the wildlife thereon.[23]

Fashion changed during the Second World War. The bureaucratic methods which were thought to have brought victory would be applied in peacetime in order to bring about a more equitable society and a more rational allocation of resources. The Labour government of Clement Attlee legislated for national parks in England and Wales as well as introducing fully subsidised agriculture throughout Britain. Darling sniffed the wind and abandoned his previous emphasis on private property. He transformed himself into one of the leading advocates of bureaucratic land management. People should be viewed in the mass, as opposed to individually. Opposition to this view was considered reactionary. In the preface to the published version of his survey, Darling wrote: 'Unfortunately there is a general antagonism to anthropological consideration of human problems in Britain. Such methods are thought to be more suitably reserved for Africans or New Hebrideans.'[24]

---

23 *A Naturalist on Rona*, F. Fraser Darling, Oxford 1939, p. 100.
24 *West Highland Survey: an Essay in Human Ecology*, F. Fraser Darling, Oxford 1955, p. iv. Darling commented on, for example, Islay's economy: 'Today a few distilleries remain and unbalance the life of what should be a prosperous agricultural island.' (p. 68) Forgetting that the distilleries provided a major market for the island's barley, Islay has been transformed from an impoverished agricultural island to a modern, prosperous society by the

After a dismal, mother-dominated childhood, Darling spent much of his life searching for a cosy Eden away from the world where he could indulge his love of wild nature. He lived on four islands at different times, Tanera Mor and Eilean a' Chlerich in the Summer Isles, Lunga in the Treshnish Isles and on Rona. Darling described the view of the north Scottish coast from the island's highest point:

> That far panorama of mountains is pale blue and remote in its beauty. The Butt of Lewis is rarely visible and the ocean remains unbroken to the eye till the rock of Sula Sgeir rises sheer, to the south-west by west, twelve and a half miles away. If I use the glass I can see the solans [gannets] flying round the gannetry on pinions gleaming white. It is on these days on the little islands that we reach apotheosis. The mighty ocean is between that far-off country that we see and this tiny reality. Which is reality and which is dream.[25]

The first thing to say about Rona is that it really is very remote, being slightly further from the nearest inhabited land than St Kilda is. The second is that it is very small, being only 260 acres in extent, less than twice the size of Queen's Park in Glasgow, and considerably smaller than Regent's Park in London. The third is that it is very lovely on a bright summer's evening. But the ferocity of the winter storms was evident when we saw the line of large stones – small boulders might have been a better description for some of them – which had been piled up all along the western side where they had been flung by the highest of the waves. This line was nearly a hundred feet above ordinary sea level.

In a cleft in the rock on the same side the sea has carved out a huge cave which rises in a semi-circular shape about 50 feet from sea level. It runs under the island for at least 200 feet, but just before the end there is a hole, possibly a yard in diameter which must act as a blowhole. When

distilleries which bring jobs, infrastructure and wealthy international tourists. Agriculture, as elsewhere, is struggling. Obviously, Darling could not have foreseen these trends, but his approach, that of central planning, is always likely to be tripped up by real life. By the time he completed his *West Highland Survey*, the Conservatives were in government and his report was rejected. Instead of re-converting to private property, he went abroad and became an advocate of State control of conservation in colonial societies, especially in Africa.

25 *A Naturalist on Rona, op.cit.*, p. 129.

the storms are raging, spray must jet up like the exhalations of a huge, rocky whale.

Immediately to the south of the cave, we found the cliff face totally covered with sitting birds. They were mainly puffins, razorbills and guillemots, and proved very easy to approach. I photographed them from every angle while sitting quietly in the sunshine watching them at their evening activities. No sooner had we set off up towards the spine of the island than we encountered quite a different sort of bird: the bonxie, or great skua. This aggressive raptor is infamous for the damage it does to both vulnerable wildlife and farm stock, especially newly born lambs whose eyes it will, like the black-backed gull, peck out before settling down to eat the guts, tongue and other delicacies. But conservationists think it 'magnificent' and so it is completely protected by law. It breeds on Rona, in substantial numbers now, having colonised the island as recently as 1965. The first we were aware of its presence was by a whooshing sound over our heads. I looked up and saw a pair of webbed feet with little claws on them, outstretched as if to grab the non-existent hair on the top of my head.

Bonxies were entirely absent from Rona when Darling was here, but his comment on the black-backs in 1939 would equally apply to them as they also attack the breeding sea-birds which are the main reason for the island's Nature Reserve status: 'If Rona were to be run by the State as a bird sanctuary it would be necessary to regulate the numbers of this predatory bird.'[26]

Needless to say, no such control is exercised today. The same point could be made about the protected grey seals which are breeding even faster than the common seals. Rona is one of the three most important breeding stations of an animal which now takes more fish from the sea than the whole of the Scottish fishing fleet. Despite their very much lower numbers at the time he wrote, Darling in his pre-bureaucratic days, advocated eating them as well as using their blubber and skins for industrial purposes.

Over the spine, on the south-facing slope, we found the original settlement, close by the shore. It is more easily distinguished by the irregular rows of the rigs than by the buildings which are almost underground. The rigs are deep and, when we visited, were covered with white clover

---

26 26 *Glasgow Herald*, 4 July 1939.

indicating fertility, while the buildings have been largely submerged by vegetation. The entrances are so low and small, presumably to keep out the wind, that the inhabitants must have had to crawl in on hands and knees. Brian did so in the building which appeared to have been the chapel, but could see nothing inside as it was pitch dark.

We then wandered up to the Toa Rona, the 355-foot hill at the eastern end of the spine. A lighthouse was erected here in 1980, the third modern structure on the island after a weather station which looked like a space capsule and an ugly square hut where we stopped on the way up to the lighthouse. That turned out to be a 'research facility' for SNH and the Sea Mammal Research Unit, who visit the island once a year to count the seals. Inside it was dry and equipped with books, rough benches and lists of rules pinned to the walls. It was provisioned for overnight stops with food and even drink. We found the last of a bottle of Bunnahabhain, which Brian and I polished off, leaving a good quantity of Ardbeg in its stead. According to the visitors' book, we were the fourth boat to have called at the island that summer, and the seventh since the current volume started in October 2000. Typical of the entries was one from Rick Livingstone, on the yacht *Breezer*, who had written two months earlier, 'One of the best and most difficult islands to bag. Even better than St K!'

I wrote, 'Ian Mitchell on *Foggy Dew* for *Isles of the North*. Glé Mhath. Enjoyed the Bunnahabhain; hope you enjoy the Ardbeg.'

By the time we had inspected the lighthouse it was getting late. We climbed down the north-west slope of the Toa in a warm evening glow. We were back aboard at about 10 p.m., just before the sun set. I agreed with Brian when he said that he would like to return for a longer stay. We decided to celebrate with a dinner of pasta in pesto sauce with asparagus and a rather expensive bottle of wine which a friend had given us on Barra.

The night was almost cloudless and as quiet as anything ever is in a boat at anchor in the open sea. We decided to leave early the following morning and try to get into Stromness by evening. I duly sprang out of my bunk at 4.30 a.m. to see that there was not a breath of wind. I decided to wait for the 5.30 forecast, so made tea and sat on deck reading. The layered cloud slowly thinned to reveal a red glow on the eastern horizon. By the time the forecast came on, the sun had appeared through patchy cloud. The Met Office predicted 'Cyclonic, variable, becoming south-east 3/4'. With an unreliable motor it seemed prudent to wait for some wind, so I made another mug of tea and settled down with my book again.

The wind stayed so light that we spent the morning working on the boat, finally raising the anchor only at 1.30 p.m. by which time, I see from my log, it was blowing south-south-east 2, which though better than nothing is not a lot, especially as it was over a hundred miles into Stromness. A shallow low-pressure system had been tracking north to the west of us, so it was possible that we might get a bit more wind. But at least we had enough to sail out of the anchorage. I was reluctant to use any battery power as what little was left should be conserved in case we really needed to start the engine. Hopefully, we would have all that sorted out in Orkney.

Before Rona dipped below the horizon, the sky had cleared completely and we had a glorious afternoon's sail. The wind picked up a bit and between four o'clock and eight o'clock we covered 22 miles without a hand on the tiller. This was the first time that it felt like a real summer's day, warm, bright and, above all, different from home. We were on our travels and thoroughly enjoying it. At sundowner time, another Ardbeg Moment seemed to be indicated. We toasted our good fortune on deck before Brian went below to prepare another of his inventive dinners. I watched a flight of six gannets gliding past in line ahead. The leader would flap its wings and the others would follow instantly. The leader would stop; so would they – a very striking sight.

As evening wore on, the wind gradually died. By ten o'clock there was a slight mist on the sea ahead, just behind the rock of Sule Skerry which lies just over half way between Rona and Orkney. In the west, the sky glowed a most fantastic red – a marine shepherd would have been delighted. As the wind dropped further we decided to try the engine. Though the battery condition meter showed 50 per cent, there was not a kick. After a certain amount of cursing and contemplation, I thought we might as well try starting the thing by hand, which had always proved impossible. But it fired up first go. Amazing!

Steering for the Hoy Sound, we motored through the night on a glassy sea which never stopped reflecting a bit of light, even at 2 a.m. An hour after that I was able to shout 'Hoy ahoy!' as cliffs began looming over the horizon fine on the starboard bow. An hour or so later, we could see the mountains around Dunnett Head in Caithness, with cloud spilling over them like cold smoke. We passed a dead gannet lying spreadeagled in the water. By the time the sun had risen the sky was clear in the west, but with a light, cirrussy layer of cloud over Orkney. Better news was that a breath of wind came up from the west and pushed us along nicely at over 5 knots.

With time on our hands and a huge pillar of rock visible in front of the immense cliffs we were approaching, we thought we would divert from the direct route into Stromness and take a look at that rock, the first part of Orkney either Brian or I had ever seen: the Old Man of Hoy.

2

ORKNEY – SOUTH

HAVING NEVER SEEN PHOTOGRAPHS of the Old Man of Hoy taken from anywhere other than the cliffs behind, Brian and I were amazed at the size of it when viewed from the sea. We went as close in as we dared to with an unreliable motor and a flukey, on-shore wind. But it was worth it. The jagged sandstone pillar rises over 400 feet from a plinth of harder rock. Why has it remained standing while the rock behind was eroded? We turned to port, heading for the Sound. From the north there is a clearly discernable face about a tenth of the way down from the top. Partly due to the hook of the 'nose' and partly due to the shape of the rock above and behind which gives the impression of a feathered head-dress, the effect is of a carving of a 'Red Indian' chief bizarrely set down in monumental form on the wrong side of the Atlantic.

Almost as spectacular was the sight of a small fishing boat setting creels close inshore under St John's Head near the entrance to the Sound of Hoy. The adjacent cliffs are some of the highest in Britain, rising almost sheer over 1,000 feet, half as high again as the cliffs on the west side of Mingulay. They are smooth and vertical. In places we could see overhangs. Though about 250 people climb the Old Man of Hoy every year – it was not climbed until 1967 – all attempts to climb St John's Head have failed.

The Clyde Cruising Club's *Sailing Directions* for Orkney say that the 'the tidal streams in Hoy Sound are very strong and entry should not be attempted in bad weather or with wind against tide or on the ebb tide ... The spring rate may exceed 7 knots.' We were off the Old Man of Hoy at about 9 a.m. and high water at Stromness was less than two hours later. We would have the last of the flood tide or slack water to pass through the Sound, and a west wind as well, so conditions seemed favourable. Yet there was still definite tidal movement in the Sound and a peculiar rolling of the sea, like small waves moving towards a gently shelving beach. Calm though it was, I could quite see how the Hoy Sound 'roost' (from the Old Norse word for maelstrom) might develop in adverse conditions.

In the event we passed through uneventfully and by 10.30 were snug alongside in Stromness harbour. The first necessity was to find a marine electrician to attend to *Foggy Dew*'s charging circuit. The harbour master could not have been more helpful. Within an hour we had been introduced to Paul Chapman of J.G. Merriman & Co. who examined the whole set-up and took the alternator away to have it tested by a friend. He said he would be back at eight o'clock next morning.

Next we needed to charge the battery. The harbour master pointed to somewhere on the other side of the dock where, if we had an exceptionally long lead, we might have plugged in our charger. But we did not have such a lead. 'There's one in the back of my car,' he said, pointing to a battered red Astra van. 'Just take it. Take the car if you like. The key's in the ignition.'

'The lead'll be fine, thanks,' I said, smiling at what I took to be jokey dig at my importunity.

'No, I'm serious,' he said. 'Take the car if you need it, if you want to do some shopping. Just bring it back, that's all.'

We paid our fee of £21 which gave us fourteen days' use of all the Orkney Islands Council's harbours, which is every one except St Margaret's Hope, and set off to get clean and unthirsty. We were turned away at the Stromness Hotel, but were very cordially received at the locally owned Ferry Inn. Later on we found ourselves in Bistro 76 in Victoria Street, where we had a memorable meal of mussels and halibut before our first full night's sleep for days.

Next morning at five to eight, Paul Chapman was standing on the quayside above *Foggy Dew* with our alternator. It worked fine after his friend removed the rusty drill-bit from inside. Quietly and efficiently, Paul refitted it, replaced the negative lead to the engine, took out a redundant cut-off switch, fitted a new indicator light and switch, replaced all associated wires and clips and tested the whole arrangement. It took him three hours. Everything worked perfectly. We were so relieved that we gave him one of our precious bottles of Ardbeg for his trouble. He said he would keep it for the birth of his first child, which was expected in three weeks' time.

While I tidied the boat up and sorted my papers, Brian went back to the Ferry Inn, where he found the Stromness Ladies Hockey Club in full match gear, raising funds by waving short skirts and collecting boxes. During our days in port, Brian paid quite a few visits to that pub. I noticed that during the day he would set off in his deck shoes, taking Max Hastings's *Bomber Command*, which he was reading on board at the time. But when he went up at night, he wore black boots and took an Iain Banks novel.

Like the Hebrides, Orkney is in many ways a world unto itself. Within a couple of days of arrival, Brian remarked that the people even looked different from Scottish folk. Trying to generalise, we agreed that, first, they were on average taller and, secondly, that they were darker, though dark in the sense that Russians or Germans can be dark, not dark in the pale-skinned way that many Irish and Glaswegians are.[1] Stromness, with its narrow, winding streets, looks more like a Baltic than a Scottish town. The food in the shops and restaurants was more varied and sophisticated than is normal in rural Scotland. The Orkney ice-cream was of positively Italian quality. We were almost abroad.

Gordon Donaldson, the late Historiographer Royal, many times pointed out that while the Northern Isles are obviously *de facto* parts of Scotland, *de jure* there is less certainty. The question arises because of the different ways in which law came to the Northern Isles and to Scotland. In the eighth century, a Pictish kingdom was replaced by what became the Norse earldom of Orkney after a battle between the armies of Maelbrigte Tusk, so-called because he had a prominent tooth, and Sigurd the Mighty, so-called because he won. Though the early Vikings lived where and how they did by right of conquest, the Norwegian administration which evolved in the later Middle Ages was based on law. That law, so far as it pertained to issues of land ownership and tenure, was quite different from the feudal system which was developing in Scotland at the same time. It was also very different from the Gaelic legal system, of which we know very little but can infer a certain amount, that existed in the realms of the Lordship of the Isles in the

---

1 In his *New History of Orkney* (Edinburgh 2001), William P.L. Thomson makes the point that 'recent DNA research into the Y-chromosomes . . . suggests that a significant proportion of the Orcadian populations are likely to be Norse . . . Genetically, Orkney lies mid-way between Scotland and Ireland on the one hand, and Scandinavia on the other.' (p. 46)

Hebrides and adjacent mainland. But Norway surrendered the Hebrides to the Kingdom of Scotland by the Treaty of Perth in 1266, following the Battle of Largs in 1263. That treaty explicitly reserved Orkney and Shetland to the Norwegian Crown, which ruled those areas for another two centuries. Today it is a little remarked fact that within its present borders, Scotland once had three very different legal systems operating. Gaelic law, which was not written down, has left no trace in modern Scots law, but udal law, which was the legacy of Scandinavian rule, has left a small but locally important imprint.

The original assumption behind feudal law was the legal fiction that the Crown owns all of the kingdom and lets out land to vassals in return for obligations of service. These obligations were later commuted to money payments. These vassals might 'subinfeudate' property to inferior vassals and so on in a theoretically endless chain of obligation. All land is held of a superior and the rights of the vassal are, to a greater or lesser extent depending on individual circumstances, limited. Udal law is quite different. The basic principle is that land is held 'allodially', that is without obligations to any superior beyond payment of a generally levied land tax, known as 'scat', to the Crown. Each landholder's dominium was said to run 'from the lowest of the ebb to the highest of the hill'. He was an independent freeholder or, in modern parlance, an owner-occupier.

A second relevant aspect of udal law was the rights of inheritance by kin. Property was subdivided on the death of the owner, all children having a right to an equal part except that the sons' shares were twice that of the daughters' and that the eldest son had the right to his father's house. Later, uneconomic subdivision was avoided by a custom whereby the land passed to one descendent who made compensating money payments to the others who did not receive property.

Finally, if an udaller, as landholders under udal law are known, decided to sell property, there were certain rights of pre-emption in favour of, first, the eldest son, then other kin (in feudal law the beneficiary of the right of pre-emption is generally the feudal superior). Land sold otherwise could be compulsorily reclaimed by the vendor's relations. This system still exists in Norway, where most privately owned rural land is held on udal tenure.

In 1468 the Northern Isles were mortgaged to the Scottish Crown by Christian I, King of the then united kingdoms of Norway and Denmark, on the occasion of his daughter's marriage to King James III of Scotland. Christian could not afford the dowry of 60,000 Rhenish florins. Orkney was to be mortgaged, or impignorated, for 50,000 of those florins, and was reclaimable on full repayment. But Christian could not even afford the remaining 10,000 florins. He appears to have paid 2,000, and mortgaged Shetland for the remaining 8,000. The 58,000 florins were never paid to the King of Scots, so the islands have since then been under *de facto* Scottish and, latterly, British rule. But, Professor Donaldson argues, sovereignty cannot have been conveyed since the pledge might, in theory, have been redeemed at any time.

It is therefore reasonable to maintain that sovereignty was never formally transferred, even in pledge, let alone by complete cession . . . The link of Orkney and Shetland with Britain may resemble a marriage by habit and repute, but it is nonetheless a legal marriage. There remains, however, one point of ambiguity. Granted that British sovereignty now exists by prescription, no one else had ventured to pronounce on the date at which such sovereignty became effective *de jure*, and it may be considered to remain uncertain whether Scotland had acquired sovereignty before 1707 or if it was acquired by the UK after that date: it might therefore be asked whether Orkney and Shetland, while legally parts of the UK, are legally parts of Scotland. At the moment this question is purely academic, but in the event of Scotland becoming independent it might conceivably have to be discussed.[2]

With a Scottish parliament once again sitting in Edinburgh and one large and two small parties committed to independence, this question is no longer purely academic. Even less academic is the other question touched upon in Gordon Donaldson's paper, namely the status of udal law in the Northern Isles today. Unlike the Treaty of Perth, which expressly mentioned that the inhabitants of the Hebrides were to be thenceforth subject to the laws of Scotland, the treaties of 1468 said nothing about law. In his paper, Professor Donaldson concludes that this 'suggests that the men of Orkney and Shetland were not intended to be subject to the laws of Scotland'. (p. 26) He then cites evidence that the Scots parliament recognised the legal distinctiveness of the Northern Isles as late as 1567. It was not until 1611 that James VI, as part of his

---

2 'Sovereignty and Law in Orkney and Shetland' by Gordon Donaldson, in *Miscellany Two*, Stair Society, Edinburgh 1984, p.19.

attempt to reinforce royal authority throughout Scotland – remember that the Statutes of Iona which were intended to bring the Highlands and Hebrides 'into line' were promulgated in 1609 – formally abolished 'foreign' law in the Northern Isles. However, even that did not end udal tenure. It merely made it a part of Scots law.[3] I was curious to know what the practical effect of this situation was, so, while Brian was in the pub, bombing Dresden and Cologne, I met Colin MacKenzie, the Sheriff of Orkney and Shetland, on the steps of the Stromness Hotel. We adjourned to his car for a chat.

I asked him how often he had to deal with cases involving udal law. Speaking quietly and precisely, he said, 'In more than a decade of my commission as Sheriff and royal judge of the bounds and the administration of the law, I have never had any udal law seriously pleaded before me. I would be absolutely charmed if something came up. I would love to do it. It's good lawyers' stuff, but it just doesn't happen.'

The reason, he told me, is that the only aspect of udal law still available for litigation is rights over land where title is not evidenced by the Register of Sasines in Edinburgh, where transactions in, and burdens placed upon, land have been recorded since 1617. Udal land is held on 'use and wont and a progression of writs according to pre-1468 law'. Many people preferred the security of a recorded title, and once a title is recorded, the sheriff said, it becomes feudal. In cases where udal law is still relevant, it is sorted out to the satisfaction of all parties by the local lawyers who know the background and seem to be able to resolve all matters without recourse to Sheriff MacKenzie's Court.

Though there is very little unregistered property left, one aspect of udal law provoked an important case some years ago when, during the construction of the Flotta oil terminal in Scapa Flow, Occidental Petroleum neglected to buy the foreshore rights from the islanders

---

3 It is a general principle of international law that the legal regime of a country over which another acquires sovereignty will continue to operate until altered by the successor state. In imperial times, Britain generally abolished the laws of non-white countries it took over, but came to an accommodation with white ones. In South Africa Roman–Dutch law was allowed to continue, as was French law in Quebec. The Code Napoleon is still one of the sources of the law of the State of Louisiana, which was bought from France by the United States in 1803.

across whose land the pipeline passed. In most of Scotland the Crown owns the foreshore, but not where udal law operates. Conversion from udal to feudal tenure does not affect boundaries so the ownership of the foreshore still resides with the relevant islanders. Following normal Scottish practice, Occidental dealt with the Crown Estate which happily took rent and said nothing. When furious locals discovered what had happened and claimed their rights, the Crown Estate had to refund Occidental's rent so it could pay the islanders.

Sheriff MacKenzie is a native of Lewis and I asked him more generally about his impressions of the people of the northern isles.

'The Orcadian is hale fellow well met, friendly anyway. The Shetlander is cooler. There are very, very nice, Shetlanders, don't get me wrong. They are as friendly as you could ever want, but, by and large, if they don't know you, you are of no interest to them. They acknowledge Orcadians as fellow members of the human race and they have heard of Lewis, I'm glad to say, but they're not that keen on certain types of Scotsman. You must not be put off by them, though. Orcadians would say they require the "second touch".'

'Meaning what?'

'For instance, if you enter a shop and go, "Ahem!" and the girl continues staring at her nails instead of serving you – the Shetlanders carry that to a fine art – you will get nothing from her. If you are so sensitive about it and you say, "To hell with this, don't bother, I'll go somewhere else," you'll get no reaction. But if you just persist a wee bit, nothing at all, just ask for some help: "Sorry, my dear, I am looking for such and such, could you tell me where that I might go and buy it?" you will be absolutely astonished at the reaction. "Well, we do sell it here but you'll actually get much better value down the road. Come and I will show you where it is." They could not be more helpful. But if you don't make the first approach to them they don't care whether you live or die. The Western Islesman tends to wear his heart on his sleeve. The Shetlander doesn't wear his heart on his sleeve. But if you make the right contact with him he will give you his heart.'

If udal law does not reach the courts, it is still influential insofar as it gives backing to a popular myth about it, namely that public rights exist in private places. Trout fishing on the lochs in Orkney has always been free, for example, and the islands have a long tradition of tolerating access. Both seem to derive from general Nordic egalitarianism rather than any rights enforceable in the Scottish courts. But they are meaning-ful freedoms, nonetheless.

I had been alerted to these issues before departure by John Hinckley, an immigrant to Orkney from Birmingham who married an islander and is now Treasurer of the Orkney Sailing Club. Helping me plan my trip he gave me an outsider's view of the situation. Orcadians, he said, are 'very independent-minded and very cosmopolitan. They are very laid back, but when people like the Royal Society for the Protection of Birds, which you may know is the largest landowner in Orkney, takes liberties they just say, "Oh no, you don't; clear off." And they do. They have to. When I first came here ten years ago, the local policeman had to come round to inspect my shotguns. I said, "This is a bit of fuss, isn't it? How many people in Orkney shoot?" He said, "There are more guns than people in Orkney." We've got more birds than you could shake a stick at, yet we've got a very active shooting fraternity. SNH know that if the Orcadians want to go and shoot something, they'll just go and do it, so they say, "Please don't shoot the birds on the important lochs." So nobody does. There's just so many wild places. If the geese were on a farmers' land, he wouldn't have any hesitation, he'd just go and blow them away. The RSPB and SNH don't have anything like as much power here as they do in some other places, and I think it is because the local populations say this is ours, not yours. You're here because we allow you to be here.'

'You mean no tradition of feudal inferiority?' I asked.

'Something like that. I'm sure the RSPB would like to have more clout, but they don't get away with it. Orkney's very much like that. If you started to say, "You can't walk here," there'd be a riot. "What do you mean we can't walk here? We can go anywhere we like, thank you very much." Just a mile from where I am sitting we have a wind-farm. There are three huge turbines there at the moment, and the RSPB were complaining recently that they didn't want another one put up and they were just told, no, I'm sorry we're putting it up. They said the red-throated divers will be flying into the wires and all that sort of stuff and I'm afraid they just lost. People are trying to be sympathetic, but practicality comes to the fore here. If the birds can't see the wires, that's tough. People don't destroy the birds unnecessarily. One of the things I like about Orkney is that it is so laid back. There's very little exertion of rules and regulations. It's very much live and let live. I guess there's room for everybody.'

One of the most immediately obvious features of Stromness is the extent to which local tourism is geared to the presence of Scapa Flow. Though interesting because of its having been the main British naval base in both world wars, it appears that it is the sunken German High Seas Fleet which brings most of the tourists in, mainly to dive the wrecks which are still lying on the sea bed. I was keen to visit Hoy, partly due to the fact that there is a naval museum there, and also to see Scapa Flow. Before leaving Stromness I also wanted to get a copy of the Management Plan for the RSPB Reserve which occupies much of the west of Hoy, around the Old Man, plus a couple of others which might help me understand the approach of the largest landowner in the islands.

This status was discussed by Lord Grimond who, as Jo Grimond MP, had represented Orkney and Shetland in the House of Commons from 1950–83. Twelve years ago, during the House of Lords debate on the Bill which brought SNH into being, he said:

> There are many sectional interests with impeccable intentions which bring about undesirable results. There is the Royal Society for the Protection of Birds, which is now the largest landowner in Orkney. I very much doubt whether it is a good thing that such an absentee landlord, run by bureaucrats, should own such a large area of Orkney.[4]

I was forced to go and meet one of these bureaucrats because the RSPB headquarters in Edinburgh told me before leaving Islay that, though the plans are public documents, I would have to lodge £100 to cover copying costs of any I wanted to see. Apart from a charge per sheet, staff time would be billed at £25 per hour for the copying.[5] The only alternatives offered were the Stromness public library, which turned out not to have all the plans I wanted, or a visit to the Orkney office.

---

4 *Hansard*, 19 November 1990, col. 585
5 Letter from Stuart Housden to the author, 7 May 2002. After asking for the plans for thirteen reserves, Housden suggested that I 'send a cheque for £100 in advance made payable to the RSPB. Once this is exhausted we can inform you and you decide what more you require.' This approach contrasts with that of SNH, from whom I requested citations for the 137 designated sites on the route I planned to take, plus Management Plans for six national Nature Reserves. Everything available was sent to me without demur and free of charge.

Inside the little cottage on Stromness's main street which is the RSPB's local headquarters, I was received by the Orkney manager, Eric Meek, a stocky, red-faced man from Newcastle, who lists amongst his hobbies 'drinking real ale'. He was closeted with his deputy, Keith Fairclough, a taller man from Liverpool who describes himself in *Who's Who in Ornithology* as 'fortyish but still sportyish'. This being lunchtime, Meek said he was free until 2 p.m., when he had to 'go into another meeting'. Why had I come here, Meek wanted to know? I said because the Scotland Director had recommended it. With ill-concealed reluctance, Meek produced the plans and asked how many sheets I wanted copied. After a thorough inspection, I said about 150. When he sighed and shook his head, I said I was quite happy to do the copying myself seeing he seemed so busy. I spent the next 45 minutes at the machine while Meek stood in the same room, apparently working, though as far as I could see actually just keeping an eye on me.

Since we were alone, it would have been awkward not to have at least ventured conversation. The least controversial thing I could think of to ask was about the changes he has noticed in his work during the twenty years he had been on Orkney. All Meek would say was that when he first came here he was a one-man band, whereas now the RSPB has thirteen reserves 'and the inevitable bureaucracy that goes with that and the staff that goes with that'. That staff is 'seven FTE jobs' – FTE meaning Full Time Equivalent.

'So you have to spend most of your time in meetings these days rather than out in the fresh air?' I asked.

He nodded gloomily.

'Which do you prefer,' I went on, 'the dirty fingernails or the sweaty armpits?'

'That's irrelevant,' he said unblinkingly. 'I'm just proud of what we've been able to do here over the years. If that means a bit more bureaucracy then that's the price we have to pay.'

On a brilliantly clear morning, we cast off from Stromness pier, intending to make a circuit of Scapa Flow, taking in the museum at Lyness and finishing on Hoy by evening. There were now three of us as my brother, Gordon, had joined the trip for a few days.

Within five minutes, it was clear that while the engine had performed flawlessly alongside, when in gear and under load, it did not. The charging circuit worked fine so long as the revs were kept up, but when they were reduced to engage gear, it flicked off and would not flick on again while in gear as the revs never reached the required level. So once again we were not charging. Not only that, the surging was much worse – so much so that on a couple of occasions the engine died completely. We had to restart it using the hand crank. This was no way to put to sea. I decided to carry on for the day, and maybe still get round to Kirkwall the following afternoon, where we could call Paul Chapman out again.

There is nothing to be seen in Scapa Flow itself other than a wide expanse of water, plus a few stationary boats above the German wrecks. There are two British wrecks in the Flow. The best known is that of the battleship *Royal Oak*, which was sunk at anchor by *U-47*, commanded by Günther Prien, on 14 October 1939. It was one of the most audacious German raids of the war. Prien took his boat into the Flow on the surface, just after midnight, navigating in the faint glow of the northern lights past the blockships which had been sunk in some of the narrower channels. At one point his vessel was caught in the glow of headlamps. The driver reported the sighting to the authorities, but they did not believe an incursion possible. Hit amidships by three torpedoes, the *Royal Oak* went down in thirteen minutes, taking 833 sailors with it, from a ship's complement of 1,400. Prien sailed out unobserved scraping, he said, barnacles from the hull of the blockship, so tight was the channel.

Less well known, but involving more fatalities was the destruction of HMS *Vanguard* off Flotta in quite different circumstances, a war before. On a still July evening in 1917, shortly after 11 p.m., with the last glow of the setting sun still in the sky, a party of officers were preparing to sing the National Anthem at the end of a night out on the fleet cinema ship, *Gourko*. A naval artificer on shore glanced towards the fleet resting quietly at anchor and, in his words, saw 'one of the ships appear to lose its true outline and quiver'. It then appeared to lift up in the middle and from this point there rose a vast column of orange-brown and slate-grey smoke. This immediately burst into a flickering pillar of fire which cast a crimson glow over the whole anchorage. The pillar of fire mushroomed out and in its light debris could be seen travelling upwards. This spectacle lasted four or five more seconds, then the silence was shattered by the sound of a terrific explosion. The ship was about five miles distant from me, but the shock wave, which took about eleven seconds to reach me, was heavy enough to momentarily stop my breath.'[6]

The smoke from the explosion covered much of the Flow. By the time it cleared there was no sign of the great ship. There were only two survivors from the nearly thousand men aboard, not surprisingly in view of the fact that the force of the explosion was such that it hurled one of the battleship's gun-turrets, weighing several hundred tons, a mile through the air. So suddenly did the ship blow up that many of the men asleep below were subsequently seen by divers investigating the wreck to be lying in their hammocks 'just as if nothing had happened'.

The reasons for Scapa Flow's popularity with divers is the German High Seas Fleet, created to challenge the Royal Navy before the First World War, which was scuttled there. It fought the British Grand Fleet, based on Scapa, in the only major naval engagement of the war, the battle of Jutland on 1 June 1916. The Germans inflicted greater losses on the British than they themselves suffered. But it was the German fleet which abandoned the field of battle. For the rest of the war the British sailed the North Sea at will while the Germans stayed in port.

At the time of the Armistice, in November 1918, the Allies ordered seventy-four German warships to be interned in Scapa Flow pending signature of the peace treaty. Rust-streaked, neglected and belching clouds of black smoke from the poor-quality Polish coal which the British navy's blockade had forced them to burn, the Germans sailed into the Flow in the middle of winter. It was a bleak scene, made bleaker for the skeleton crews aboard by the fact that the High Seas Fleet had been designed for forays against the Grand Fleet and so did not have the sort of accommodation which a blue water navy like the British, equipped for long voyages, provided. The Germans were forbidden from going ashore; indeed they were not allowed to visit each other's ships. British personnel were ordered not to shake hands with them. Official hostility compounded the impression of bleakness, poverty and isolation which Scapa Flow in winter must have made on them. One German

---

6 Leading Mechanic Percy Ingleby, quoted in *Scapa Flow*, Malcolm Brown and Patricia Meehan, London 2002, p. 109. The cause was almost certainly unstable ammunition, but rumours of sabotage quickly began to circulate among the lower-deck. The Navy did nothing to check them as it felt it better for Fleet morale to believe in enemies within than that ships could be death-traps for their crews while lying peacefully at anchor.

sailor commented, 'The houses of the natives are about as high as a good German dog kennel.' Another said of the 'god-forsaken' place, 'If the English have stood this for four years they deserve to have won the war.'

Seven months later, on a day as blue and bright as we were enjoying, a strange sight could be seen: across the otherwise empty Flow – the British ships guarding the Germans were at sea that day for torpedo practice – Imperial German Ensigns were flying for the first time since the British had ordered them to be struck on 21 November 1918. The Germans were also seen to be launching boats, another forbidden act. Finally, and most mysteriously of all, the ships appeared to be settling in the water. 'Some wobbled, some rolled over on their sides, many sank stern or bows first, many were enveloped in a cloud of steam,' wrote an eyewitness.

By the time the British battle fleet returned, at tea-time that day, the sparkling blue waters of the Flow were almost empty but for debris floating on the surface, amidst blue oil slicks, and the masts of some of the ships which had sunk in shallow water. The British authorities were enraged, accusing the Germans of a breach of 'honour'. A not untypical press comment about this 'dastardly trick' was to ask, 'Who can analyse the German mentality? It is a thing apart; and savours much of the mentality of brute creation.'[7]

In the longer term, though, brute creation was kind to Orkney, providing 200 jobs for the next twenty years while Metal Industries Ltd., a commercial salvage operator, lifted most of the wrecks from the seabed. They were either cut up for scrap on the spot, or towed to other ports – mainly Rosyth – where they were converted into a total of 327,000 tons of high-quality steel, much of which was sold back to Germany where it was used in the Nazi re-armament programme. Seven of the larger ships were left on the sea bed where depth made salvage uneconomic. Today they provide one of the main tourist attractions in Orkney. We saw three boats out while we crossed over to St Margaret's Hope on South Ronaldsay, diagonally opposite Stromness.

We lunched alongside the pier in the bay where, in 1263, Haakon Haakonsson, King of Norway, had assembled a fleet of 120 longships for the expedition to reassert control over the Hebrides which ended

7 Quoted in *This Great Harbour: Scapa Flow*, W.S. Hewison, Kirkwall 2000, p. 150.

unsuccessfully at the Battle of Largs. Until the Grand Fleet arrived in 1914, this was the largest naval force ever to have sailed into Scapa Flow. We arrived at Lyness mid-afternoon, putting into the very well-constructed small harbour where the fleet tenders used to be based. The museum was a disappointment. The display conveyed little of the drama, poetry or tragedy of war, in contrast to the excellent museum in Stromness, which has quite a large display of wartime artifacts. Not only that, it closed so early we hardly had time to look around.

We were soon at sea again, heading for the pier at Moness, near the RSPB reserve. Under lowering skies we motored unevenly on a dead calm sea. The clouds came down over the treeless, heather-covered hills of Hoy, much the highest on Orkney. Nothing appeared to move on land or sea. It was not hard to imagine just how bleak this area must have looked to the servicemen marooned here for long periods of wartime service. The population of Orkney was about 25,000 in 1914. By 1916 it was 125,000. The proportion was similar in the Second World War. There was little for the new arrivals to amuse themselves with amongst the low, bare hills and low, dog house-like dwellings. Concerts at Lyness and in Kirkwall helped, but even they lacked appeal, at least if the author of 'Bloody Orkney', Captain Hamish Blair, is to be believed.

> This bloody town's a bloody cuss –
> No bloody trains, no bloody bus,
> And no one cares for bloody us –
> In bloody Orkney ...
>
> Everything's so bloody dear,
> A bloody bob for bloody beer,
> And is it good? – no bloody fear,
> In bloody Orkney
>
> The bloody 'flicks' are bloody old,
> The bloody seats are bloody cold;
> You can't get in for bloody gold
> In bloody Orkney
>
> The bloody dances make you smile,
> The bloody band is bloody vile,

It only cramps your bloody style,
In bloody Orkney

No bloody sport, no bloody games,
No bloody fun, the bloody dames
Won't even give their bloody names
In bloody Orkney

Best bloody place is bloody bed,
With bloody ice on bloody head;
You might as well be bloody dead,
In bloody Orkney

Almost everyone who has written anything about Orkney has quoted this poem, or parts of it. Rather nicely, W.S. Hewison, the Orcadian who has written the most comprehensive book about Scapa Flow, *This Great Harbour*, adds the following footnote:

Oddly enough in spite of this diatribe, quite a few of these probably homesick troops risked 'the bloody clouds and bloody rains' after the war to come back for holidays, some of them staying for good. And a few went even further, turning the other cheek to those 'bloody dames' who wouldn't 'give their bloody names' by marrying them and giving them new names. (Appendix II)

One of those who served in Orkney during the Second World War and who came back, if not to live, but to buy most of the island of Hoy and spend his summers there, was a Norfolk farmer called Malcolm Stewart. In 1973 he handed his estate over to the Hoy Trust, chaired by Laura Grimond, the wife of the then sitting MP. The aim was to try to halt the population decline. Ten years later the Trust made the rather odd decision to sell nearly half of its holding to the RSPB – odd because it is hard to see how population regeneration might be assisted by trans-ferring ownership to a body whose slogan was 'Birds come first'. I was intrigued to know how the experiment had fared.

We had difficulty tying up at Moness as the tidal range is nearly 10 feet and the rocks at the base of the pier seemed uncomfortably close to the surface. To be sure of the exact depth, I sounded manually. We would have no more than 2 feet to spare at low water. The pier is a small but recently constructed concrete structure which is used by the ferry which plies out of Stromness, calling at the island of Graemsay opposite. By the time we were all snug, the dripping mist had solidified into a thin drizzle. We snacked quickly down below before I was collected by a man called Jack Rendall, who had agreed to show me around the area of the reserve. There is a pub on the island, but it is open only on Wednesdays and Fridays, so Gordon and Brian settled down to tackle the remains of a very foul-looking bottle of gin which had been left on board.

Jack is more than just a native of Hoy; his family have lived on the island for as long as records go back. He now owns land in the township of Rackwick which nestles in a lovely glen, above an unforgiving look-ing bay, on the west side of the island. In 1973 Malcolm Stewart gave the few remaining tenanted crofts to the crofters. The grand old man of Orkney letters, George Mackay Brown, wrote at the time, 'It is wonder-ful that something is going to be done at last for Hoy. Mr Stewart's foresight and generosity will be remembered among the truly altruistic deeds that happen from time to time in the north.'[8] At that time, Jack was the only resident of Rackwick, though Peter (now Sir Peter) Maxwell Davies, the famous Mancunian composer, had moved to a small house high above the village, overlooking the Atlantic, in 1971. Though miles from the nearest settlement, Davies was preoccupied with the role of the artist 'in society'. He set some of Mackay Brown's poems to music and, in 1977, inaugurated the now famous St Magnus Festival in Kirkwall.

Jack told me that there had been 150 people living in this valley in the 1880s. 'Many of them left to get jobs,' he said. 'There are very few jobs on this island now, especially for young people. Some of them went to sea. There was never more than ten at the school after my mother started teaching there, and that was a long time ago. We did not get electricity until 1980. We had our own generators up until then. It was just all oil lamps in the war. Later on we had a 12-volt generator, but it was so weak that if you wanted to do the ironing you had to switch the fire off.'

I asked if the naval base helped with the employment problem.

'A lot of folk got work at Lyness,' he said. 'But then they closed it down. It was move to a job in Rosyth or go. That helped depopulate the island. A few have come back, but not many. Some of the incomers are

8 *Letters from Hamnavoe*, George Mackay Brown, London 2002, p. 138.

Scots, but mostly English. Property is so much cheaper here than it is down south. They can afford to buy an old croft and do it up. A few have good jobs in Kirkwall and they commute every day on the ferry.'

Jack told me that he was ten years old before he visited the south end of the island, though he used to walk the four miles from Rackwick over to Moness on the old track to go to church. The new road was built to open up the peat banks in the 1930s. On the way back, Jack pointed out where the eagles used to live.

'The whole hill went on fire,' Jack explained, 'in 1984, a year after the RSPB bought the ground. A pair of golden eagles nested here and they were very keen to protect them. Very few people knew where the actual nest was. Perhaps it was better not knowing. If anybody asked me, I said I didn't know. Occasionally, you saw them. I mind once – there was a very thin mist that night – coming round a corner and there were the eagles sitting on the top of the Hydro poles. That's the closest I have ever been to them. Then all that hill went on fire. There was only one seen the year after and they have never made a nest there since.'

After Jack dropped me back at the pier, I walked up to see a farmer who, I had been told, had more experience of the RSPB's operations on Hoy than most. Living on ground his family has occupied for five generations, Terry Thompson is Chairman of the Hoy Partnership which is a cross-community group, including the RSPB, SNH and the Hoy Trust, whose remit is development of the island.

Looking at the Ordnance Survey map, I was struck by the names of the natural features around north Hoy: Howes of Quoyawa, Santoo Head, Candle of the Sneuk, Genie Fea, Moi Fea, Nose of the Bring, Glifters of Lyrawa, Tuaks of the Boy, Iron Geo, Geo of the Lame, The Witter, Black Nev, Rinni Gill, Withi Gill, Too of the Head, Hendry's Holes. The RSPB owns 10,000 acres of this exotic environment. The Management Plan calls it a 'wilderness area' with 'magnificent landscape features [which] convey an aesthetic appreciation of natural unspoilt wilderness'.[9]

The most frequently mentioned priority in the RSPB's plan is the necessity for successful co-existence with the local community: 'It is

---

9 *Hoy RSPB Reserve Management Plan* T. Prescott and J. Plowman, Sandy 1998, p. 4. A striking point about the reserve is the lack of interesting wildlife. The list of birds is unremarkable and the full complement of mammals is as follows: otter, mountain hare, pygmy shrew, wood mouse, hedgehog, rabbit, brown rat and feral cat. (p. 25)

essential for the smooth running of the reserve and the implementation of this Management Plan that the Warden integrates his/herself [*sic*] into the fragile and isolated community on Hoy.' (p. 4) 'Main management Prescriptions and Projects . . . (p. 9) 'Maintain good PR with the local community.' (p. 6) 'Main Conservation Management Achieved . . . Objective 7: Good PR with the local community' (p. 31) 'Future Wardening: It is essential for the protection of the site that the warden and the RSPB are respected by and integrate with the local community.' (p. 40) 'Main Factors Influencing the Management of the Site: Internal: The requirement of the staff to be aware of the problems associated with living and working with small rural communities in remote locations . . . External: Maintenance of good PR with the local community and their representatives' (p. 41) 'Operational Objective 5.11, Project ML30/01 Liaise and Integrate with the Local Community: Excellent PR and goodwill with the local community is paramount . . . Be approachable and integrate with the community by becoming part of it by participation and gaining respect . . . Primarily maintain and enhance the excellent PR and goodwill that has existed between the RSPB staff on Hoy and the Local community.' (p. 63).

Sitting in his warm and spacious kitchen, drinking a pint of home-brewed ale the strength and colour of sherry, I asked Terry whether he thought that the RSPB had achieved its aims as far as 'excellent PR and goodwill' is concerned.

'When they get the job here,' he said, 'it seems that they are told not to mix with the locals. When we get a new warden here I say, "Come in for a coffee, drop in." He says "Oh yes, we'll come in." They never do, none of them. They do not come and visit. There was one, he's the second in charge in Orkney now, Keith Fairclough, if you met him socially he was all right. He was in our darts team, played pool, good craic in the pub. But mention birds and the RSPB and you're cut off instantly. No, they certainly don't communicate with people.'

'How do the rest of the people on Orkney view them?' I asked.

'Well, I have never heard anyone boosting the RSPB other than themselves. We try to get on with them because they are here. We are stuck with them. Even people on the Hoy Trust, who sold them the property, say that they should never have sold it, rather kept it under Orkney control. But it was too late and that was it. I don't honestly see any benefit to the place whatsoever. None.'

'Not even through "green tourism"?'

'We do get the green-type tourist people who come here. I drive a seventeen-seater bus and I check the people coming off the ferry and when I see the hiking boots and the green wellies, I don't look for a bus-fare because the green tourists want to walk. They don't want to spend any money, just walk about looking. The ranger takes them on guided tours and off they go. It's nobody's fault, but they are kill-joys. They bring their own flasks of tea and their own back-packs. They don't stay in bed and breakfast, or drink in the pub. Green tourism doesn't bring in any money. Locally we don't benefit at all.'

The Management Plan gives an idea of the sort of welcome awaiting anyone who engages in non-green tourism, or 'unsympathetic visitor recreational activities' as the RSPB puts it: 'One new phenomena [*sic*] was of a parascender "flying" over the lower slopes of Ward Hill. He subsequently had a bad fall denting his pride, breaking his leg and deter-ring himself and hopefully others.'[10]

By contrast, the only activity that is written about with enthusiasm in the plan is 'the experience and rush of adrenalin when being dive-bombed by bonxies' (p. 38). I asked Terry about these controversial birds.

'We used to have several marsh harriers, sparrow hawks, owls – there were a lot of owls – but they have all gone. There were ground-nesting birds that have gone. The only thing that we have in abundance is the great skua which the RSPB are doing their damnedest to save. But they kill all other bird life. They even go for black-backs, even though the bonxie is smaller. They kill calves. If your cow is calving in the field, they go straight down. The first thing is they bite the soft feet and the calf cannot stand up. Then, if the head comes out with the tongue hanging out, they bite the tongue and take the eyes. It is the same with lambs. They take the tongue and maybe the eyes so the lamb can't feed and so it dies. When it dies, they come back and eat the carrion. Very clever, but not much good to the farmer. Every time the RSPB are talking to a farmer they're told "We'll shoot any bonxie that gets in range, no matter what you say." '

'How do they react to that?'

'I'll tell you,' Terry said after a pause to scratch his beard and take a long draught of his ale. 'I was at an RSPB meeting one day. A lot of

_____
10 *Ibid.*, p. 29.

officials up from England, sitting around the table and this guy – I won't tell you his name, but he's a farmer from the mainland – comes in and says, "Ah! I have just killed about 5,000 black-backs this morning." And they all laughed, thinking he was winding them up. And he said, "You think I am joking? I killed 5,000 black-backs at least." "How could you possibly kill 5,000 black-backs?" He waved his walking stick. "Since 5 o'clock this morning I have been poking every egg I found in every nest in the hill." There was just a hushed silence. And sure enough, no chicks. He had broken every egg. They didn't say a word. You could have cut the air with a knife. They were totally, totally speechless. And so he said, "What are you going to do?" They never said a word, they just changed the subject and carried on the meeting as if he had never come in.'

'But they're not so good themselves at looking after the birds, if Jack Rendall is right about the eagle.'

'He is right. When they came here first, twenty-seven years ago or so, we had seven different types of birds of prey, including the golden eagle and buzzards. All sorts, you would see them everywhere. After a couple of years of the RSPB being here, we found these birds dead and Eric Meek said, "I don't think it very funny you farmers in Hoy poisoning all these birds of prey." I said, "We are not poisoning birds of prey." "Oh, you must be poisoning the birds of prey and I don't know what your reason is." I said, "Eric, if we wanted to poison the birds of prey, why did we start it now? Why didn't we do it thirty years ago?" I said to Keith Fairclough, "It is no wonder that the eagles have gone. You are always trying to ring the chicks. You are always pestering them. You trap the birds and ring them." I said, "The bird doesn't say, 'It's all right, I won't be frightened because that's an RSPB person.'" To them you are a human being and you're a predator. No matter what you do if you keep going into their area on a regular basis, they are going to take off. I said, "Why do you always take dogs with you? You have always got dogs. No ordinary farmer ever takes dogs when he goes to his peats. Dogs are left at home. But you guys take the dogs into the hill. Why do you do that?" "Oh, it's to raise birds," he said. I said, "But you are just harassing the birds." They don't understand that and they don't accept it but that is precisely what they are doing with their dogs and their mist nets and all the ringing. They are terrorising the wild life.'

'Just thinking about the Hoy Partnership,' I said, 'and its aim of trying to regenerate Hoy, does the RSPB presence help with that?'

'An awful lot of people want to come and live here, but the RSPB are against all that. We know these hills. We don't class it as wilderness. Wilderness is somewhere where there is nothing. This is full of life, and it would be full of visitors in the summer if the RSPB did its job properly.'

'In what sense?'

'Let people enjoy themselves. The RSPB are seriously officious. Boy, do they have rules and regulations! And they wonder why people make fools of them.'

'One thing I noticed was that, when I went into the office to get this Management Plan, I met six people and they were all English. Why is that?'

'I think the Orkney people are deliberately excluding themselves because it is the RSPB,' Terry said.

'Why?'

'Because it is the RSPB and all that implies. You don't get local people. They only employ a warden for six months of the year. I thought that'd be a nice sideline for me. I know as much about birds and tourists as they do. So I spoke to Eric Meek. He says we have to get someone with qualifications, you know, a bit of paper. I said, "I've got bits of paper." He says, "But not in countryside management." I said to the guy who got the job, "You must know about birds?" ' He said that he hadn't got a clue about birds. "I don't know one bird from another. I just applied for a job and got it." Because he was an incomer, they gave him a job. That's their policy as far as I can see. The RSPB gets so much money in from people – wills, estates, wifey's dowries and things – and they have to spend it so they employ all these people and give them wages. They are no good to themselves, the community or anything else.'

One of the 'operational objectives' in the Management Plan shed some light on why the RSPB preferred outsiders, and possibly also why their attempt to integrate into the local community is less than wholly successful. 'Patrol the reserve and the whole of the Hoy SSSI regularly. Document any breaches of SSSI PDOs and inform SNH' (p. 48). An SSSI is a Site of Special Scientific Interest, and a PDO is a Potentially Damaging Operation which, on an SSSI, may not be undertaken without informing SNH. Each landowner who has an SSSI on his ground is served with a PDO list by SNH. As the Hoy SSSI is considerably larger than the RSPB reserve, this means that RSPB staff are officially instructed to walk over other people's ground to see if the landowner is breaking any rules which the government has imposed – hardly a recipe for cordial relations with hard-pressed farming neighbours on a small island.

Although it was not much more than a mile back to the boat, Terry insisted on giving me a lift in the bus which he uses to take visitors around the island. Down at the pier, I invited him to come aboard for a wee Ardbeg. We had an enjoyable hour, with Brian and Gordon in high spirits having polished off the gin between them. Apart from asking about the engine – Terry was as mystified as we were, and suggested new filters – I inquired about sailing out of the Hoy Sound by going from here round to the west of Graemsay rather than taking the much longer route round to the east. I had noticed on the tourist map that the ferry does a full circuit of the island. But the chart says that the Burra Sound, between Hoy and Graemsay, is blocked with wrecks, the remains of the blockships sunk during both World Wars. Could we Günther Prien it?

The largest of all the ships sunk round Scapa Flow, the 9,000-tonne *Inverlane*, still blocks part of Burra Sound. The remains of five other blockships still lie in the Sound. During the war they were connected by a thick hawser, anchored at one end on Graemsay and at the other on Hoy to reinforce the barrier. That was dismantled in 1945, and the wrecks blown up by the army in 1962. Nonetheless, substantial parts of these ships still litter the sea bed, with potentially disastrous consequences for the incautious mariner.

Terry told us that part of the *Inverlane*'s superstructure was above the water until just a year or two back, when it was finally demolished in a storm. Now it is visible only at low water. He also said that the best thing would be to ask the ferry skipper for directions as there is a deep channel, but it is very narrow. The Admiralty's *North Coast of Scotland Pilot* advises that passage through the Burra Sound 'should not be attempted without very good local knowledge'. Terry told us the ferry comes in at 8.10 in the morning. We should meet it and ask the Captain, Stevie Mowatt, for advice.

Next morning was still and bright though lightly overcast. A silvery glow shone through the thin cloud, like exceptionally intense moonlight. The rain had washed away and the air had the feel of warm weather to come. The midges were out. I watched the MV *Graemsay* steam straight through the supposedly blocked channel. Though small, it looked heavily enough built that it must have a draught at least as much as *Foggy Dew*'s 6 feet.

Like most Orcadians we met, Captain Mowatt turned out to be very helpful. He said that if we were careful we could get through, adding rather surprisingly that we should only attempt the passage at *low* water. The reason for this was that due to the way the wreck was disintegrating, there is actually quite a deep passage between it and the rocks on the Graemsay side, though that channel is very narrow. He had himself attached a buoy marking the south-westerly limit of the clear water to the most north-easterly part of the remaining superstructure of the wreck. Because the space is so tight, the rope on the buoy has to be short or swirling tides could give a misleading position, with potentially disastrous consequences. But the tidal range in Orkney is so wide that a buoy on a short rope will only be above water at the lower extremity of the tide. Hence the instruction to attempt the passage only at low water, when the buoy can be seen.

Captain Mowatt told me that we should leave the buoy no more than the beam of his boat – 20 feet, at the most – to port or we would risk running on to the reefs on the Graemsay side. The only difficulty would be to know the exact time of slack water as the tide in the Burra Sound runs at up to 7 knots. The tides around Orkney are amongst the strongest in the British Isles. Slack water is therefore very brief. We did not want to be too late as we might not be able to push against the force of the flood. If we were too early, we would catch the equal force of the ebb and be cascaded through so fast that, particularly with an engine not giving full power, we might not have enough manoeuvrability to avoid either the wreck or the rocks if our initial angle of approach were not perfect. We might not even see the buoy at all, which could be catastrophic.

It was therefore with a certain apprehension that we cast off from the pier at 9.20, having calculated low water to be about 9.30 and estimated the distance to the wreck would require about 10 minutes' motoring. The engine started first time and seemed to be surging much less than the day before. Captain Mowatt had said, 'Just look out for a dirty, flat-topped buoy with a lifting ring on top.' He said we should have no trouble seeing it, even though only 6 inches would be visible above the water at the bottom of the tide.

With Brian on the helm, I stood on the boom at the gooseneck with the binoculars, conning. Though my head was 12 feet above the surface of the sea, I could see nothing except a very sinister-looking part of the wreckage sticking a foot or two above the water in mid-channel. At least that would give us the distance. But the buoy was nowhere to be seen. It seemed better to throttle right back and put Brian on the bow. But after a minute of that, I decided that, as the tide was still flowing strongly and we needed speed for manoeuvrability, we should put the throttle down.

I soon realised that we should have left 10 or 15 minutes later because we were travelling far too fast – almost too fast to turn round and retreat, had we wanted to. We were committed. The tide was still running at 3 or 4 knots, judging by the vortex around the buoy when we actually passed it. At that moment, *Foggy Dew* was at an angle of about 20 degrees to the direction of travel, so hard had I been trying, on absolutely full throttle, to make another few yards off the wreck in the 15 seconds or so which elapsed between spotting the buoy – with only 3 inches visible – and shooting past it at 8 knots or so: a most uncomfortable experience.

Once beyond the buoy we were in the clear. So great was the relief that we celebrated by tearing all our old bread into short strips and throwing it to the bonxies which were swooping and diving about the boat – sharing the gift of life, I suppose. When the bread was finished, Brian tried a couple of clothes pegs – a gift of civilization – which they fought over just as ferociously.

Outside there was a breath of wind, so we raised the mainsail. After an hour or so we cut the motor and were able to make 2½ knots in a westerly 2/3. The barometer was standing at 1053, which is very high. It had been around 1020 when we left Islay and had stayed steady until we got to Barra, when it moved up to 1030 or so for a while, then up closer to 1040 as we sailed to Stornoway. It went back down to around 1030 while we were on Rona, but had climbed back up to 1036 by the time we berthed in Stromness. Now it had shot up even further. Clearly we were going to have good weather ahead – at least 'good' if you like hazy sunshine and have plenty of diesel on board. In other circumstances, I would have preferred a bit of a breeze, but with the boat in the chaotic condition it was, perhaps high pressure and calm seas were best.

Three hours later we were off Marwick head where, in a violent summer storm on 5 June 1916, just four days after Jutland, HMS *Hampshire* was torpedoed while carrying the British War Minister, Lord Kitchener, to Russia. Horatio Herbert Kitchener is best remembered for his finger-pointing recruitment poster captioned: 'Your country needs you'. He was a tall, cold-eyed, brutal and morbidly ambitious man who never married. His hobbies included interior decoration, flower-arranging and porcelain collectin – or stealing, if the owner of the pieces he coveted did not hand them over willingly. His father had been a vicious martinet who, while living in Ireland shortly after the famine, would horse-whip tenants during evictions, then set fire to their houses. He was unpopular even with the Anglo-Irish gentry. Once he was badly beaten up by a neighbouring landowner at the Tralee races. He was also a didactic hypochondriac who thought blankets so unhealthy that he slept under sown-together sheets of newspaper.

The younger Kitchener grew up equally odd and inhumane. He made his name as the savagely efficient Commander-in-Chief of Imperial forces in the second half of the Boer War, where his indifference to civilian casualties resulted in tens of thousands of Boer women and children dying in 'protective' British captivity. Their descendants consider this to have been an attempt at genocide. That is probably unfair. Kitchener did not want Boers killed; he simply did not care if they lived or died so long as British war aims were achieved. Small nations did not count. After the war, a grateful country gave him a viscountcy and £50,000 (perhaps £10 million today). He chose for his coat of arms a camel, presumably to symbolise his earlier slaughter of the Dervishes at Omdurman in 1898, and a blue wildebeest. The strapline was not some affected Latin motto, but a single English word: 'Thorough'.

Kitchener was by far the most popular military figure in Edwardian Britain, which was one of the reasons why, at the beginning of the First World War, he was taken into government. His greatest achievement was partly due to this popularity: recruiting 3 million men by voluntary enlistment before conscription was introduced in May 1916. But the Dardanelles fiasco and the shell crisis on the Western Front were both felt to be partly his fault and the war cabinet started to circumscribe his authority. He arrived at Scapa Flow on 5 June 1916 a star in eclipse, but also one in a hurry. Apart from a natural impatience, Kitchener thought that if he stayed away from the centre of power too long he might not have a job to go back to.

He had travelled from London on the night train to Thurso and had been ferried over to Scapa in the morning. He was determined to leave that afternoon. He lunched with Admiral Sir John Jellicoe on his flagship the *Iron Duke* which had, just four days earlier, led the Grand Fleet into action at Jutland. But a storm had blown up that morning. It threw into question the route out of Scapa Flow which Kitchener might take on the cruiser, *Hampshire*, which had been assigned to convey him to Archangel, escorted initially by two small destroyers.

Initially, the storm came from the north-east so Jellicoe decided that his important guest, who hated cold water and rough seas, should sail west round Orkney rather than by the easterly route, which was the normal route and therefore continually swept for mines. But, to everyone's surprise, the wind backed to north-west during the afternoon. We now know that a very deep depression must have passed from west to east to the south of Orkney for the wind to have shifted in the way that it did. But meteorology was much more primitive then than it is today.[11] No change was made to the sailing plan.

By the time the *Hampshire* slipped her moorings in the Flow, at about 5 p.m., the wind was blowing force 9 ('severe gale'). Even in the protected waters of the naval anchorage, waves were washing over the decks of some of the smaller vessels. There was so much spray in the air, and the rain was so thick that, despite it being late afternoon just two weeks before midsummer, one eye-witness talked of the 'gathering darkness'. The *Hampshire* sailed south out of the Hoxa Sound, then turned to starboard and started up the south-west coast of Hoy, beating into the teeth of the gale with its two tiny escorts in attendance. Once they rounded the headland beyond Rackwick and had the Old Man of Hoy abeam, the seas were mountainous. In calm water, the *Hampshire*'s top speed was 22 knots and that of the destroyers 30 knots. But the sea state was such that the cruiser could not make more than 14 knots and the destroyers not even that. Since the main threat to the *Hampshire* was considered to be U-boats and the best defence against them was speed, the commander of the flotilla, Captain Savill, decided that he ought to send the destroyers back to base rather than reduce speed to allow them to keep station.

---

11 It was then only half a century since the term 'forecast' had been coined for weather predictions. Forecasts were a result of the introduction of the telegraph which enabled observer stations throughout the British Isles to send information to London quickly enough that a synoptic chart could be plotted and inferences drawn as to the likely weather in the near future. It was not until 1916 that Norwegian scientists identified the phenomenon we call 'weather fronts'. Meteorology did not take the highly technical form we know it today until the Second World War, when flying made accurate forecasts crucial.

So the *Hampshire* sailed on alone with the War Minister down below, seasick. At about 7.45 p.m. there was a huge explosion for'd. The ship lost way and started going down by the head. Men streamed aft up onto the quarter deck. Kitchener was seen climbing out of the hatch with his greatcoat on. Captain Savill tried to beach his ship, but he could not steer her as the electrical system had failed. Kitchener was last seen on the bridge deck, without his greatcoat, apparently resigned to his fate in the element he hated and feared. Within 15 minutes, the *Hampshire* rolled over to starboard and sank, the whole underwater section for'd of the bridge having been blown away by a German mine probably laid only days before.

Men plunged into the sea. Quite a few made it to the shore, but were killed when thrown against the cliffs by the huge seas. Others managed to clamber out of the surf but died of exposure in the fierce wind before help arrived. Local people who tried to render assistance were turned back by armed guards on 'security' grounds. Permission to launch the Stromness lifeboat was repeatedly refused. Of course, if the two destroyers had still been sailing in convoy with the *Hampshire*, they could have picked up many of the men in the sea. As it was, only twelve survived from the ship's complement of 622. Kitchener's body was never found. In a war of 'chateau generals' he was the only senior military figure on either side to die a violent death.

Though the sea between Marwick Head and the Brough of Birsay does not look much different from the sea anywhere else in the area, the dark faces of the cliffs that run most of the 5 miles from Brough Head down to the Bay of Skaill (where the Neolithic settlement of Skara Brae is) look forbidding even in calm weather. This is where most of the men would have died. I had always imagined the place of Kitchener's death grey, mysterious, remote – the Bloody Orkney phenomenon, possibly. But the wreck lies within 2 miles of smiling farmland, where Orkney cheese and other delicacies are produced. A less impatient man might have lived to enjoy them, along with his porcelain and flower arrangements.

By the time we had weathered Brough Head and were in the entrance to Eynhallow Sound, the wind had died completely. We took the sails down and motored to Evie, where I was to meet a photographer from the *Sunday Times* who wanted a picture of me and the boat. Gordon left us there and hitched a lift into Kirkwall with the photographer. As I rowed back out to *Foggy Dew*, I could see the slender fronds of seaweed standing motionless in the clear water below me.

Brian and I raised the anchor and in an early evening chill motored south-east to Shapinsay where we had a dinner appointment with an Orcadian by the name of Richard Zawadski. His family owns Balfour Castle and much of the farmland round about it. The castle was undoubtedly the most bizarre building we saw during the whole trip. But then Shapinsay is an island with an unusually interesting history, and Richard is far from being an ordinary Orcadian.

3
ORKNEY – NORTH

LOOKED AT ON THE MAP, Shapinsay is unique in the islands of Scotland in that its roads and farms are on an almost completely rectangular pattern. Approached from the sea, the island is unique in Orkney in having an enormous, 'Scottish baronial'-style castle visible over the low, grass-covered cliff by the shore. The reason for both is that Shapinsay was the focus of the nineteenth-century agricultural revolution which changed much of Orkney from being a poor, chronically exploited relic of Norse civilisation into one of the most productive farming areas in Scotland.

Unlike on the mainland, the estate system vanished almost completely from Orkney during the twentieth century, creating a relatively classless society of owner-occupiers, not dissimilar to Norway's. This is a recent development, not a hangover from the Viking era. From the Middle Ages to the end of the First World War, owner-occupancy declined to a point where more than 90 per cent of Orkney was tenanted ground. But after that war, the big estates were broken up much more comprehensively than elsewhere. Orkney's historian comments:

> It is doubtful if even the Vikings brought about such a rapid change in landownership as occurred in the 1920s . . . In Scotland as a whole owner-occupancy increased from 8.2 per cent of agricultural land in 1919 to 21.1 per cent by 1930. That was certainly a large increase but much less than the change in Orkney from 9.4 per cent to 65.8 per cent owner-occupancy in the same period. After 1930 the trend towards owner occupancy continued, reaching 86 per cent at the close of the twentieth century.[1]

1 *History of Orkney, op. cit.*, pp. 416–7. Today in Scotland as a whole 69 per cent of agricultural land is owner-occupied and 31 per cent farmed by tenants. In his book *Who Owns Scotland?*, Andy Wightman gives only two

In an unpublished paper, the same historian calls the owner-occupier revolution 'the single event which most altered Orkney society', commenting that 'the buying of farms released a burst of energy . . . Leadership passed to the go-ahead farmer . . . Estates simply faded out of the reckoning and a new feeling of self-confidence developed.'[2]

In 1919, before the ownership revolution, the largest landowner on the Valuation Roll was Colonel Balfour of Shapinsay. The rectangular fields are evidence of the reason for his pre-eminence, and the baronial residence a consequence of it. It was his father's half-brother, David Balfour, who led the revolution in agriculture fifty years before which brought Orkney out of the Middle Ages. The *Old Statistical Account*, published in 1792, paints a colourful picture of farmers of Shapinsay before the age of improvement:

> They plow [*sic*] their fields in spring, cover them with some seaweed, sow them immediately, and as soon as the seed is committed to mother earth, they carelessly fold their arms, satisfied that they have done their duty, and leave the event to divine providence. Neither are they more enlightened or industrious in regard to the use or application of manures . . . Even the dung of their cattle, which is at their hand, and which is so generally considered as an excellent manure, rather than be at pains to carry to their fields, they in some places throw into the sea, by way of a peace offering to Neptune, in order to render him propitious in casting ashore for them plenty of seaweed, which is the only substance they consider as a valuable manure . . . [the island was] a dreary waste, interspersed with arable lands ill-cultivated, a few miserable hovels thinly scattered over its surface, under the name of farm houses or cottages, which were not fit to shelter from the rigours of the climate a few ragged inhabitants, dirty through indolence, lean with hunger, and torpid by despair.[3]

---

holdings larger than a thousand acres in Orkney, one on Rousay and the other the RSPB's estate, which he quotes as 15,500 acres but today runs to 20,500 acres. He does not mention the Zawadskis' 1,200-acre holding.

2 *The Owner-Occupier Revolution: the Break-up of the Earldom Estate in Orkney, 1920–1926*, William P.L. Thomson, undated, pp. 28–30. Part of the reason for this was that the Fleet at Scapa Flow created an immense demand for farm produce which made the tenants financially solid enough to be able to offer competitively for their holdings when they came on the market.

3 *Old Statistical Account, Orkney XVI Shapinshay* [sic], Rev. George Barry, Edinburgh 1792, pp. 229–31

The author thought the cure was the importation of 'resident heritors' who would 'set an example of industry' and 'by the combined influence of their money, their authority, and example, they point out to [the rest of the population] the road to happiness'.

The first such man had already arrived on the island when that view was expressed: Colonel Thomas Balfour of Elwick. His grandson was David Balfour, the greatest agricultural innovator in the Northern Isles. With the aid of government loans for drainage and other improvements, he transformed Shapinsay and set an example for landowners all over Orkney and beyond. He replaced runrig cultivation with fixed-field boundaries on a rectilinear pattern and introduced five-year crop rotation. He built roads, schools and other infrastructure, including the pier at which Brian and I tied up that evening in Elwick Bay. He also built Balfour Castle partly, it is said, to provide a sense of stability to a community unsettled by the rapid and far-reaching changes he was forcing on it.

Like Fettes College in Edinburgh, Balfour Castle was designed by David Bryce, one of the inventors of the Scottish baronial style. The effect is familiar: crow-stepped gables, corbelled turrets that could have been copied from a medieval Book of Hours, and a conscious asymmetry which was intended to suggest an ancient building agglomerated over time. In fact the whole, 52-roomed structure was put up in 1847, complete with a stone taken from Westray which carried the date '1725'. In his *History*, William Thomson comments:

> David Balfour destroyed the real middle ages by his ruthless squaring of the landscape while at the same time creating his own medieval dream world. He decorated his private gasworks with fake fortifications [and] he collected ancient music to which he set abominable verses . . . His grandfather's village of Shoreside was renamed 'Balfour', and when he persuaded the Post Office to change the name of its office on Shapinsay to Balfour, he possessed the most imposing of addresses: David Balfour of Balfour, Balfour Castle, Balfour.[4]

Though both married and obsessed with lineage, Balfour died childless. The estate passed to his half-brother, whose son, the owner in 1919,

---

4 *Op. cit.*, p. 403.

also died childless, despite having had two wives. He was succeeded by his cousin, David Hubert Balfour, who had no fewer than four wives but also died childless. In an eccentric inversion of the earlier David Balfour's obsession with heritage creation this one, the last of the line, had his ashes scattered by the grave of his dog.

In 1961 the estate was put on the market. The buyer was a neigh-bouring farmer, a refugee Polish Lancer called Tadeusz – known locally as Teddy – Zawadski. He had come to Britain after escaping from the death march of the Polish officer corps to Katyn, where 14,000 men were murdered by Stalin's commissars in 1940. It was his younger son, Richard, whom we were dining with that night.

I had not met Richard before and did not know what to expect. *Foggy Dew* was hailed from the pier by a tall, slim, dark-haired, athletic-look-ing man with the bearing of a Polish Lancer. He introduced himself, showed us to his Land Rover and made us the gesture most appreci-ated by yachtsmen after food and drink, namely a bath, up at Balfour Mains, the farmhouse where he lives. Afterwards over drams and a deli-cious dinner of woodcock and snipe, followed by bramble pie, he and his Danish wife, Berta, explained how they live there. The family runs the castle as a hotel, while Richard organises the wildfowling holidays which attract many of the guests. Teddy Zawadski was a soldier and his father a lawyer, so the family has no background in farming. But they have nonetheless made a success of it.

On the in-hand acreage, Richard mainly grows barley, having sold his beef herd in 1995, just before the BSE epidemic erupted. Many farmers are wedded to their stock, and think of farming more as a way of life in which personal amenity is at least as important as commercial success. Richard is more detached. Despite that, he admits it was a wrench to part with a herd which had been built up since his father started farming half a century before. Now that agricultural subsidies are substantially environment-orientated it makes commercial sense for farmers to reduce their exposure to the uncertainties of the food market.

Richard's passion is wildfowling. As quarry species, he offers his customers widgeon, mallard, teal, greylag and pinkfoot geese, snipe, woodcock and golden plover, as well as home-bred pigeons, ducks and pheasants. He has twelve ponds which he feeds, 160 acres of winter stub-ble and a scatter of skerries and off-shore islands where ducks are hunted during dawn boat trips. Though not a shooter myself, I can think of few more romantic ways of wielding a gun than flighting ducks from an islet in Shapinsay Sound as an autumn sun rises over the empty North Sea.

After dinner, Richard took Brian and me on a tour of his part of the island. We ended up at Mill Dam, the RSPB reserve nearby, because I was keen to see how bureaucratic conservation, as practised by the RSPB, compares with market-driven conservation as practised by the Zawadskis. In an article in *The Orcadian* entitled 'So *that's* what the bird-ieman does', Eric Meek wrote, 'We are very proud of a fabulous wetland site at the Mill Dam on Shapinsay . . . Perhaps, more than any other habitat in the islands, it is wetland that is currently most under threat.' (23 May 2002)

Meek is correct to observe that much of Orkney has, like a lot of agricultural areas throughout the world, been drained for farming purposes. Globally speaking, the only important crop which requires standing water is rice. But paddy fields are not considered 'wetland' by conservationists because they are simply wet land. The term 'wetland' applies to a habitat classification, not a degree of saturation of soil. Wetland is undrained land in its natural state, which a paddy field is not. By the taxonomic gymnastics of the conservation industry, a dam is wet land when in use and wetland when not. Thus the area of Mill Dam was wetland before construction, wet land after it, and is wetland again now that it is no longer productive, even though the dam itself is still there.

The structure was erected in the 1880s by the Balfour Estate to provide motive power for a mill. In 1961 the main spindle broke and was not repaired. Improved transport made it more economical to mill grain in large, centralised factories. The dam and sluice were left to rot, so they and the surrounding area of semi-saturated soil acquired 'heritage' potential. While in use, the dam had interrupted the natural operation of the ecosystem on its site. Once abandoned, aspects of that ecosystem could reassert themselves. The water level fell and the floor of the little valley started going 'wild' again. That is the state in which Richard knew it as a boy. He loved wandering over it, he told us, looking at the birds, and from time to time shooting them.

When the RSPB purchased the property in 1993, they repaired the sluice and raised the water level in order to make the land more 'wet'. It is now as artificial an ecosystem as it was when built, with a larger area of open water than twenty years ago and a much smaller area of swamp, mire and marsh. When in use the dam was 'development'. As unproductive amenity it is now 'heritage'.

As the main bird population of Mill Dam is wildfowl, Richard and the RSPB have similar interests, at least as far as numbers go. To judge the success or otherwise of the Reserve in the RSPB's own terms, I wanted to know how things had changed since the Society bought the ground.

Inside the RSPB's hide overlooking the dam, Richard said, 'Since they've raised the water level, the islands dotted all over the marsh, which is where the birds used to nest, are now submerged. The young chicks have nowhere to hide and are taken by predators. On open water, they are sitting ducks, as it were.'

'So they're less protected than before?' I asked.

'That's right. I don't see that what the RSPB has done has actually benefited any bird. In the winter the surface is just a mass of waves. The implication of the fact that this is a bird reserve is that the birds are only here because of the RSPB. The truth is the opposite. There were many more birds here before they raised the water level.[5]

'This piece of ground is right next to yours,' I said, 'so when it came on the market, did you try to buy it?'

'Yes, I did,' Richard said. 'I approached SNH to ask if I could get a grant. I said, "If the RSPB gets grants, why shouldn't I, as a private individual, be given the same opportunity?" They weren't very forthcoming on that. I also said it would be very much appreciated if the RSPB did not get to know about this conversation. They said, "Given the nature of the people involved it is very unlikely that that would not happen." Somebody would be bound to tell the RSPB that I'd been in there trying to get a grant. That's human nature and it doesn't surprise me. Needless to say, I didn't get the offer of a grant.'

Back in the Land Rover, I asked about access and shooting on Orkney generally.

'There's almost an unwritten law in Orkney that if you're keen on shooting you can go and shoot anywhere. There are exceptions to that, but generally most farmers will take a tolerant view of people who want

5 Taking figures for the main breeding species on the reserve from 1993 to 1998, the only Red Data species present in 1993 was reed bunting, which had vanished by 1998. Of the Amber species the total definite breeding pairs of all listed species in 1993 was 62. By 1998 that figure had declined to 59. (*Mill Dam, Shapinsay: Management Plan,* RSPB, Sandy 1999 p. 11)

to shoot. They certainly have done up until now. They would expect you to give them a couple of ducks, and to ask permission, but otherwise they're not too fussed. That's probably changing now that we have so many outsiders moving in. Previously you knew most people who might be interested, or knew someone who knew them, so there was an element of good neighbourliness in it. Now that is changing, so, sadly, the tolerance is likely to be less in future.'

'What about access to places like Mill Dam?' I asked.

'If you walked past the hide at Mill Dam and down to the water's edge and somebody in authority saw you, they'd tell you to get off.'

'Do they have the power to do that?'

'I don't know. They're just a group of people who have bought a bit of land. That's no different from any other landowner. There are no rights associated with it. It's not a local nature reserve designated by the Council; no by-law has been passed to prevent you going. It just goes with the territory: RSPB, get off.'[6]

'From an urban perspective,' Brian said, 'the thing that would worry most of the people I know is that you can't go anywhere on RSPB land. Why have they got a different set of rules from the Duke of Sutherland or whoever? He can't stop you from walking on his land as long as you don't damage it. Why do the RSPB think they can?'

At that point Richard stopped the vehicle and pointed out into the gathering darkness. Though the shore was not far down to our left, it seemed there was a moor on the other side. I couldn't see anything other than the dark heave of a low hill in the middle distance. A wandering night breeze came and went through the open windows. The land was cooling after the heat of the day. We could hear the slow wash of the sea on the rocks below, but not much else.

'An interesting aside,' Richard said, 'is that there is quite an area of heather up there where we have always had grouse. The few people on this island who shoot had a verbal agreement that none of us would shoot the grouse because there weren't that many of them left. One farmer bought part of this hill and reseeded it. I bought a bit and the Scottish Naturalist Trust or whatever they're called bought a bit to prevent it being reseeded. Anyway the grouse have died out, probably because

---

6 This is stated explicitly in the Management Plan: 'Main Management Prescriptions and Projects . . . 3. Minimise disturbance to site by restricting access . . .' (p.5)

there are too many bonxies and gulls. Nobody's made any fuss about that. The RSPB haven't said that the vanishing population of red grouse on the island of Shapinsay was causing concern. I don't even know if they're even aware of it. Now they're extinct.'

I asked about hen harriers, which are the main species which conservationists wish to preserve on heather moorland. The two main areas for harriers in Scotland used to be Orkney and the Isle of Arran. It is a startling fact that Orkney, which has thirteen RSPB reserves, has suffered a crash in the hen harrier population, while on Arran, where the RSPB does not own a single acre of ground, harrier numbers are at a historic high.

'I'll tell you a story about that' Richard said. 'I've got a farming friend on the mainland here and he has about 1,000 acres of land designated as a Site of Special Scientific Interest for hen harriers. They like long heather to nest in. So old rank heather, particularly high up on the hills, was designated to protect these nesting sites. The annual payments are large. Despite that, it now transpires that the decline in the hen harriers is "continuing to cause concern", as the conservationists say. One of the reasons appears to be increased predation but the other thing they have discovered is much more interesting. Part of the management agreement on the SSSIs was to reduce the numbers of sheep on the high hills so that the heather would not be grazed too far down. What did the farmers do? Because they are on a headage payment, they do not want to get rid of the sheep altogether, so they put them down the hill, over the fence onto the semi-improved ground – which is exactly what you'd expect them to do. That is now more heavily stocked and has been eaten down, but that, ironically was the area where the Orkney voles lived. They are the main food of the hen harriers, particularly when they are feeding chicks and want to fly a short distance to catch food quickly and bring it back to the young. So they're flying over what used to be rankish vegetation, lightly grazed, with lots of vole tracks in it. Now it's as bare as a billiard table so there's no voles. The harriers can't feed their young, so they're dying out.'

'While all the money is still being paid out to save them,' Brian said. 'That's incredible.'

'I don't really blame anybody for it,' Richard went on. 'It's just ignorance. But if this had all been managed by people who were slightly more "with it", they might have anticipated this. They just thought, take the sheep off. They didn't say, where are they going to go? I think if I were a single mother with two babies in Harringay or somewhere like that, I'd be pretty pissed off there's a hen harrier out here in Orkney getting thousands of pounds instead of me.'[7]

We returned to this subject back at Balfour Mains where Richard offered us a nightcap before running us down to the boat. He asked Brian for his impressions as an outside observer.

Sipping a glass of port, Brian said, 'What comes across to me for organisations like the RSPB and SNH – all these people with ecological backgrounds and their knowledge of nature – they do seem to be rather incompetent.'

'They're not country people in the main,' Richard said. 'That's the trouble.'

'If they don't understand the issues properly,' Brian said, 'how do they manage to portray themselves as being competent?'

'Because the people who support them don't understand the issues either,' Richard said. 'And there is always a scapegoat. Take, for example, the decline in the song-birds, which is in the news these days. What is the RSPB line? The RSPB line is it is all down to farming practices, pesticides etc. Obviously they have had an impact, but there are a helluva lot of people who live in the countryside, who do not have a doctorate in ornithology but who see what is going on around them, and they think that a big part of it is the increase in the sparrowhawk numbers. A sparrowhawk will only eat small birds; they don't even catch mice on the ground. They only eat birds. They catch things on the wing. A kestrel will eat beetles; other raptors will eat carrion. But a sparrowhawk will only eat birds. What are they eating? They're eating little birds, including songbirds.'

It was late by now. I was getting tired and I could see the glass in Brian's hand beginning to lean over. But before leaving, I wanted to ask the Hoy PR question: 'How do you think Orkney people view the RSPB?'

'I don't think they're very happy about them,' Richard said.

'Why?'

'It's not something you hear people talking about very much.

---

7 It has subsequently been announced that the Scottish Executive is to spend £1,046,684 on the Orkney Hen Harrier Scheme, paying farmers to 'manage their land in ways that will help sustain and enhance the island's hen harrier population.' (*Scotland's Natural Heritage*, SNH, no. 22, Spring 2003)

Orcadians are not very communicative people in that way. They tend to form their opinions from a gut feeling. They are unlikely to debate that sort of thing with you, but I can tell you that the RSPB as the biggest landowner is not popular. They are very popular with some people, of course, and it would be true to say that most people here are actually indifferent: they wouldn't even think about the RSPB for one second in one year. But the numbers who do think about the countryside and who question what they are up to is growing. Instead of looking at a bearded northerner giving a reason on TV why some catastrophe is happening in the bird world and taking it in, they are nowadays a little bit beginning to think, what actually is this bloke's agenda?'

Next morning we woke to warm but hazy sunshine and the ghost of a breeze from the north-east. After a full night's sleep I was more than ready for the thick bacon sandwiches with mustard which Brian prepared for breakfast. We ate on deck, enjoying the peace of the quiet, very sheltered harbour. We both felt ready for a relaxing sail out to the island of Copinsay, where we had been invited to attend the sheep clipping, and a subsequent barbecue, by the tenant of the owner, who happens to be the RSPB. Not wishing to waste battery power by starting the engine, I decided to sail out.

With the bow facing the sea and the wind pushing us gently onto the pier, we had only to get round the end before we could sail. We rigged a slip line from the stern of the boat for'rd to the end of the pier which would enable Brian to move us parallel to the pier while I pushed like a rugby forward to keep the boat off. We had raised the mainsail before casting off, so once we were round the pier we were able to sheet in and get steerage way almost immediately. To my relief we completed the whole operation without a single dunt. We unfurled the genoa and slid quietly down past Helliar Holm and out into Shapinsay Sound. There, the wind was less blanketed by the land and *Foggy Dew* picked up speed. Soon we were clipping along under what was by then a strong and very bright sun.

It was a glorious day for a sail. Brian took the helm and I settled down by the stern rail to read about Copinsay. The island is a slanted plateau of about 150 acres, with the west side at about sea-level and the east 200 feet above it. The ground is sufficiently fertile that it was used for the breeding of farm horses in the nineteenth century. It supported a full-time farmer, and his thirteen children, until the early 1950s, after which it was used for sheep grazing only. In 1972 it was acquired by the RSPB. An appeal was organised by the World Wildlife Fund to raise the £6,000 which was eventually paid for it. The intention was not to buy Copinsay specifically, rather to acquire a 'seabird island' to commemorate the work of James Fisher, the ornithologist who had recently been killed while drunk-driving on the M1. It just happened that Copinsay was on the market at the time.

Now a forgotten name, Fisher was one of the great and the good who took up the cause of nature conservation in the period, starting in the 1920s, when Britain abandoned its Kitcheneresque, imperial stance in the world and began to turn in on itself. The result was the 'new Jerusalem' mood which reached a climax after the end of the Second World War. Most of the bureaucratic initiatives which are with us today directly date or indirectly derive from the first post-war Labour government. Fisher spent the war years in Oxford researching the eating habits of the rook hoping afterwards to be appointed director of the Edward Grey Institute of Field Ornithology there.[8] Passed over, he turned to publishing and broadcasting and made a name for himself as a pipe-smoking naturalist who was thought of in the same breath as Peter Scott, Maxwell Knight and, more recently, the pipeless David Attenborough.[9]

8 Ironically, the Institute is named after Sir Edward Grey (later Lord Grey of Fallodon), who in 1914, as Foreign Secretary, took Britain into the war which destroyed the imperial ideal forever. A quiet, domestic man, Grey was a keen bird-watcher until his eyesight failed. In retirement, he headed the appeal for the first major conservation land purchase by the English National Trust, for the Farne Islands, in 1925. His brothers retained the taste for wider horizons. Both went out to Africa to hunt. One was killed by a lion and the other by a wounded buffalo.

9 George Waterston, the ornithologist who brought the RSPB to Scotland, claimed in the Society's magazine that Fisher's 'crowning achievement was to influence the Services to annexe [sic] Rockall for the British Crown'. (Birds, Jan–Feb 1971) This was nonsense, as he would have known if he had read Fisher's book about the island. Rockall was seized by the Royal Navy in 1955, at the time the rocket testing range was being constructed on Benbecula. The fear was that the Soviets might annex it – which would have been quite lawful as it was legally terra nullius – and install missile monitoring equipment there. It was formally incorporated into the United Kingdom, as an outlier of Harris, in 1972, when it was first thought that there might be substantial oil reserves in the surrounding sea. This was the time when Exclusive Economic Zones were being recognised internationally as applying up to 200 miles from land – hence the 'cod war' with Iceland.

Though the RSPB calls Copinsay 'a memorial island to James Fisher', their published justification for the acquisition was that, 'We need places like Copinsay with its wild whirling seabirds and their wild cries, where, for a while, the crazy modern world can be left behind.'[10] As Brian and I came in sight of this strange-shaped hump of rock, rounding Mull Head on the peninsula of Deerness, the wind died. The motor fired up nicely and we chugged on a glassy sea into the roadstead off the little jetty.

We ghosted in, with the engine in gear though idling. The depth sounder showed a consistent 10 feet of water, but we could see seaweed beneath the surface ahead, meaning rocks below. I took the engine out of gear and was about to tell Brian to throw the anchor overboard when, *bang!*, the keel hit something hard, and we stopped dead. It is a horrible sensation, hitting underwater obstacles in a boat. I put the engine into reverse, but we did not move; then full ahead and we slowly swung round, though still not moving. Brian and I hung onto the shrouds and rocked the boat from side to side as hard as we could while the propeller churned. Eventually, inch by inch, we eased off. What a relief! The tide was ebbing and we could have got nastily stuck. We motored 50 yards further out before anchoring on smooth sand clearly visible through the unclouded water.

By the time we stepped ashore, the barbecue had finished. We accepted a couple of beers and offered a few drams of the Ardbeg to the shearing party, which had done its work for the day. For the next hour and a half a small boat conveyed the clippers in three journeys back to the mainland while we sat on the pier and chatted in the sunshine with those still waiting to go.

Mardi Jenkins, the wife of the tenant, Richard Jenkins, told us how intelligent her sheep are. 'The purer the breed, the closer you get to the Shetland, the cleverer they are, and the harder to gather. Cheviots stick together. They are much more easily controlled. The Shetlanders stay split-up to give themselves the best chance.'

As an isolated island colony, British sovereignty would not confer control of the surrounding shelf. Only full title would. This was the first accession of territory to Scotland since the transfer of the northern isles from Denmark in 1469.

10 *Birds*, May–June 1973, p. 240. Fisher himself thought in similar terms, describing the history of ecology as a 'battle between the conservationist thinkers and the rash, greedy exploiters and disturbers of nature.' (*The Times*, 24 October 1970)

'Is that really true: Shetland sheep are more individualistic?'

'They really are. I swear they have a brain, a strategic brain.'

Richard, who had stood for parliament as a Conservative on a number of occasions, told me about the pragmatic approach of the people to the presence of the RSPB in Orkney. They are seen as little different from the soup manufacturers or cotton kings who bought estates in the nineteenth century. He was mildly critical of those who thought that something radical ought to be done about such concentrations of land-owning power.

'In the end it becomes every polemicist, once he has nailed his victim to the sampling table, to come up with solutions,' he said. 'We all have to find ways of getting along with them. We are not going to drive them out of the islands; they're not going to disappear. Nobody's going to rob them of their money or their charitable status. We're all just going to have to find ways of dealing with them, just as we dealt with all the other big landowners.'

After the last of the clipping team had departed, with a final wave of hats in the clear evening light, Brian and I walked up to the light-house, hoping to find out what is so different about an island where the corncrake is king – or at least the main focus of the owner's land-management policies.

The corncrake chronology on Copinsay is interesting. The RSPB took over the island in 1972, when there were numerous birds breeding on the island and it was intensively grazed by sheep. Seven years later, the sheep were taken off and a further seven years after that the corncrake bred on the island for the last time. Today the RSPB says this was 'due to the degradation of suitable corncrake habitat'.[11]

In 1990 sheep returned to the island and the RSPB used them 'as tools in our corncrake management work'. Enclosures were created, with

---

11 *Copinsay Management Plan*, RSPB, Sandy 1998, p. 3. I subsequently asked Eric Meek why the RSPB had allowed the habitat to 'degrade' in a corn-crake-hostile way. He refused to answer personally, saying, 'We are happy to provide published material at cost, but there is a limit to the amount of time we can devote to answering your queries.' (email 14 May 2003) I subse-quently received an answer from the RSPB's Glasgow office which effectively shifted the blame onto the Orkney farmers: 'A lack of interest by graziers to stock the island during the late '70s and the '80s resulted in habitat changes.' (email 4 June 2003) The lack of interest is not explained and is therefore puzzling as these were boom years for sheep farmers.

crops and cover in them, to entice the birds back to the island. Oats, grass and nettles have all been tried. The sheep have been excluded from some parts of the island, then let into those parts and excluded from others. But none of these methods has worked. The 1998 Management Plan gave a target of 2 calling male corncrakes in five years' time. When Brian and I visited, four years later, not a single bird had been recorded, despite this extravagant application of machinery and manpower. Yet on other parts of Orkney corncrakes continue to appear. Indeed Richard Zawadski told us that Shapinsay had two breeding pairs that year, neither of them on the Mill Dam reserve.

Copinsay is a lovely island to wander round on a sunny summer evening. The sight of the seabirds sitting in their thousands on the almost sheer face of the cliff beneath the lighthouse was spectacular. They comprise the largest such colony in Orkney. Far down below us I could see a bonxie eating a dead bird which lay spreadeagled on the surface of the water.

We weighed anchor at eight o'clock and ate a 'boatfood' dinner of corned beef, beans and naan bread as we motored in windless conditions all the way back to Kirkwall. It took two and a half hours, and by the time we had rounded Mull Head and were into Shapinsay Sound, the setting sun was dead ahead. There was a strong red glow under the clouds and on the sea below. The land stood out dark and austere in the evening chill.

We discussed the odd feeling that Copinsay has become somehow detached from life on the islands all round. I pulled out my notes and read Brian this sentence from the visitors book we had seen in the farmhouse: 'A three-night visit to listen for corncrakes [and make repairs]. It's wonderful sitting here at 11.45 p.m. in my old armchair, writing in front of a huge fire with the hiss of a calor lamp in my ears. NB Despite doing my best corncrake impersonation, there was no response. I'll have another go at 1 a.m. then it's off to bed. Keith Fairclough, RSPB 11 July 1997.'

Fifty years ago the farmer would have sat in front of the same fire with thirteen children milling around while uncounted corncrakes crekked away outside. Now the place is deserted. To what purpose? The best answer I could come up with was to quote from one of the 'bibles' of the conservation movement which we happened to have on board, on the last page of which the author gives a brief statement of what he calls

'The Mission': 'To change the fundamental outlook of, first, a nation and then the world, from greed and materialism and continued striving upwards, to gentle coasting into an infinite and comfortable future.'[12]

This was such a depressing vision that Brian and I, almost without speaking, agreed that as soon as we tied up in Kirkwall we would go ashore and find the scruffiest and noisiest pub we could see near the waterfront and get drunk. We did.

Next morning we arranged for Paul Chapman to come back to the boat for another go at the charging system. This time he was successful, and by late morning I was ready to go and have a look at the town.

Kirkwall has the same crowdedly cosy, semi-Hanseatic feel that Stromness has, though with a less attractive waterfront. I had to squirrel around to find the BBC Radio Orkney studios where I was to give an interview about the trip. I let the interviewer have an unvarnished view of the conservation industry and the danger it poses to life on small islands through bureaucratisation and centralisation of power. The stifling of open scientific debate is a wider danger. The interviewer seemed both shocked and excited. She said, 'I think a lot of folk on Orkney would agree with you.'

Since there is a curry house in Kirkwall, Brian and I decided we would eat there that evening. Before doing so we went for a couple of pints of Dark Island Beer at the Sailing Club, to which visiting yachts are given a key by the harbour master on arrival. It is situated in the Girnel, an attractive stone building, dating from 1640, which used to be a corn warehouse and is therefore right next to the quay. There is a well-appointed bar and excellent showers. We were approached by a chatty Norwegian woman who was with two men off a boat which had tied up along side us. They were from Kristiansund, it transpired, and were on their way home after visiting the Faeroes.

'Is there a restaurant where we can get steak?' she asked. 'I have two hunters aboard.'

Next day we woke to a clear wind, blowing a grand clip from the north. It was cool but very bright as I walked out to the Haston Industrial Estate. There I talked tourism – Kirkwall is the second

---

12 *A History of Nature Conservation in Britain*, David Evans, London 1992, p. 257.

most popular cruise-ship destination in Europe – and yachts to the Chairman of Orkney Enterprise, the Managing Director of D.A.G. Kynoch Ltd, a Director of the Orkney Tourist Board and one of the prime movers in the Orkney yachting marinas project, all of whom are Mr Brian Kynoch. I walked back into town for an appointment at the Orkney Museum in Tankerness House. The director had been called away unexpectedly so I was asked if I minded seeing another member of staff, Tom Muir. This turned out to be a stroke of luck. Tom is a chatty, black-clad, boot-wearing native of Tankerness, the peninsula between Kirkwall and Deerness.

The museum building was once the town house of the Baikes of Tankerness, who were major landowners for 300 years. Part of it is devoted to a display of how the house would have looked during Baikes's occupancy. The rest contains exhibits of Orkney life from Skara Brae times to the present day. The large garden behind has been maintained beautifully. From the first floor window I saw groups of people sitting chatting on the lawns in the sunshine, amidst gloriously colourful flower-beds.

Tom's spare-time interest is in story telling. He had just published the second in a series of books of folktales for children, *The Hogboon of Hellihowe*. Hogboons are creatures from prehistoric Orkney who lived in earth mounds. Story-telling as a formalised activity was new to me. They have meets all over the country and, to my amazement, a national headquarters at the Scottish Storytelling Centre on the Royal Mile in Edinburgh. We quickly got onto the subject of the story of 'The Bloody Orkneys'.

'It's a poem which you find often in areas where troops are stationed,' Tom said. 'It is not a specifically Orkney thing, though obviously different versions have different words. Strangely enough in the late 1970s there was a punk poet called John Cooper Clarke and he wrote a piece called "Evidently Chicken Town". It's basically the same thing: "The bloody flats have bloody rats / It bloody gets you bloody down, / Here in bloody chicken town", or something like that. When I heard it I'm sort of thinking, wait a minute! This guy comes from Salford!'

'Who was Captain Hamish Blair?'

'There have been several people who have claimed to have written 'The Bloody Orkney's. Hamish Blair, who was a Canadian pilot, was one person that it was attributed to. There are two other people who contacted the *Orcadian* in the 1990s saying, "I wrote that." There has been a scramble to claim credit for it.[13]

Orkney Museums have two internationally known themes, Skara Brae and Scapa Flow. From an administrative point of view, the former is a static situation, whereas the latter is far from it. New finds and gifts of exhibits come in all the time. The latest is possibly the largest after the Lyness base itself.

'We were gifted recently the gun battery and war-time huts at the Ness battery in Stromness,' he said. 'I'm not sure what we're going to do with that yet. It was owned by the Ministry of Defence until a few months ago. The local TA used it as a camp. The Council got very excited. But we've got more than we can cope with as it is, and we've got no budget for it. At least it is a derelict building. That might help.'

'How?'

'Because the Heritage Lottery Board are not funding new projects.'

'Why's that?'

'Two reasons. One is we are a local authority and they are not keen on giving money to local authorities, the other is that museums are out of favour after the Olympics. Britain did well in the medals board as a direct result of Lottery funding. They are now thinking, oh yeah we'll put money into sport and everything else will get cut back.'

'Might that change?'

'It could do, if Britain does badly in the Commonwealth Games.'

The buildings are substantial wooden huts, but the main feature is the set of murals which are painted round the walls of the mess hall.

'They are of idealised English country scenes,' Tom said. 'There's a cottage with the roses round the door. The windows have diamond-shaped panes. You can open them and it is the serving hatch where they got food and booze. The notice-board is done as a billboard leaning against a country fence. There's Romany caravans in a clearing in the woods, a village pub with the old sign hanging from the post and all this sort of stuff.'

'What was it for?'

---

13 It was first published in *The Orkney Blast*, a paper started by Major Eric Linklater for the forces stationed in Orkney during the Second World War. Gerald Meyer, who was editing the *Blast* when the poem was published, did not know who the author was. 'Several people claimed to have written it,' he told me recently, 'but I just dismissed them.'

'Making the troops feel more at home, I suppose. They're stuck in an alien landscape, they want to see something that reminds them of home, but also I think, more importantly, reminds them of what they're fighting to preserve. I think there's more to it than meets the eye. People have got this cosy image that we don't do propaganda in Britain; it's not British. We leave that sort of thing to Dr Goebbels and Lord Haw-haw. But that's not always true.'

After returning home, I spoke to the main expert on the Ness Battery at the Royal Commission on Ancient and Historical Monuments in Edinburgh, Geoffrey Stell. He places the scenes in the English Midlands, and thinks they must have been done with official sanction. 'It cannot have been an exercise in graffiti because it covers the whole wall space of the canteen,' he told me. 'But there is one section missing. Apparently that was on a martial theme. It had paintings of warships above the stage at one end of the hall. There was a banner which said "Let them come from every quarter/And we will blow them out of the water", which has a sort of McGonagallesque ring. The interesting thing is that now we have identified this one, we are finding murals all over the place in military canteens. It is turning into a sub-scene that folk are taking up. But none of them are as well preserved as this one, which is both very expertly executed and pretty well intact.'

I asked Tom if it would be possible to go and see the display but he said the whole site is wired off and the Museums Department did not yet have permission to let members of the public in. There was a story attached to it, though.

'A friend of mine, Archie Bevan, the English teacher in Stromness, said that he was up there a couple of days after the war started,' Tom said. 'A cargo boat was heading in through the Hoy Sound. The battery had to stop it for inspection. They signalled but it carried on. So they fired a warning shot across its bows and the ship stopped. This was the first shot fired in anger in Orkney during World War Two. That was fine, but they didn't know what to do next. The battery commander, who was a local farmer, scratched his head. He had no instructions. So he asked Archie, who was kicking around there as a boy, to peddle back down into Stromness on his bike and get a guy called Captain Porteous, who happened to be his uncle, to take his boat out and board the incoming ship. If the crew had been a bunch of armed Nazis, he'd've had it. Captain Porteous took his boat out anyway, went on board and said, who are you? It turned out it was a Dutch ship that was blissfully unaware that there was a war on. They had left South America before war had been declared. Still, the battery commander had to come up with a decision on what to do in the future. If anything like this happens, what is the procedure for stopping ships and inspecting them? We can't keep sending Archie down to Stromness on his pushbike to get Captain Porteous.'

'I suppose it's the opposite of the Japanese soldier found in the Pacific jungle who hadn't realised that the war had stopped,' I said. 'These people come to an island and don't realise that a war has *started*.'

'Well, this is it. There was a German wheat ship, the *Borkum*, which was attacked by the RAF and ended up drifting ashore on Westray at the beginning of the war. Again, it left from, I think, Argentina before war was declared and the first that they knew about hostilities was when bombs started raining out of the sky.'

Tom explained that though Orkney had a quiet war from late 1940 onwards, it was the opposite before that. 'With the naval base here,' he said, 'it was the case that while folk in the south were having the phoney war, we were having the crap bombed out of us. At the beginning of the war there was air raid after air raid after air raid. The first British civilian casualty of World War Two was on Orkney. Six weeks into the war there was a big air raid and the *Iron Duke* was holed and nearly sunk. The first German aircraft to be shot down by anti-aircraft fire, the first one to crash on British soil, and the first bomb to fall on British soil, were all on that day, 17 October 1939. After that there was a lot of big air raids. They strafed the whole length of the main street in Stromness. There were people killed in Sanday, Tankerness, South Ronaldsay, Stenness.'

'These can't all have been military targets, surely?'

'No. There was a bairn who was strafed in a field in the middle of agricultural land. Luckily he dodged and wasn't hit. But the only thing in this whole area was this boy. They were obviously deliberately targeting him. There was a woman killed in a field lifting neeps, so they weren't just too fussy where they were dropping their bombs.'

'How long did this continue?'

'The British invented something in April 1940 called "the Scapa Barrage", where every anti-aircraft gun based around Scapa Flow and every gun on every ship fired everything that they had to explode at the same range, on the same bearing, at the same time. It produced a blanket of shrapnel right in the path of the incoming bombers. The shrapnel came down like rain. They did that for three minutes solid. It was claimed to be the loudest sustained noise ever heard in Britain. The German pilots just couldn't get through it. After three minutes the guns went back to individual firing, but that's what broke up the attacks. There was a huge one which came in on 10 April 1940. About sixty bombers came over, but up went the Scapa Barrage and eight were shot down straight away plus dozens of others damaged. It would have been a devastating raid if they had actually achieved their objective. After that they never came back.'

Finally, Tom told me a story about the blockship in Burra Sound we had sailed past.

'The *Inverlane* used to sit high and dry until a few years ago, on top of a skerry,' he said. 'She was an old oil tanker. Early in the war, she was hit by a mine off the north of England and the stern section sank. They towed the bow section into Scapa Flow and they beached her at Lyness where she was used for several years by the firecrews to practise their drill on. Shortly before she was moved to the Burra Sound, there was a man killed on board during the fire practice. They couldn't find his body and they assumed that he must have been incinerated in the intense heat inside the ship. As it happened a couple of guys from Hoy were in the ship a few nights later stripping the non-ferrous metal out – they were plundering the ship – and they stumbled across the badly charred remains of this man. They thought, what the hell do we do? We should really tell the authorities that there's a corpse out there, but if we do, that's us in trouble: what the hell were you doing on board the ship? They agonised about this, then after a day or two the problem was taken out of their hands when the ship was towed out and sunk as blockship, with the man's body still aboard. For many years, until it rolled over in a storm, off the skerry, she was a popular base for divers. They were presumably unaware that there were the remains of a Second World War fireman down below.'

Back aboard ship, I entertained Kath Gourlay to tea, a bite of fruit cake and a smallish Ardbeg. Kath is Orkney's best-known freelance journalist. Her father was a Gaelic-speaking army major from the Western Isles so, though she grew up on Orkney, Kath does not consider herself fully 'local'. We discussed at length the issue of incomers on Orkney, or 'white settlers' as some people call them in the Hebrides. The issue has provoked a body of research of which Orkney's historian, Willie Thomson, recommended one piece in particular to me, partly because it describes the general problem most vividly and partly because it is specifically about Orkney.

The author, Diana Forsythe came to Orkney from the University of Aberdeen in the late 1970s to study emigration from the islands, but discovered that the real story was the opposite flow: immigration to the islands. Such were the sensitivities of her conclusions that she had to disguise the island she was referring to, creating one called Stormay for her purposes. This is a 'small island of several hundred inhabitants located in the northern half of the archipelago', but it is typical of Orkney as a whole.[14] Thus:

> The majority (68 per cent) of the urban migrants are English in background . . . Most moved to the island directly from urban centres. They invariably explain their move by asserting the superiority of rural over urban life [and] have no ties of kinship or marriage with any member of the receiving community . . .
>
> Orcadians share a distinctive style of public behaviour. Socialisation on Stormay is in effect socialisation for independent but non-leadership behaviour. Islanders take pains not to draw attention to themselves, not to exert authority over other people in public, and not to overtly express conflict. Even when disagreeing with each other their speech is quiet . . . The urban migrants on the other hand are used to a more assertive, explicit style of communication and to more formal methods of decision-making. Many of them react to the Orcadians' indirect style as inarticulate or even backward, and in response become even more directive themselves. The islanders respond to their directiveness with silent non-cooperation. Despite the incomers' desire to fit into the community, leadership qualities

---

14 14 Urban Incomers and Rural Change: the Impact of Migrants from the City on Life in an Orkney Community, by Diana Forsythe, *Sociologica Ruralis* 1980, p. 287 *et seq.* See also: Contrasting English and Scottish Residents in the Scottish Highlands and Islands by Paul Boyle, *Scottish Geographical Journal, 1997* p. 99; and English Migrants in the Scottish Countryside: Opportunities for Rural Scotland? by D. Short and A. Stockdale, *Scottish Geographical Journal 1999*, pp. 183–4.

which may have stood them in good stead in an urban setting impede communication with the islanders. Since the incomers are insensitive to the islanders' indirect methods of social control, and the islanders resist the more direct methods of control practised by the urban migrants, a self-perpetuating gulf in communication divides the two groups, causing frustration and irritation on both sides . . .

One result of this struggle has been the replacement of consensus decision-making by voting at general meetings. But most islanders are more interested in social contact than administrative detail on their 'nights out', and their attendance at meetings is low . . . A politically active group among the incomers has exploited the Orcadians' tendency to avoid public conflict. These individuals maximise their voting strength by organising slates of candidates before meetings, and then attend as a bloc to vote each other in. Through this method, they have succeeded in taking over the entire leadership of certain important local organisations . . .

This conflict represented a direct confrontation between two ways of life: the personal orientation, informal control, and reliance on local standards characteristic of a small, face to face, community, and the impersonal orientation, formal control, and standardised rules characteristic of urban life . . . The incomers have no allies but each other; they have no place in the island's kinship network, nor are their ties of friendship with local people strong enough to redress major conflict between immigrants and the receiving community . . .

One island woman summed up the situation in the following way: 'When they come they think us delightfully old-fashioned and quaint. But no sooner are they established than they want everything that's part of the rat race. A new way of life is being imposed on Orcadians. It's just like the English in India.'

I asked Kath if she thought this picture of incomers in Orkney was fair.

'The funny thing is that those who are most vociferous against the incomers today are those who came in the 1970s,' Kath said. 'They were the white settlers, the initial incomers. These are the ones who are now shouting, "Get these ferryloupers out of here!" '

'Ferryloupers?'

'They walk off the ferry. White settlers have cars.'

'I've heard of white settlers,' I said. 'But not ferryloupers.'

'Ferryloupers are the ones who come with their heads full of butter-flies and think, oh wonderful, let's live off the land and be happy ever after. There was an awful lot of that in the Northern Isles. My sister had a lot of classmates at school with names like Andromeda. Sanday was full of hippies. The white settlers came in the 1970s, have been here for about thirty years. It is they who seem to dislike the ferryloupers most.'

'So you've got the white settlers versus the ferryloupers?'

'Yes, and the Orcadians somewhere in the middle, saying nothing.'

The number of incomers is partly a function of the nature of land-hold-ing on Orkney in that there has always been property to buy. Shetland, by contrast, like the Western Isles, is largely crofted and so ground has been far harder to come by for incomers with no local connections. This has had both positive and negative results.

'Shetlanders are completely different,' Kath said.

'Why is that?'

'They just have a completely different nature. They're much more assertive, more confident. If you phone up the Shetland Islands Council you'll be answered by a voice with a Shetland accent, even if you are talking to a head of department. You phone up here and ask for the director of a department you will not hear an Orkney accent. The thing is, Orkney was taken over in 1914 and 1939. It has never gone back. The people don't have the same sense of identity, though they would like to. When I was at school you were brought to task the whole time for your accent, and I think that has bred generations of Orcadians who think, "I'm not good enough." The doctor, the teacher and so on never had Orcadian accents. They were the learned ones; they were the clever ones, the ones the people looked up to. A lot of that still exists. But Shetlanders never had that. Maybe because they were further away. They never had the experience of being over-run in two world wars.'

'Presumably the upside of this lack of assertion is partly to be seen in the way Orcadians are so friendly,' I said.

'That's right. There is a much more laid-back attitude here. It is not so aggressive. Orkney tends to realise that its bread is buttered by tour-ism. That started thirty years ago. Shetland has been cushioned by oil. Orkney didn't become so reliant on oil revenue as Shetland. Now that things have started easing off, Shetland is feeling the pinch.'

*   *   *

Next morning, being a Sunday, it seemed right to visit St Magnus Cathedral, by far the most majestic public building in any of the Scottish islands. In size, it is half way between St Giles and St Paul's, but older than both. It had been in use for 500 years before Christopher Wren started designing the latter. Sadly the Reformation saw the wholesale destruction of the rich decorative embellishments which used to adorn the interior. Now it is rather plain, especially in the nave.

I took my seat just before 11 a.m. in a three-quarters full house. The choir was dressed in red and the Minister, the Rev. Fraser Macnaughton, was a vigorous, red-haired, man in early middle age who spoke in a powerful voice with a semi-Morningside accent. A Norwegian bible lay open on the lectern in front of the lower altar.

We were given the parable of the sower (Matthew 13:24–30), which concerns the undesirability of separating weeds from wheat before harvest-time in a field sown with both, lest the wheat be uprooted with the weeds ('tares' in the King James version). Christ explained to his disciples that the farmer represented the kingdom of heaven and that at harvest-time the mature wheat is gathered into the barn while the fully-grown weeds are collected and burnt. Segregation is easy at harvest-time, but difficult earlier in the growing cycle. That is as far as St Matthew goes. But Mr Macnaughton went further.

'This is about tares,' he began loudly. (I have abbreviated, but I hope not misrepresented, his text.) 'I have to disillusion you because that means weeds. This is the parable about the field that God plants in the hope of gaining a rich harvest of blessing for himself and the world He has made. We are the field of God. We are the ground that God works, the people upon whom He rests his hope, the folk He plants his seed in, the congregations that He anoints with his purpose.

'For many people the idea of a good God is ridiculous, a mystery, because if He is good, why does He allow so much evil to exist in the world? Why does God, if He is an almighty creator, allow evil to exist?

'As you may know, I have been on holiday in Australia for the last four weeks, and part of our holiday we spent in the tropical zone, north of Cairns. And one of the mornings, when I woke up, I wondered why mosquitoes were ever created, as I scratched my ankles and other exposed parts of my body.

'I don't know if you've seen that mad Australian, Steve Irwin, on the television, the one who plays with crocodiles and snakes? We went to visit his zoo. In the reptile house he had the ten most poisonous snakes in the world. There was one snake, the *most* poisonous in the world, the taipan, whose one bite can kill 100,000 mice. Now that might seem to be a bit of an over-kill, a bit ridiculous. But there are enough nuclear warheads in the world to blow ourselves and the whole world up about 250 times.

'Why have poisonous snakes on this earth? Why have nuclear blasts? Why is there drought in one part of the world when another part is suffering from floods? I've often wondered why God created all the opium poppies which, processed, cause untold misery for millions and millions of people who are heroin addicts, and their families.

'Again and again, we find ourselves in the situation of asking the question, why? Why do we have all these evils in the world? Why had God allowed them to be?

'The fact is that we humans are not even capable of seeing the tips of our own noses. We think we know it all. Our western, rational culture of the last 250 years has made us think that we humans are in control of our own destiny. But we are not able to understand a lot of the purposes of God. One such is the great mystery of evil.

'Whatever we study, we see that every culture has resolved those great mysterious questions by describing life as a constant battle between the forces of good and the forces of evil, the forces of light and the forces of darkness. Even an eclipse of the sun was seen as a tiny victory of evil over good.

'And even though we have a liberated, rational, western way of thinking, and we think we're all very clever, the reality is that this is just like all so-called primitive cultures. We mostly see things in black and white. We always see contrasts. We imagine conflict everywhere. Society is a dark tunnel. Economy is the work of the free market laws; it's the will of the powerful.

'And then we see that God, the creator of the world, accepts this. It is God who said, let the seed and the weeds grow together till harvest time. Don't separate the bad from the good. In other words, God awaits the repentant sinner. God gives strength to those who acknowledge their weakness.

'God calmly recognises there is evil in the world, but He knows there is no need to sound the alarm. Evil, God knows, cannot stop good because God is supreme. God will always have the last laugh.

'Our care for the good seed should not make us take drastic steps to uproot the weeds because, at the end of the day, the weeds do not stop the good seed from bearing fruit.

'We came back on Friday from our holidays. The growth in our back garden is enormous. I keep discovering things in it. One of the things I discovered was a patch of strawberries entirely overgrown with weeds. But despite all the weeds, yesterday our friends and our family enjoyed a bowl of strawberries in the Manse garden.

'Despite the weeds, the strawberries had ripened for us to pick on our return from holiday. In other words, even in the midst of evil, in this case personified by weeds, there was much of the good.

'What the parable is telling us, what Jesus says, is that if we see weeds among the good seed we need not get alarmed. Let us not over-exercise, or over-worry, about the mischief of evil. It is a fact of life. After all, weeds are just wild flowers growing in the wrong place. Amen.'

After church, Brian and I sailed for Stronsay in a clear, fresh northerly. We anchored off the wide, sandy sweep of Holland Bay, where, on going ashore, I was amazed to see a monk in flowing black habit strolling amidst the dunes. We were there to meet John Holloway, a human incomer who moved from Kent to observe the avian incomers.

Stronsay is one of the most easterly of the Orkney islands and so is regularly visited by rare birds blown off-course while migrating. John and his wife, Sue, are a quiet couple in late middle age who have escaped from the rat race to run birding holidays from their home, which was once a farmhouse but is now the centre of a weed-intensive garden which offers food and cover for exhausted migrants. Their customers want to see these rarities.

'In the spring and the autumn when there's an east wind we get loads of birds from the continent,' he told me as we drove around the island in his battered British saloon to see the best birding spots. 'Our visitors love it because you can come and look in our garden – we call it a bird reserve – and most likely see something. If there's nothing there, you can go up the road and look at the next garden.'

'Sounds ideal.'

'It is, in a way,' John said. 'But there is a problem. We rely on the good-will of our neighbours as the birds are on somebody's ground – unless they're on the road, which is unusual. The professional conservationists have let us down so many times that I don't tell them about sightings any longer. As a consequence they deliberately try and destroy our records by rejecting official submissions for rarities records when they have not seen them personally. That's the whole essence of what's going on in British ornithology today. It's blackmail, basically. If you don't tell the authorities, they won't accept your sightings as official records. Our business depends on my reputation for having my rare bird sightings officially authenticated, which they always used to be.'

'What is the problem about telling the conservationists about your sightings?' I asked. 'So what if they also see them?'

'I'll give you an example,' John said. 'In 1989, when the RSPB were having a day-twitch to raise funds for their centenary, they asked me to find a corncrake.[15] Stronsay was one of the last strongholds and I found one in one of the last regular places where they nested. It was in a small paddock of about an acre which went to a narrow point by a wall. On those day-twitches it is an unwritten rule that if you hear a rare species you can count it. You don't have to see it, so you don't disturb rare nesting birds. I took a party of them out and there was a corncrake crekking away in the corner. They jumped out of the car and said did I mind if they went in to see it. I said I'd rather they didn't, but they totally ignored me. They formed a line across this paddock, walked up through it and the bird eventually came out of its corner and flew over the wall. They said, "Yes! there it is," and they were happy. It was never in there again. I said to Sue that I'd just about had enough of these people.'

'But surely that's not birdwatching in any meaningful sense at all?' I said.

'Exactly. My idea of birdwatching in the 1950s was just to get out in the countryside with a pair of binoculars and see what I could find. But then it changed. In the 1970s, with transport being much better and everyone being on the telephone, it became easy to find out where birds were and get there. Most birdwatchers sit by the phone on a Friday evening and find out what's the rarest bird about and go and see it the next day. Most of them have pagers. They can edit their pagers so that only the birds that they need to see on their list will come up. It just

---

15 'Twitching' is the word for bird spotting when the observer is not interested in seeing the bird, only in recording the fact that he has caught sight of it. The observer is a 'twitcher' and the sighting is a 'tick'. A day-twitch is a competition to see which twitcher gets the most ticks in a single day.

shows how shallow the attitude is. Thirty years ago nobody who was a keen birdwatcher would work for the RSPB, now keen bird watchers have realised it's the only place you can get paid for doing your hobby. Good luck to them, but my worry is that now they have infiltrated all the committees, they control all the sightings. Sue and I depend for our living on my reputation for rare sightings. That is now under threat from so-called bird lovers who want to see birds so badly that they will break the rules.'

'Are they mad, bad or sad?'

John laughed. 'Look at it like this,' he said. 'We, who still prefer looking at birds, are considered mad, or at least old-fashioned. Most people these days are listers. They have lists for counties, lists for each year, lists for all sorts of things, even for birds they've seen on the television. The most interesting one was a visitor we once had who wore a different coloured hat each day and he had a list for every coloured hat that he had. He'd put his blue hat on one day and go out and he'd got a list he'd seen in his blue hat. He'd say, "Oh I've never seen one of those" – maybe something fairly common – "in this hat." He maintained his enthusiasm like that. It's like train spotting.'

I asked John what he thought of the resources expended on Copinsay attempting to entice migrating corncrakes back there.

'It's futile,' he said. 'There's millions of the birds in Russia, as you know. They might as well forget it. I'm the last person to want them to go, but I'm a realist. If they don't fit in with farming, then that's the end of it. Stronsay was covered in corncrakes fifty years ago. Thirty years ago there was still a lot: thirty or forty pairs in the 1970s, when we first came here. What has happened since is that the grazing and silage regime suits curlews better than corncrakes, which preferred the old hay-fields. Now hay-fields are uneconomic and there's at least 200 pairs of curlews nesting on Stronsay, whereas there were none in the 1970s. Today, every 20 acres of grass supports a pair of curlews. But all the RSPB go on about is how the corncrakes have declined. To me it's a hard life. I don't think it is right to ask the farmers, a lot of whom are struggling, to farm for corncrakes – what they call "environmentally friendly farming" – if it is going to be the difference between not surviving and surviving.'

'How is it more environmentally friendly to have corncrakes than to have curlews?'

'That's right. It's not. Conservation-wise there is a huge dilemma, because if you tried to go back to a regime which attracted corncrakes, you'd have to accept the loss of all the curlews.'

John suggested we go back to his house for tea. Just at his road-end he stopped the car and said in a whisper, 'Just look at that garden. I ask you to keep this to yourself for the moment. There's actually a pair of icterine warblers in there. Only the second ever record in Britain. They breed in northern Europe, but always on the other side of the North Sea.[16] Nobody can understand why they have never colonised Britain, but they never have. You'll just see a yellowy bird, about sparrow size, in that sycamore. And look! There's the chick. It's just come in to feed.'

Using his binoculars, I could just about see a small, yellowy bird, but what I found much more impressive was John's ability to spot the bird itself, and see that it is an icterine warbler, at a range when it was hard to tell with the naked eye that there was a bird there at all.

Sitting at his kitchen table, with a mug of tea and a digestive biscuit in front of me, I asked about bird ringing.

'If ever the word passé was appropriate, it is for bird-ringing,' John said. 'It's absolutely ludicrous. They all have lists, just like twitchers. It's the same competitive thing. They catch birds, just to be the first one to ring them. It's a total waste of time, normally. I'm not against it if a population is being studied, and they can justify it, but the trouble is I know a lot of the people involved. They come to Orkney more than they used to because in the south there is so much opposition to it from the public, who think it is a bad thing, that they are shut out of a lot of places they used to go.'

'So it is as much a competition as birdwatching?'

'That's right. They say they are gathering data, but it's rubbish. They've already learned almost everything you can learn from ringing. In my view, ringing is promoted mainly to keep the ringers themselves in business.'

'What harm does it do to the birds, apart from obvious distress at being unexpectedly handled? It is less harmful than shooting, obviously.'

'I don't agree with shooting either,' John said. 'It depends on the species and the individual. A red necked grebe came ashore on the Fair

---

16 First British breeding record 1992; Russian population estimated between 1 and 10 million pairs (*Birds of Western Palearctic,* ed. D.W. Snow and C.M. Perrins, Oxford 1998, vol. 2, p. 1 283)

Isle once while I was there. Nobody had ever ringed one before. It kept trying to come up on the beach. Clearly it had had it. It is a completely aquatic bird. It just about gets on to a platform to nest and that's it. Apart from that they live on the sea. They can't walk properly. Everyone knew it was nearly dead. But that evening the ringers went out in a small boat, and kept it diving until it was exhausted and they could catch it to ring it. The next day it was found dead on the beach. But it was a record for the ringer, and that was all that mattered.'

'That's sick. You can't even eat it.'

'Yes, but it's a competition. I've never regarded bird watching as a competitive sport. But for a lot of people twitching or ringing is the only thing they compete at. When you get that competitive edge, everything else goes by the wayside, honesty, good behaviour. It just becomes a battle. It's a macho thing. It's the ringer that counts, not the bird. There's also the fact that a lot of people just have to handle things. They're not satisfied with just watching. We call them "fondlers".[17] There was a classic example of a Pallas's grass-hopper warbler which the Fair Isle Reserve warden was showing around. He was a meticulous and excellent warden, and he was holding this out for all the observers to see and suddenly from about three rows back this hand was thrust out under somebody's armpit and it went forward to touch this bird. That man had got a touch list.'

John ran me down to Whitehall, the main village of Stronsay, which is little more than a large row of substantial houses, most of which have seen better days. Walking the last of the way through the village, I came upon a group of youngish people hanging out by the harbour wall. Amongst them was a shaggy-haired South African smoking a joint. He was saying to an admiring couple of girls, 'You guys have really crazy weather here, eh! You go round the corner and you've got to put your jacket on. You go round the next corner and you've got to put your overcoat on. Then you go round another one and you've got to take them all off again. In South Africa we've got a climate but, boy, you guys have got weather!'

---

17 One authority has gone so far as to suggest an erotic element to birding. In his book *Birders* (London 2001), John Cocker quotes a Yorkshire twitcher who exclaimed after seeing a rarity: 'It were so good I nearly creamed me pants.' (p. 52)

A hundred years ago Whitehall was the biggest herring port in Orkney – hence the substantial houses. It had fifteen fish-curing stations, thirty pubs and 1,500 'fishwives'. Today the main local interest lies in the new owners of the island which made Whitehall such a sheltered anchorage for the herring fleet, Papa Stronsay.

Situated 50 yards from the Stronsay shore at its closest, this fertile island was abandoned by its owner in the late 1990s because of the difficulties in crossing over in winter to get his daughter to school. The isolation was part of the attraction for the new arrivals, who are monks from the Transalpine Redemptorist Order. This is an ultra-traditional group which celebrates Mass in Latin and despises the worldly Benedictine Order 'with its cream teas, visitor centres and green lawns', as one Redemptorist put it. The order opposes the current, papally inspired ecumenical drive by the mainstream Catholic Church.

The Redemptorists bought Papa Stronsay in 1999 to complement monasteries in France and Kent. They intend to revive the island's monastic tradition, inaugurated by the Culdees 1,500 years ago, by founding a new monastery which they have called Golgotha (an Aramaic word meaning 'skull'). The monks spend part of the year travelling the world evangelising, and part of it working, largely in silence, on their own island farm where cheese-making is planned to be the main income generator.

I had come to talk to Bill Millar, a Stronsay man who spent thirty years in the Metropolitan Police, most famously leading the hunt for the perpetrators of the Brinks Mat bullion robbery at Heathrow in 1980. In the spacious sitting room of his modern house overlooking the anchorage, I was introduced, by coincidence, to the monk I had seen walking on the beach at Holland Bay four hours before. He was Brother Columba Marie, a tall, lean figure, with disorganised teeth and a far-away look in the eyes behind his round spectacles. A young Irishman, he had thrown up a career in computing to give his life to God. He said almost nothing during the hour and half I spent there, except to describe progress with the monastery's cheese-making enterprise, which was about to expand with the locally controversial purchase of the largest farm on Stronsay.

Apart from John Holloway's biscuit, I had eaten nothing since lunch, so I gratefully accepted Bill's offer of sandwiches – sadly not made from Golgotha cheese – and a glass of wine (unconsecrated).

We chatted mainly about the new building works, for which Bill is the foreman. After a successful £2 million fund-raising appeal, thirty centrally heated cells for postulants are now under construction as the first part of the larger programme.[18] Larger cells for the monks will be constructed later, along with a chapel, library, cloister and other communal facilities. The only personal property allowed is underpants and spectacles, everything else is shared. Each New Year the monks move cells so that they do not get too attached to any particular living space.

Collectively, they seem to be fairly attached to their island space as the order insists that nobody may go ashore without permission from Father Michael Mary, the New Zealander (of Orkney extraction) who runs Golgotha. Bill told me that some canoeists who had landed recently to have a look around were 'soon sent packing'.

It is not just the identity of visitors which the monks seek to control, but also their mode of dress. Archaeologists excavating the medieval chapel on the island have been told that the women amongst them must wear ankle-length skirts, long-sleeved tops and some sort of cover on their heads. Curiously this rule applies only to those under thirty years old. 'It can be very difficult telling women over thirty what to do,' Father Michael Mary said. He explained his position on the under-thirties by saying, 'If you are going into a church, there is usually a dress code. The whole island is our church. T-shirts and jeans are very inappropriate. The sacredness of the island must be respected.'

The reason Brother Columba had interrupted his silent labours on the island was to show Bill and some other guests a video of a BBC Newsnight Scotland programme about the monastery. We all watched it. The reporter said of the order:

They believe the Vatican has gone soft and should not seek reconciliation with other faiths . . . When the Pope recently kissed the Koran, they considered it a scandal. 'The Pope is the successor of St Peter and kisses the book which we have always judged to be a book of heresies and a book that is not going to lead people to heaven [said

18 Sadly, not all postulants have proved apt for their vocation. Two days before my visit, the *Orcadian* carried a story about one who had asked for a private room in the Kirkwall cybercafé, where he had accessed homosexual material on the web. He was disciplined for 'internet sin'. (25 July 2002)

Father Michael Mary]. You are making people think this is a good thing, that those who are Muslims should carry on being Muslims. Catholics have never, never, never believed this before. We believe they should be Catholics.

Rowing back out to the boat a few hours later under a darkening but still clear sky, I described the order to Brian, whose father had been Catholic and mother Protestant.

'They're a strange sort of Catholic because they refuse to accept the authority of the Pope in all matters,' I said.

'That makes them Protestants,' he said rather nicely.[19]

Next day dawned overcast and blustery. The glass was still high, at 1042, though the wind had shifted in the night to west-south-west. We were now lying parallel to the beach rather than bow-in. Occasional rain squalls washed in across the headland to the west of Holland Bay. Our destination that day was Westray, since I had been told that at Pierowall there is the best fish and chip shop in the world.

But I had decided to finish with the bird business by taking a detour to the island which is the headquarters of the RSPB's British corncrake experiment, Egilsay.[20]

It was on Egilsay, in 1117, that Earl Haakon was murdered. Subsequently canonised as St Magnus, the great cathedral in Kirkwall is named after him. His remains were discovered in 1919 entombed within the cathedral. They showed that he had died from two axe-blows, one of which split his skull and the other one his face, coming in just under his nose, as the upper jaw is severed from the rest of the

19 I subsequently contacted the Catholic hierarchy to ask their view of the Redemptorists' status. The Right Reverend Monsignor Peter Smith, Chancellor of the Archdiocese of Glasgow, told me 'These Redemptorists are not in communion with the Church and do not recognise the authority of the Pope. If you ask if this makes them "Protestant" – no, is the simple answer . . . They are effectively a group of excommunicated Catholics, hence Catholics should not have anything to do with them apart from encouraging them back into the Church.' (email 14 July 2003)

20 'What're you at, Ian?' a friend asked me one evening in the pub when I was back on Islay and busy writing this chapter. 'Egilsay,' I replied. 'What's that?' he asked. 'It's an island in Orkney,' I said. 'Oh right. It sounded like a testicular disease.'

head. This act is commemorated in a little roofless church close to where it happened.

Egilsay is an island of white settlers, lightly admixed with ferryloupers, the native Orcadians having mostly left in the 1960s and '70s.[21] In 1996 the RSPB launched an Appeal which raised £221,000 for corncrake research and the purchase of 30 per cent of Egilsay for corncrake production. A further £330,000 was raised in a subsequent Orkney Isles Appeal, some of which was used to buy more land on Egilsay. Success on Coll, where corncrake numbers have increased on the RSPB reserve[22] was to be repeated in Orkney. As science is not science unless it is repeatable, this project would test whether there is anything scientific about the RSPB's approach to corncrake 'production'. Since the main justification for the Society's immense landholdings in Scotland – it is the sixth largest landowner in the country – is its 'bird science', the Egilsay experiment could be said to be a key indicator of the validity of the RSPB's whole *raison d'être*.

The management states the Egilsay reserve's main aim: 'To increase the breeding population of the corncrake on the reserve from three to up to ten calling males'. The next highest priority is 'to increase the corncrake population on surrounding land on Egilsay from one to ten to twenty calling males . . . [Egilsay] is central to the corncrake recovery programme in Orkney . . . This reserve will be developed as the core area for corncrake management by the RSPB . . . It is known that there is sufficient habitat to support at least ten corncrakes on the reserve.[23] If the habitat is so appropriate and its control in the hands of the RSPB, the figures for corncrakes on Egilsay must be a fair indicator of the RSPB's effectiveness in bird preservation. Starting with the first full year of RSPB control, to the year of my visit, the figures for corncrakes on the island are as follows:

21 An RSPB document notes: 'Today there is only one Orcadian on the island. The population is cosmopolitan and is made up of six English families, three Irish families, two Scottish families and one each of Welsh, Canadian, Anglo/Orkney and Anglo/Norwegian', *Corncrake Newsletter, 1996*, Tim Dean. The RSPB also researched the islanders' finances, noting that of the families on Egilsay 'income is supplemented by the DHSS in seven houses [out of fifteen]'.

22 See *Isles of the West*, pp. 47–56.

23 *Onziebust RSPB Reserve, Egilsay, Orkney: Management Plan*, RSPB, Sandy 1998 *passim*.

Year	Egilsay total	RSPB reserve total
	7	4
	4	3
	4	2
	4	2
	0	0
	0	0

In the light of this failure, the third priority in the Management Plan is interesting: 'To use the Reserve to demonstrate corncrake management to other farmers and land managers.' The RSPB's Director, Scotland, is confident in the Society's ability to attract corncrakes to suitable ground:

> I believe we have cracked the problem for the corncrake. We now know that careful management of crofts and farmland in their strongholds is leading to a recovery. In time these illusive (*sic*) birds could return to some of their traditional haunts . . . The crucial discovery was that numbers declined because of changes in farming practice.[24]

Prodded by the RSPB, the British government uses corncrake production as an indicator of its own ecological virtue. 'Only through actions at home can the government have authority to be heard in the global debate,' said Barbara Young, then Chief Executive of the RSPB, in an article arguing for state action on the basis of the agreements made at the Rio Earth Summit in 1992.[25] She tied this directly to the issue of the corncrake:

> This winter sees the first gathering of the states that signed the Convention on Biological Diversity since the Rio Earth Summit two and a half years ago . . . In 1994 the corncrake became extinct in

---

24 RSPB Media Release 'Corncrakes Turn the Corner', 1 December 2000. These words were published almost verbatim in the *Scotsman* and the *Herald* on 4 December. The relationship between corncrake numbers and agricultural practices was first suggested over half a century ago by C. A. Norris in a ground-breaking paper: Summary of a Report on the Distribution and Status of the Corncrake, Part I. *British Birds* vol. 38 (1945), p. 142; Part II *Ibid*. vol. 40 (1947), p. 226.

25 *Birds*, Winter 1994, p. 5. Miss Young is now Baroness Young of Old Scone, and Chief Executive of the Environment Agency.

Northern Ireland. Numbers fell in Britain . . . The reasons have been identified, practical solutions tried and proven: we [the RSPB] have played our part. The question now is how the government intends to act to save the corncrake and to encourage more of them, in accordance with our commitments to the Convention.

In 1995 the UK Biodiversity Steering Group published its recommendations – including 'costed action plans', most of which were not costed – for 116 species and fourteen habitats considered to be at risk. Each of these species and habitats was allocated a public body to organise its revival. Thus English Nature got the Sandy Stilt Puffball (*Batterraea phalloides*) and the Ministry of Agriculture Fisheries and Food the Black-backed Meadow Ant (*Formica pratensis*), while the National Trust was awarded Maritime Cliff and Slope. The only species allocated to the Scottish Office was the corncrake, 'reflecting Scotland's special responsibility for this globally threatened bird,' as John Randall, the head of the Countryside and Natural Heritage Unit in the Scottish Office put it to me. Randall's Group had two sub-Groups, the Core Group and the Consultative Group. Together, they form the Steering Group, to which the RSPB was corporately appointed as Secretary.

The first meeting of the Core Group of the Corncrake Steering Group of the Scottish Biodiversity Group was held on Islay on 14 July 1997. The top priority in the official Remit of the Corncrake Action Plan Steering Group was to develop a Biodiversity Costed Action Plan for the corncrake, on which regular reports were to be made to the Costed Action Plan Sub-group of the Scottish Biodiversity Group, itself a sub-group of the UK Biodiversity Action Plan Steering Group. A subsidiary task was to 'develop awareness' of the work of the Steering Group through the Public Awareness Sub-Group of the same Scottish Biodiversity Group.

Throughout the period when the committee structure was being set up, I corresponded with Dr Rhys Green, who was the RSPB's scientific advisor to the Core Group. I wanted to find out how important Scotland's 500 or so corncrakes are in a global context. My question was simple: how many of these birds are there in the world? Green replied very briefly: 'I know of no estimate of the world population of corncrakes.'[26] I wrote back asking how the species could be considered

---

26 Letter, 11 February 1997.

'globally threatened' when no estimate of its global numbers had ever been made. He replied saying, 'I know of no estimate of the world population of corncrakes and think it unlikely that one exists which is reliable . . . The conservation status of extant species is assessed against criteria defined by the World Conservation Union which include estimates of world population, when available, but do not necessarily require them.'[27]

What I was not aware of was that at that time Green was helping to publish revised estimates of the Russian population of corncrakes which were 1,400 per cent greater than those which had been presented to the Scottish Office. Since Russia is thought to hold nearly 90 per cent of the world's corncrakes, this was of immense significance. In 1999 Green himself published a paper in the main German ornithological journal in which he said that the corncrake is 'a widespread species with a large world population'.[28]

Not only did Green say nothing of this to me, he did not advise the Corncrake Steering Group of the revised population estimates. The Scottish Office officials laboured on, trying to help a bird which they thought was rare when their scientific advisor knew it to be 'widespread and numerous'.

In 1999 the Scottish Executive, as the Scottish Office was now called, held a Corncrake Biodiversity Action Plan Seminar in Inverness. Andrew Dixon was in the Chair, having replaced John Randall, who had been promoted to Registrar-general of Scotland, and was busy organising the 2001 census. Rhys Green made the keynote presentation, once again saying nothing about the new research on corncrake numbers in Russia. In the question session afterwards I asked him about the paper he had published two years previously: 'Have you advised the Scottish Executive of any change in the status of the corncrakes in the last couple of years in terms of global population numbers?'

'Have I advised them on that?' Green said.

'Yes.'

'No,' he answered.[29]

---

27 Letter, 18 March 1997.

28 *Die Vögelwelt* 118, (1997), p. 132 Corncrake numbers in Russia were revised from between 10,000 and 100,000, to 2.5 million. Other eastern European countries also were shown to have hugely increased numbers.

29 Transcript of Annual Corncrake Seminar: Corncrakes in Context, 28 October 1999. Green did say that he had told SNH of his new knowledge, but not the corncrake group.

Dixon looked shocked, as well he might have been because the work and expense of running the Corncrake Biodiversity Action Plan Steering Group was not insignificant.

Next year John Ramsay, a rubicund Scot with a direct manner, took over as Head of Biodiversity at what was now called the Scottish Executive Environment and Rural Affairs Department (SEERAD). No more seminars were held under its aegis. I asked him why. He said, 'I am trying to reduce unprofitable bureaucratic business.' The Scottish Executive subsequently put the RSPB in sole charge of the Corncrake Biodiversity Costed Action Plan Steering Group.

In May 2000 I published a long article which described the controversy over corncrake numbers.[30] The RSPB responded a year later with a paper in an RSPB scientific journal which attempted to answer my point that a 'widespread species with a large world population' cannot, in the natural and ordinary meaning of the words, be 'globally threatened'. The answer was that 'the reason that the corncrake is listed as globally threatened is not rarity, but the history of large and rapid declines in many countries and the prospect that these could happen elsewhere.'[31]

The RSPB sponsored a book about the status of the corncrake in Russia published by the Russian Bird Conservation Union in 2000, a year before the paper mentioned above. It was edited by the scientists who had produced the new, larger figures for the bird in 1997. They conclude that, 'Corncrake should undoubtedly be *excluded* [emphasis added] from the list of Globally Threatened Species . . . As there are no serious human-caused limiting factors for corncrake, no special actions are needed now for species conservation throughout the whole range in Russia.'[32]

The RSPB paper, which was published a year *after* the Russian book, concludes the opposite: namely, that the corncrake *should* be considered

---

30 *The Times*, 13 May 2000.
31 The Global Status of the Corncrake, by Norbert Schäffer and Rhys Green, *RSPB Conservation Review* 13 (2001), p. 22.
32 *Corncrake in European Russia: Numbers and Distribution*, Soyuz Okhrani Ptitsi Rossii, Moscow 2000, p. 169. An example of Russian abundance is that the Moscow administrative district – by far the most intensely developed in all Russia – contains more than *five times* as many corncrakes as the whole of western Europe from Spain to Finland. The Director of the survey, Alexander Mishchenko has subsequently told me, 'The corncrake population in Russia is in good condition.' (email 5 June 2003)

'globally threatened', even though the RSPB authors' information on Russia comes from the Russians. The RSPB make no mention of the Russians' conclusions and therefore offer no reason why their reasoning should be ignored. There can be no argument that the RSPB knew of the Russian work because they, Rhys Green and Norbert Schäffer, are explicitly thanked in the Russian book's Acknowledgements – two of only four individuals mentioned. It is hard to resist the conclusion that the RSPB chooses the science that suits its political and/or fund-raising purposes.

A small final point is that while the first attempt to count corncrakes in Britain was not made until 1979, the Russians started keeping an eye on the bird half a century earlier. The oldest data set mentioned in the Russian book, for Izmailovsky Park in Moscow (roughly equivalent to Hampstead Heath in London), starts as long ago as 1928. In the 1950s, part of the park was drained and ploughed up for vegetable gardens. But neither that nor its proximity to the centre of a city which now has a population of 8 million, nor heavy recreational use, has affected corncrake numbers there. The author says, 'Presented data suggest the exceptional stability of the corncrake population for seventy years in this developed area.'

At about twenty calling males in each of the surveys over the last seventy-five years, there have been more corncrakes in the middle of Moscow than there are today in the whole of Orkney. Even more significant is the fact that, despite the expenditure of what must be a seven-figure sum on buying and managing land for corncrakes, in 2002, the RSPB *did not have a single calling male on any of its Orkney reserves!*

That, perhaps, is the truly appropriate context in which to assess both the failure of the RSPB's experiment on Egilsay and the questionable nature of its science. Add in the harrier failure, and it has to be asked what remaining justification there can be for the RSPB's huge estate on Orkney?

Brian and I sailed out of Holland Bay, round Rothiesholm Head, into a wet and gusty westerly breeze. Just off the headland we grounded very lightly, which was another unpleasant experience. Then we laid a course north-west for the southern tip of Egilsay. Under a heavy sky, the northern islands had a forbidding look. More luminous patches of cloud were visible here and there, low on the horizon, giving hope for better weather to come. Though the glass was still up at 1042, nothing much changed in the three hours it took us to tack up to Rousay Sound and then reach in to the ferry pier on the western side of Egilsay.

After two hours ashore – the St Magnus Church was interesting; the RSPB area boring – we cast off for Westray. Shallows make it interesting work getting out of the north end of Rousay Sound, but the sight of a largish fishing boat coming south gave us valuable clues. We took it slowly until well through, then set all plain sail and headed north-east for the little gap between Weather Head at the south end of Westray and Faray Holm. By now the clouds had lifted slightly and we had a dry, easy sail round to the east side of Westray and up towards Pierowall. Then the wind got up a bit and, coming due west, forced us to tack as we headed into the bay. Heeled well over, we raced in as far in as the fish farm before I thought it prudent to fire up the engine and lower sail.

We tied up alongside a wooden Norwegian sixty-footer, which had a young family aboard on a round-the-world cruise. Within five minutes of doing so, the harbour master arrived with a leaflet explaining the delights of Westray, including details of where we could shower (the showers were excellent), the times of the meals in the hotel and how we could have fresh bread sent down to the boat in the morning – a charming welcome.

Westray is the opposite of Egilsay in that of all the islands in Orkney it has retained the highest percentage of its Orcadian population. It has become a by-word in Orkney for the will to survive. Up until very recent times, Westray was an important fishing island, mainly due to the relatively sheltered harbour at Pierowall. But as the white fish trade contracted in the early 1990s, the island was threatened by economic stagnation and population decline. But, as we were to discover, the community is fighting back.

On our way up to the hotel for our fish and chips, Brian and I were picked up by one of the people I had arranged to see, a retired fisherman called Alex Costie who now farms for birds after SNH imposed an SSSI on his ground.

'If everybody ran their farms like mine,' Alex said to me with a sigh, 'the whole community would collapse. I don't need fertiliser, so I don't need a haulier to bring that stuff in. I've no cattle to go out to the mart in Kirkwall, so I don't need the ferries. It's grand for me, but it's no doing much for the community. When I was arguing with SNH I used to tell them that when I die and go to heaven I am going to be asked, "Did you farm that land to the best of your ability to feed the starving children in the world?" I'm going to have to answer, "No I got more money for keeping birds." So that'll be me doon the road.'

By contrast, Alex said, the fishermen were doing well, even if there were far fewer of them on the island than twenty years ago, when he was at sea. His current interest was trying to devise ways of making money from what might be called the by-products of biodiversity. What started him thinking, apparently, was admiration for the neighbour who had sold the cliffs at Noup Head to the RSPB. 'It's quite a good trick, yae ken, to sell somebody a vertical cliff,' he said.

But he wasn't so happy when that principle was applied to farmland. 'With the money that RSPB paid for the cliffs you could have bought any farm on the island at that time. RSPB are inclined to buy any small farm that comes up for sale, so the price goes up. Its very fine for the folk that's selling it, but for a chap like me that's wanting to buy a piece ground, it's not so good.'

'What of the future?' I asked.

'You can only shoot a seal once, but you can charge folk to see it any number of times. That's what I tell the fishermen when they complain about the number of seals. It's quite an easy way of making a pound or two. I just wish we had whales as well because whale-watching is a really lucrative thing.'

'Really?'

'God, aye. I was on a trip in New Zealand one time and they took about $80 off me, and there was three bus loads of us.'

Next morning – yes, the fish was excellent, and also very cheap – the weather had turned cool and damp. I had arranged to meet Stephen Hagan, the Councillor for Westray, Papa Westray and Eday,[33] on the pier as he was going to try to give me some idea of how the island was dealing with the disease of centralisation which is so effectively killing life on so many Scottish islands. Westray is known in Orkney for being the most go-ahead of all the islands and Stephen, or Steve as he prefers to be known, was directly involved in founding the Westray Development Trust which has been the main instrument for turning round the island's economy.

Steve is a tall, smartly dressed, red-haired Ulsterman who met and married a Westray girl when they were both students in Edinburgh,

---

33 In May 2003 he was elected Convenor of the Orkney Island Council.

he of engineering and she of nursing. Sixteen years ago they moved to
the island. In 1998 a conference of all parties and people interested in
the future of the island was called. A staggering 400 people turned up
for the two-day event, a figure higher than the island's adult population. A report was published which made the main point that Westray,
and by implication all islands in a similar position, were being depopu-
lated because people left either for further education, which was both
inevitable and desirable, or for employment, which was neither. The
result is that Westray has more or less full employment but a declining
population.

One of the reasons so many of the fishermen, who were once, with
the farmers, the backbone of the island's economy, had left for ports
like Kirkwall was so that their wives would be able to get jobs of the
sort which are not easily obtainable in smallish islands. Modern outdoor
work is largely done by men, leaving women with few employment
options outside urban centres. Partly for that reason and partly due to its
neglected state in the past, tourism was the focus of the main recommendations made at the end of the conference, though two other schemes
were also discussed. First was a care home for the elderly of Westray who
at present are shunted off to Kirkwall. Secondly, there is the fish factory
which now runs very successfully above the harbour. It is said to be the
second largest crab-meat producer in Britain.

Steve not being a local, the talk naturally got round to incomers. 'The
Chairman of the Community Council on Eday is an incomer and he
said to me, "I didn't come to Eday to look out on a fish farm." Generally
speaking it's the local people who want to move ahead. The incomers do
not seem to realise that if you don't develop the place it's slowly going
to die.'

'You say Westray is the most go-ahead of the Orkney islands,' I said,
'and it is also, proportionately, the most indigenous. Do you see a
connection?'

'I think there is. People who have lived here all their lives have seen
what happened to the farming and the fishing and they realise that
something's going to have to change to keep the island alive.'

'Presumably there are examples of incomers who have given the place
a boost?'

'Absolutely. When we set the Development Trust up I chaired it for
the first couple of years and I was aware that those people will come to

the fore, whereas a lot of the locals tend to be a little reserved. They'll take a back seat if they can, so you really have to try and encourage them to get involved. I was very keen that at least half, if not more, of the trust's directors were locals. Otherwise I think it loses its credibility. Westray has needed the mix. The incomers have helped to draw the locals out their shells a little bit. A lot of them have really helped drive the trust forward. The chairman at the moment, for instance, is a Church of Scotland minister. He's a really go-ahead guy. What's happening here really is that the community itself, both incomers and locals, is taking the initiative. We haven't had agencies like Orkney Enterprise telling us what to do. They can give you professional advice and can help you to draw up business plans and all that stuff, but you have to have the ideas coming from the ground.'

Steve took me for a quick trip round the north end of the island, explaining as we drove that his wife's family had come from Papa Stronsay in the 1930s. We ended up at the archaeological dig above the beach at Aikerness. On the broad, pebbly strand it is easy to imagine Vikings hauling their longboats up above the high-tide mark before handing out the day's fish or distributing loot from the last raid. Throughout the summer the Pierowall Hotel does such a brisk trade accommodating young archaeology students that the proprietor – who, incidentally, was the enterpriser who sold the Noup Head cliffs to the RSPB – has established a hostel for them. While the students fiddled around with paint brushes and teaspoons in the foundations of what used to be a Viking feasting hall, the master-in-charge – or so I could not help thinking of him, so youthful-looking were the diggers – explained to us some of their finds. Amongst them had been some very large cod bones, suggesting that fish were much larger in Viking times than today.

'It's funny the things the press picks up on,' the archaeologist said. 'Overfishing was one unlikely one. This reporter came out and interviewed a local sea-captain and myself. We looked at these bones and compared them with the bones of the modern cod, which is about 50 centimetres long, and this archaeological find which was massively larger. The reporter goes, "Don't you think this is clear evidence for overfishing in modern times?" The sea captain turned to him without a moment's hesitation and said, "No. It's clear evidence for *under*-fishing in the Viking age." '

Steve handed me over to Sam Harcus, who is the island's Development Officer and, as such, in charge of implementing the plans conceived by the Development Trust. A total contrast to Steve, Sam is Westray born and bred. He drove a dilapidated van and looked like a village mechanic on a 'dressing down' day. He had been chief engineer on an oil-rig supply vessel until retiring from the sea a few years previously. Down at his smartly modern house, we discussed the different types of tourist the Westray Tourist Association are trying to attract. They get about 5,000 visitors of all sorts in an average year, but the ones they want more of is yachtsmen. The reason is that they spend lavishly – partly because they have no accommodation expenses – without taking up bed-space. At the other end of the scale are bird-watchers who occupy hotel beds while spending very little.

Sam was interested in the differing psychology of the two types of visitor. We agreed that a likely explanation is connected with the fact that most birders are, in John Holloway's term, 'listers'. People who collect specimens must be 'retentive characters', I said, trying to be tactful. Sam just laughed and called them 'mean'.

Finally we discussed the one type of tourist whom Westray had so far failed to attract: sea anglers.

'What can you catch around here?' I asked, knowing little of the sport.

'Shark.'

'Shark!'

'Shark, aye, porbeagle sharks. They pass by here quite a lot. They like tidal headlands. There was a local fisherman who retired from the white fish trade and bought a work boat and went out fishing in his spare time. He found he got loads of sharks. They started selling them in the hotel; they may be still on the menu, I don't know. You could get a porbeagle steak.'

'What does it taste like?'

'It's quite fishy, but stringy like chicken or beef.'

It was obvious that the next person I had to visit was the shark fisherman. Willie Sandison lives in a large house overlooking the harbour where he made his money. He told me he had caught only two sharks the previous year. They had become entangled in nets he had put out for other fish. One of them weighed 14 stone and the other 20 stone. He showed me photographs of them and I would judge them to have been 8 and 10 feet long. They go after herring and mackerel and are quite common off the northern isles in the brief season. I asked Willie how he caught them.

'You catch them with hooks but you will need a lure of some kind. Sharks are very sensitive to smell, they can smell blood an awfa' piece away. A guy tellt me if you're catching sharks, be very careful and not let the blood of the shark go over the side, because if you do all the sharks in that area will disappear. Whatever you are doing don't pump the bilge with the shark water in it.'

'Is there a market for their meat?'

'Aye, very good. One guy here tasted it and said it reminded him of veal.'

'Why did you give up the ordinary fishing?' I asked. 'Not enough fish?'

'It wasnae lack of fish, lack of getting leave to catch them.'

'Really?'

'Yes. Plenty of fish about.'

'Is this all to do with the quotas?'

'It's all to do with *politics*,' he said with disgust. 'Anything you see on the TV is absolute garbage. There's plenty of fish in the sea. There was so much fish in here this year that the one guy burst his net. He has been at sea for fifteen years and he said it is the most fish he has ever seen round these islands.'

'So why do we get the message that there's no fish?'

'It's the scientists, they don't have a clue what they're doing. Fish don't go to the same piece every year. You can't go to the same piece and get fish. You have to go aboot looking for them. There are different areas that they come to. You'll find them somewhere in that area, but what the scientists do is they go to the same spot every year and if they don't get fish there they think the fish are gone.'

'That doesn't sound very sensible.'

'I wouldna say that. The scientists don't want folk to think there's fish in the sea. If they can't go aroond every year doing their tests they're out of a job.'

By tea-time I was tired of talking and walked back to the boat for a rest. By now the sun was out and it was hot. I could not resist the temptation to go up to the fish factory and buy myself a small feed of crab, which I ate with a can of lager while relaxing in the sunshine on deck, watching the Norwegian children playing around as if they had lived on boats all their lives.

At seven o'clock Brian returned, as had been arranged, clean, shaved and after-shaved. This was his birthday and I had decided we should celebrate by dining at the Cleaton House Hotel, which is known for having the best food in the northern isles of Orkney. I had booked for eight o'clock but thought it would be pleasant to walk the two miles beyond the town to where the hotel, which used to be a Church of Scotland manse, sits on its own amidst the fields. So we had a small Ardbeg while Brian opened the single birthday card he had received, from the skipper.

It is a lovely walk up to Cleaton House, especially if you take a half-overgrown farm track which cuts off quite a bit of the distance. Twenty years ago the house was bought by Alex Costie for conversion from a Church eventide home to a family home. Alex sold it to a Westray family who had been away from the island working for some time. As we were to discover 24 hours later, their name, Stout, is common on the Fair Isle, from where the family had come in the nineteenth century. Today Malcolm Stout – dark-haired, bearded and, believe it or not, stout – runs the hotel to what quickly proved to be the very highest standards.

We started in the sitting room with a couple of Scapas, the new Orkney malt, and bottles of Red MacGregor, a beer which is also produced in Orkney. By the time we took our seats in the dining room, I was so caught up in the quiet magic of the place that I ordered us a bottle of fizz. The dining room has only five tables in it and the atmosphere is that of a home. There was an elderly pair of holiday makers at one and two Scottish matrons obviously on a jaunt at the other. Apart from that we were alone.

While we were eating, a dense cloud came up from the west. There was a heavy shower which lasted ten minutes or so and was followed by an amazing double rainbow. The ladies lifted themselves out of their seats to get a better view at the windows. The smooth fields of silage which lead down to the sea glowed a rich green in the low evening light, while the sea beyond them, being still in shadow, was grey and wind-swept-looking. The sky was equally divided with a cold but clear evening blue above us and the dense, dark cloud out to the east. The rainbow divided the two. If the weather kept in that quarter, I thought, we would make excellent time to the Fair Isle in the morning.

The meal was absolutely delicious. We both ate sirloin steaks. My only regret was the unavailability of an item I had seen displayed on a sample menu when we arrived: 'Pan-fried fillet of porbeagle shark, resting on a pink peppercorn, port, brandy and cream sauce.' Afterwards, we drank port with our coffee in the drawing room while chatting to Malcolm Stout. At about midnight, he hopped into his Volvo and drove us back to the boat. A perfect way to say farewell to the unbloody Orkneys.

4

FAIR ISLE

AFTER THE KALEIDOSCOPE OF exotic drinks the night before, Brian and I were not at our freshest when hauling ourselves out of our bunks at 6 a.m., in order to catch the flood tide which flows west to east around Orkney. But it was a sunny morning and as *Foggy Dew* slipped past Papa Westray and headed for the open sea an hour later we both began to feel a little more human.

One thinks of the Fair Isle as being north of Orkney, but from Westray we steered more east than north to pass south of the island. The wind was north-west and steady, so it looked as if we would have it on the quarter all the way, which was ideal. We raced past North Ronaldsay with the GPS showing 11.5 knots, suggesting nearly 6 knots of tide. But I got a shock when, a mile off the lighthouse, I looked overside and saw the water rushing back from south to north. This was clearly undertow, implying shallow water. We were over the seal skerry, a wide shelf of rock which I had thought we were clear of. Brian was below, catching up on his sleep. With the wind free, I would have needed the autohelm rigged to have left the tiller. Though *Foggy Dew* will easily hold her course with the helm lashed on a reach or going to windward, downwind it is a different matter. I had been reluctant to wake Brian just so that I could check the chart again in what looked like open ocean. Never again.

Approaching the Fair Isle, the wind got up a bit and the sky clouded over. We passed a large trawler heading north into the swell. Sheets of spray were flying up towards its bridge deck, though we were sailing dry. Off the south end of the island, we ran into a steep chop near the Röst of Keels where the tide boils past a scatter of skerries. Sleeping in the port, and therefore now windward bunk, without the lee-cloth up, Brian was at one point catapulted onto the cabin sole with a crash which looked painful. For some reason he climbed back into the same bunk again, probably without having fully woken.

Once we were through the turbulence, I had time to get the binoculars onto the island, which looked pleasantly lived-in rather than bleakly deserted as I had expected. Turning up the eastern side we rounded into the wind and became aware of its strength. Not only that, rain started pelting down, so we had an uncomfortable half-hour approaching the North Haven. Close in, we furled the headsail and started the motor. The wind eased and the rain turned to a near-vertical drizzle. The sailing directions warn of rocks on both sides of the entrance so we dropped the mainsail and poottered in very gingerly, not wishing any more collisions.

Recently, a breakwater has been constructed of huge boulders so that the harbour is now relatively sheltered – in summer at least. For winter, there is a cradle and slip with which to winch the island's ferry, *Good Shepherd IV*, completely out of the water between its weekly trips to Shetland. We tied up alongside a modern concrete quay at about 2 p.m.

After lunch, I took my turn at catching up with my sleep then set off to walk the short distance to the north end of the island. There the landscape is hilly. Arctic skuas, a bird I had not seen before, strutted around amongst the clumps of heather like big lapwings. From the lighthouse I could see the southern tip of Shetland clearly, even though the visibility was not particularly good. I explored the buildings then took some pictures of the myriad seabirds on the Stacks of Skroo. Soon after I set off to walk the mile and a half back to the boat, the only car I had seen all evening drew up and offered me a lift. The driver was a friendly, bright-eyed woman with tight, curly hair. She told me her name was Clare Scott and that she lived at the south end of the island where she made silver jewellery. I asked her if I might come and see her workshop. We arranged to meet next day after lunch. She dropped me off at the famous Bird Observatory which stands immediately above the harbour and which played such an important part in rescuing Fair Isle from abandonment in the 1950s.

The history of Fair Isle is not known in much detail until the eighteenth century, when it was first bought and sold. It was mentioned by the writers of the Viking Sagas and appears to have been inhabited since at least 1000 BC, if not earlier. It peeped into world history when the *Gran Grifon*, one of the King of Spain's transport ships for the Armada in

1588, went aground there after losing its bearings in an autumnal storm while sailing back to Spain. Many other ships did the same. It was not until 1892 that the lighthouses at the north and south ends of the island were built – by Alan Stevenson, son of the man who erected the Dubh Artach light.

These lighthouses were indirectly very damaging to Fair Isle because they facilitated inshore trawling, which became such a threat to local fishing that for many years there was sporadic talk of evacuation, St Kilda-style. The development in the late nineteenth century of steam-powered boats, equipped with winches powerful enough to handle huge nets, changed the balance of advantage in fishing communities to the benefit of those where capital was concentrated, like Aberdeen and Peterhead, and to the disadvantage of smaller places where the local people had been accustomed to make a subsistence living by hand-hauling fish, often in open boats. The easiest place to trawl is in shallow, inshore waters, which have the added advantage of being where many of the fish shoal. The concurrent development of railways expanded the market for fresh fish from towns served by the new network. Always geographically peripheral, places like Fair Isle were now economically marginalised because of that.[1]

It was soon clear that new technology threatened fish stocks so, after a public outcry, Britain declared a three-mile limit in 1889, inside which trawlers were not permitted to fish. Perhaps predictably, the state did not unduly exert itself to ensure rules made to help largely powerless crofters in the Northern Isles and the Hebrides were enforced against powerful

---

1 An example of the power of capitalist compared with subsistence fisheries was the response of the former to the attempt by the British government to help small coastal communities in the late nineteenth century by closing the Moray Firth and the Firths of Forth, Tay, Clyde and others (including Loch Indaal on Islay) to trawlers in the 1890s. Several countries refused to recognise the enlarged limits, so some trawler owners re-flagged their boats, enabling them to continue to fish in waters now closed to Scottish trawlers. Little effort was made to prevent foreign boats ignoring the new restrictions. Some people thought that 'the real reason was that by this time English trawlers were fishing in a big scale off the coasts of Iceland and north Norway and that there was a powerful behind-the-scenes lobby which wished to retain the British right to fish close to the coasts of other countries'. (*The Sea Fisheries of Scotland: a Historical Geography*, James Coull, Edinburgh 1996, p. 151)

industrial fishing interests of the east coast. Fair Isle fishermen tried to resist by reporting illegal fishing. Trawler skippers were convicted in the Lerwick Sheriff Court when the culprits could be identified, which was not always possible, since they took to fishing at night, which would have been very hazardous without the guidance of the island's two powerful lighthouses.

On one occasion, some Fair Isle men rowed out to discover the identity of a trawler working inshore and were pelted by the crew with lumps of coal. They returned fire with the ballast stones from their open yoal to such effect that the trawler's wheelhouse was smashed. It had to return to Aberdeen, where the damage instantly revealed the boat's identity with the result that the skipper was prosecuted. But this was an isolated victory in a long, unsuccessful war.

The slow death of traditional fishing threw the Fair Isle boatmen back on lobster creeling. But there was no substantial export income to be earned without regular transport to the markets in the south. At the same time, agriculture was suffering from the long depression which afflicted most British farming between the 1870s and the Second World War. The future for the island looked bleak until the flamboyant Prince of Wales, later King Edward VIII and later still the Duke of Windsor, played golf at St Andrews in 1920 in what came to be known as a Fair Isle sweater. Royal example gave the island's industry a considerable boost. While shears clipped on the hill in the summer, needles clicked by the fireside in winter. But that trade, too, was hindered by the remoteness of the island. In the long run, what was needed was not so much to bring Fair Isle to the market, but to bring the market to Fair Isle. That has been the great contribution which the twentieth-century fad for bird-watching has made. The man who effected the transformation was a young, unworldly Edinburgh suburbanite called George Waterston.[2]

Waterston was the fifth generation of his family to be involved in the Edinburgh stationery business which was started in 1752 and went into receivership in 2003. But he was more interested in birds than printing, so got involved in founding the Isle of May bird observatory, the Midlothian Ornithological Club and the Scottish Ornithologists' Club. The Isle of May stimulated his interest in migration studies and it was that which first took him to the Fair Isle, in 1936. He later recalled that

2 See chapter 3,

Previous page: Sailing from Islay to Mingulay

Top: At anchor off the beach on Mingulay

Right: Callum MacNeil's lobster ready to eat in Stornoway harbour, with mole grips to crack the claws

Bottom: Up the mast in Stornoway

Top: Approaching Rona

Below: Razorbills, puffins and guillemots on the west cliffs of Rona

Right: The Old Man of Hoy

Bottom: Stromness

Top left: Early morning tea in Stromness Harbour

Top right: Morning at Lyness pier

Above: St Magnus Cathedral, Kirkwall

Top: Approaching Fair Isle

Upper middle: North Haven, Fair Isle

Left: Jimmy Stout, captain of the Fair Isle ferry

Below: Brian walking back from the shop on Fair Isle

Top left: Foggy Dew after arriving in Foula, before the mist lifted

Top right: Farmhouse on Foula

Middle: The cliffs of Foula. Note the size of the fishing boat, lower left

Bottom: Leaving Foula

Top: The North Haa, Westsandwick, Yell, Shetland

Middle: Brian and Robert in the kitchen at the North Haa

Bottom: Crossing the North Sea, before the wind got up

Top: Crossing the North Sea, after the wind got up

Middle: Måløy in the morning

Bottom: The Horneleset on Bremanger, from the mainland

Top: The bedroom in Bremanger

Lower left: Øle Stingbak and his hangar on the fjord

Lower right: The seaplane from behind

Left: The bar at the restaurant in Kalvåg

Middle: The waterfront in Kalvåg – a considerable contrast to Castlebay

Bottom: 'With the sails goose-winged in a following wind, we headed for the interior at a relaxed 5 knots. Another Ardbeg Moment seemed to be indicated.'

Top: The village of Kandall. Oddrun's home is at the lower left

Middle: The hydro-electric station for Kandall: a pipe, hut and free power for life

Left: Nick with a dram in the mountain pool near Voss

Above: Early morning alongside Jens Skjerdal's pier at Skjerdal on the Nordfjord

Left: The *Fiskebas* at Florø

Below: The bridge deck of the *Fiskebas* at 3 a.m. Nick, the ex-banker, is staggered that all this is financed purely out of retained profits

Top: The Bergen to Måløy ferry at speed – eat your heart out CalMac!

Left: A seahouse on Svanøy

Below left: Hannah Wood preparing my cappuccino on Lygra

Below right: Øle Svanoe outside his café-pub

Above: Foggy Dew alongside the pier on Lygra at sunrise

Right: Foggy Dew tied up alongside the town pier in central Bergen. No formalities; no security; no problem

Below left: Whalemeat at the fishmarket in Bergen

Below right: A dram before lunch on Røvaer

Left: The inner basin of the north harbour at Utsira

Middle: Brian and Reidar Klovning enjoying a beer in the sunshine

Bottom: Leaving Utsira at dawn, on course for Inverness

he and his friend Archie Bryson were the only visitors to the island that year.

In 1941 Waterston travelled to Crete as part of a rather larger expedition which, though he spent some of his time birdwatching, had the more serious purpose of trying to help destroy Nazism. He was taken prisoner and spent the next two years in enemy captivity until an incurable kidney disease allowed him to be repatriated in exchange for wounded Germans. Before that, in the comfortable Oflag at Eichstätt, a former German officers' barracks situated amongst the woods and rolling hills of lower Bavaria, he studied wrynecks in company with Peter Conder, later to be the first Director of the RSPB, who spent his time looking at goldfinches. Waterston also helped the Director of the Berlin Museum compile a paper on the migrant birds of Crete which was published in 1943. Luckily there are no jokes in the birding word or he might have suffered the fate of P.G. Wodehouse, who made light of his experiences as an internee in Germany in broadcasts to America and was very nearly tried for high treason at the end of the war on account of his flippancy.

The first part of Britain that Waterston caught sight of on his voyage home was the Fair Isle:

> There on a beautiful still October morning in the sunshine was the island I had been dreaming about all the time I was in the prison camp. You can well imagine the extraordinary effect it had on me. I felt if this wasn't a good omen for the future, what was! [Later] on my first convalescent leave I went straight to Fair Isle. I had to pull a few wires to do this ... [From Kirkwall] we set off for Fair Isle in an air-sea rescue launch which burned about 70 gallons of high octane petrol an hour and sped north up to Fair Isle and landed there during the war when the army were in occupation and stayed there about a week or a fortnight. My plans then began to mature for the future Fair Isle observatory.[3]

Initially, the Army would not release Waterston, but he pulled some more 'wires' and arranged for his friend James Fisher – he of Copinsay – to get him a job on his Oxford rook research project until the end of the war. After that, the next hurdle was to avoid returning to the world

---

3 *Birds* September–October 1972, p. 116.

of commerce. Fisher helped again by arranging part-time employment for Waterston as the first RSPB officer in Scotland, with a room in the National Trust for Scotland headquarters in Edinburgh. Then in 1947 Sumburgh Estates put Fair Isle on the market. Waterston raised an interest-free loan of £3,500 from a friendly peer and bought it. The following year the newly established Fair Isle Bird Observatory Trust opened for business, housing paying guests in wooden huts which the navy had left intact above the North Haven. Waterston married the secretary of the Glasgow branch of the Scottish Ornithologists' Club and settled down to the life of a landowning bureaucrat.

These were years of optimism in bird-watching circles, not least because of the feeling, reinforced by the war, that bureaucracy would be important to the efficient organisation of civil society in the future. This was the 'new Jerusalem' era of the planned economy. There was to be no return to the unregulated freedoms and widespread inequality of the 1930s. Part of this programme involved bringing the countryside under public control. The new Labour government founded the Nature Conservancy and legislated in England for easier recreational access.[4] Young people wishing to get out of doors for a few years no longer 'went east' on behalf of the Empire – India was given its independence in the year Waterston acquired Fair Isle – but into their local woods, fields and hedgerows in the interests of 'science'. The atmosphere was co-operative, earnest and plain – very different from both the 'anarchy' of the inter-war years and the self-advertising competitiveness which John Holloway regrets in ornithological circles today. An authority on modern birding describes this approach:

> In the postwar years there were observatories at a number of key birding locations [including] Fair Isle. Until the 1960s they were probably the principle focus for birding activity, and they were usually a cheap

---

4 Ironically, it also took farming under state control (by converting comprehensive wartime regulation into a regime of permanent, state-directed subsidies) and legislated for the modern planning system, two measures which were eventually to undermine the public freedoms which other measures were intended to create. Within a couple of decades the national view of the countryside had changed from a place of food production and personal refreshment to a ruthlessly exploited development resource, which, after the abolition of tax on planning gain in 1953, provided one of the few respectable ways of getting rich quickly under the post-war regime of high taxation on earned income.

hostel-style accommodation where amateur ornithologists came to share in the advancement of scientific knowledge. As an institution the observatory has its origins in the communal ethos of an older Britain, and nowadays that collective spirit towards pastimes seems both old-fashioned and quaint.[5]

Visitor numbers at the observatory increased rapidly. Bird-watching ceased to be the preserve of vicars and dotty lairds like Lord Grey, or John Buchan's son, Lord Tweedsmuir, who piloted the Protection of Birds Act through parliament in 1954. Instead it became a mass participation sport for the indoorish middle class. There were two main reasons for this. In the 1950s 'hands-on' activities, like bird-nesting by children, were criminalised while, at the same time, television introduced new techniques, including the insertion of cameras inside nests, which brought the domestic world of birds into the sitting rooms of suburbia. The expansion of interest was dramatic. In round figures, the RSPB had a membership of 3,000 in 1940, 5,000 in 1950, 10,000 in 1960, 70,000 in 1970, 320,000 in 1980 and 820,000 in 1990.[6] These were largely suburbanites, as the Society promoted the 'passive spectator' approach to wildlife which was very different from the active involvement of, say, the

---

5 *Birders, op. cit.*, p. 80. In a recent letter to *British Birds*, Christopher Helm, an ex-council member of the British Ornithologists Union and a major bird book publisher, wrote of 'today's young birders' that 'no longer are they all working a local patch in their spare time, but they are more likely to be consolidating their world lists in Thailand or Australia. Nor, I believe, are members of the current generation such good all-round naturalists as their parents or grandparents . . . the central focus of attention for young birders has switched to identification.' (vol. 93, September 2001, p. 443)

6 In 2002 it was 1,022,000, though all recent figures are misleading because about 140,000 of those are not members of the RSPB at all but members of a young persons' organisation called Wildlife Explorers (formerly the Young Ornithologists' Club). It is also debatable whether a husband who included his wife in a family membership at little extra cost over a single one has actually recruited another member, if that term is understood to imply personal commitment. After television, the biggest single boost to membership was the Chernobyl explosion in 1987, which saw dramatic rises in the membership of all 'green' organisations. Growth slowed considerably in the mid-1990s; since then it has practically stopped, despite ever increasing resources devoted to recruitment and publicity. It would probably be true to say that on a constant effort basis public commitment is now in decline.

industrial workers who raced pigeons at weekends or the landed gentry who shot pheasants during the week. Conservationists denigrated both classes' sport.

Rapidly rising numbers of bird-watching visitors to Fair Isle meant that the observatory eventually outgrew the war-time naval huts. In 1969 a purpose-built structure was erected, also above the North Haven. It was of an uninspired, cuboid design, but clad in what looks from photographs to have been reasonably tasteful wooden boarding. However, for some reason the trustees disdained Shetland builders who had experience of the local climate and employed a Devon firm whose work was so shoddy that within less than twenty years the weather had reduced the building to an almost uninhabitable condition. So a prefabricated concrete jacket had to be built outside the wooden walls, which is what gives the building its unappealing 'new brutalist' look today.

Though the observatory was a success, management of the island required resources which the new laird did not possess. So, in 1954, Waterston sold the island to the National Trust for Scotland. But the natives were restless. Three of the twenty families then resident were thinking of leaving. Many others believed the community was not viable in its present, run-down condition. There was serious talk of evacuation, as there was at the same time on Foula, our next stop. Amidst considerable publicity, the people of Soay, near Skye, had been shipped to the mainland the year before.[7]

To try to chart a way ahead, the Trust organised a Fair Isle Conference in 1956, not unlike the Westray one of 1998. The upshot was that the islanders asked the Trust to advertise for new settlers, whether returning islanders or incomers. But the disadvantages of life on the island were considerable, even by the standards of the day in the Shetland isles. After the announcement of the conference, *The Times*, noted that, 'at present maternity cases have to spend about six weeks in Shetland, mostly at their own expense, or in an emergency endure five or six hours in the hold of a 27-ton fishing boat in open seas and rough tideways on their way to hospital.'[8] An editorial in the *Glasgow Herald* said of island evacuations generally that they were 'distasteful to the romantic', and of the Fair Isle in particular that 'it is agreed that the first essential is a pier with a deep-water quay'.[9]

---

7 See *Isles of the West*, pp. 95–97.

8 23 March 1956.

9 9 June 1956.

A few later milestones will illustrate some of the difficulties facing prospective settlers. In 1962 electricity was first installed on the island. In 1967 the first patient requiring urgent medical treatment was flown to hospital, an air service to Shetland having been introduced the previous year. In 1975 the electricity provision was improved so that power was available for two hours every morning and from dusk to 11 p.m. every evening. It was not until 1992 that the breakwater at the North Haven was built, creating something approximating to a harbour for the first time. In 1993 the first house was built by an independent owner since the Trust took over the island. In 1998 the first house was painted a colour other than white. In 2001, just two weeks before Brian and I arrived, a bar on the island opened – in the observatory, which I discovered after Clare dropped me there.

Brian and I went in for a couple of pints of Guinness, which we drank outside watching the observatory staff and guests playing cricket.

Next morning I walked up to talk to Deryk Shaw, the observatory warden. He is a dark-haired, dark-skinned Celtic supporter from Galloway. Increasingly, he said, the guests at the observatory are not birders but 'empty nesters' wanting a bit of peace and quiet in an unusual location. That is why the trustees applied for the drink licence. Serious birders arrive on the plane, get their 'tick' and leave on the next flight, staying for as short a period as possible. Waterston's vision of an island full of amateur ornithologists eagerly comparing sightings every evening over plum duff and custard has faded, leaving Fair Isle with something half-way between an adult holiday camp and an inexpensive hotel.

I asked Deryk what the main work of the observatory is.

'The year is divided into two bits,' he replied. 'Spring and autumn is counting and trapping migrants. We census the island every day, counting all the birds, and send all the data into the British Trust for Ornithology. The other aspect of the work is seabird counting. We are one of five sites in Britain which do this work.'

'What are the other ones?'

'Skomer and Skokholm, and–' he tailed off. 'I can't remember the other ones. We do that in the winter season.'

After he showed me the ringing arrangements – they get twenty sightings from the two thousand birds they ring each year – I asked if there were any other major categories of work.

'No. Running this place here is the other major issue because people staying here provide the income to fund the research. As bird observatories go, this is like the Hilton.'[10]

Today, the observatory has largely forgotten its founder, who is chiefly remembered in the island's museum, which is called the George Waterston Memorial Centre. Housed in what used to be the island's school until that moved to purpose-built premises in the 1980s, it houses an interesting display, the most intriguing part of which is undoubtedly the examples of north Siberian ('severno-siberskaya') and Scandinavian knitting patterns. They are strikingly similar to the angular Fair Isle designs. The link between northern Siberia and Scandinavia must be the Lappish reindeer herders, who would have wandered back and forth between the North Cape and Yakutia. The Vikings, with the Sami influence which John McAulay described, presumably brought them to Fair Isle. The patterns are quite different from the fluid, curvilinear Celtic designs which inform most decorative art in the Hebrides.

I was shown around the museum by Stewart Thomson who, without my having asked, drove up to the observatory to collect me as it was a beastly day for walking, blowing a stiff 6 from the south with intermittent but heavy showers and a cloud ceiling of about 1,000 feet. Stewart makes traditional-style chairs from oak and oat straw. For the latter, he uses Shetland oats, a strain which has more or less died out on Shetland but which he grows on his croft. Every autumn, he has to 'thrash enough seed' to plant a crop the following year. Like the remaining knitters, he has a good market in the people who come ashore from the increasing number of cruise ships which visit the island. They probably now bring more income to the islanders than the observatory does. Their interest is more in traditions than birds.

After showing me his workshop, Stewart drove me up to see his sister, Anne Sinclair, who is the island's representative on the Dunrossness Community Council. Anne lives in a smartly-appointed house with an almost Scandinavian interior: strong colours, polished wooden floors and a Jøtul stove. The atmosphere of modernity struck me as curious when

---

10 A recent article in *Scottish Bird News*, the Scottish Ornithologists' Club magazine, by a temporary warden on Fair Isle gave five categories of work which he would do in a 'typical day'. They were: 'taking guided walks, photocopying, leaflet folding, stile building and general visitor liaison'. (Winter 2002, p. 18)

contrasted with the aims of the National Trust, which are to preserve the past. I asked Anne what is it like to live in a museum.

'We don't live in a museum,' she said, looking slightly needled. 'People here look forward; we don't look back. We use what's behind us and learn from it, but we are not living in a museum.'

'How does the relationship with the National Trust work?'

'It works *quite* well,' she said. 'We have a quarterly meeting and everyone who is a householder is a member of this quarterly meeting. It is a very good system because you all get together in the hall and you have the chance to talk about things that concern you, therefore nobody has the excuse to moan as they have had the chance to talk openly and publicly. And when you've got that kind of chance it takes the feet out from under the people who might not want to talk about things openly.'

'Do people really discuss these things?' I said. 'Do you not have the reticence as I was told about on Orkney?'

'Yes, we do, because we've had the system for a long time and people know that if they don't bring things up at the meeting they will not be given much credence. I think it's very important because we want to survive as a community.'

'What does the word "community" mean in practice? People obviously do not live in each other's pockets.'

'No,' she said, 'and that's very important. Being a community means working together when you have to, but giving each other space.'

'But in the modern world, even on islands, there are fewer and fewer activities which need to be done communally.'

'We do the sheep communally,' she said, hesitating slightly as if searching her mind for other such activities. 'The church and chapel are communal,' she went on. 'What we do here is take the best of both worlds. We do not live in a museum. We are quite open to all mod cons and most of us have computers and work on the internet and we all listen to the news, but we still live in a community where we can leave our doors open, where the children go from house to house and are not afraid.'

'If you wanted to build another house, how would that work?'

'We have to consult the Trust. Most of the time they are really quite amenable. You can have hitches, though, because the National Trust are not famous for being quick off the mark. But as landlords go we could have worse. Many of the problems come because of their conception of a traditional house being a 1950s one – which is a nonsense. But compared with the way landlords function in Sutherland, for example, we are quite lucky. They are *fairly* open to reason, I would say.'

Looking out at the ferocious gloom of the sky on what I had to remind myself was a summer's day, I wondered what it must be like in winter. 'Do you feel the need to take holidays to get away from the winter when it is dark and dingy?' I asked.

'It is never dingy,' Anne said smartly. 'It is dark, but never dingy. The light is changing all the time, the colour of the sea and the colour of the sky. It is not dingy. I love weather. I can't speak for anyone else, but I don't find it oppressive. I would find it oppressive to live in a suburban street. And because the Trust owns the island, we have no pressures to fill the place up with holiday homes, because that destroys communities. It is a very big plus for us.'

'You sound pretty pleased with life,' I said.

She laughed. 'We are not happier than anywhere else. We are just full of human beings, with the good side and the bad side. One thing that does help is that we encourage young folk who want to live here to go away first so when the come back they know what they are not missing.'

'So what are the major flies in the Fair Isle ointment?'

'We can't get milk anymore,' Anne replied immediately. 'We can't even give it to each other, never mind sell it. Things like that. It's a nonsense. We are not allowed to slaughter livestock on the island. The conservationists will not let us cull things, yet they will quite happily cull things themselves. We have got the birds, we've got the flowers and we've got them *because* of what my ancestors did – not despite them. Take the bonxies: I used to go up the hill and get berries and stuff. I certainly wouldn't take my grandchildren now because they would be attacked all the time. Sometimes if they're near the road I get very anxious because children going on bikes can get a bad fright or occasionally get hit by bonxies diving and I don't like that. They will scare small children. They will hit you. That is a product of the rise in numbers. When there was only ten pairs it was different. Now there's eighty or ninety pairs they are fighting each other for space, so they have become more belligerent. It's like rats: when they're overcrowded they become more aggressive.'

That answer provoked an opposite thought. I wondered if the amount of space here made the humans more law-abiding. 'When was the last time the police came over to the island on business?' I asked.

Anne thought for a minute then said, 'Nineteen fifties, maybe. Two people fell out and were hitting each other on the head. I can't think of anything which the police have been involved with since then.'

Astounded, I said, 'The last time there was a conviction for any sort of crime on Fair Isle was nearly half a century ago?'

'No,' she said, 'there was no conviction then, just a warning. I think the last time anyone was taken to court was the 1920s when they were prosecuting trawlers for fishing inside the three-mile limit.'

Stewart returned to run me down the road to see Clare Scott's workshop. On the way we passed a newly built house painted daffodil yellow and another pair right next to each other which were equally colourful. One had been painted a deep, solid blue and the other a rich red that was half-way between ochre and ox-blood. I remarked how nice it was to see such bright colours.

'But the National Trust wanted to write into all the leases that you painted your house white,' Stewart said. 'Quite a few people said why should we paint our house white? Why can't we paint it some other colour? It became quite a thing. Then SNH started to get involved, insisting that we all painted our houses white. Eventually I got a letter from the Trust saying that because of the annoyance and arguments that were going on that they would allow us to paint our houses in a neutral colour. So this chap went out and painted his houses blue and red – not exactly neutral, but they haven't tried to stop him.'

After returning to Islay I asked Angus Jack, the National Trust area officer for the Fair Isle, about the house colour controversy. He sent me a memo he had written on the subject in 2001:

The National Trust for Scotland Fair Isle Housing Policy, 'Housing Design Standards', states the Trust's preference for white, which is considered to be the traditional colour for external render. However the tradition of rendering and applying colour to these vernacular buildings only dates back to the end of the nineteenth century when white limewash became readily available, principally through the construction of the lighthouse. Scandinavian history and culture influences Fair Isle more so than Scottish tradition and vibrant colours are used extensively in Norway, Iceland and the Faeroes.

Should we intervene in something which is doing no harm and only affects us when we visit the island, or should we leave it up to the players, those who live there and view it every day?

'Do you have a lot of those sort of impositions?' I asked Stewart.

'Quite a bit. See the Trust again, in 1995, refused me permission to build a wooden house. I was going to build my own house because at that point my daughter was thinking about coming home. SNH said I could only have so much ground with the house, plus it had to be white.'

'Why were SNH involved in how much ground you have?'

'I don't know,' Stewart said. 'Maybe because this is categorised as an Environmentally Sensitive Area. Then the Shetland Islands Council even, the planning people, said that it had to be white and that it had to face the road, which meant that it was going to be at right angles to all the other houses on the island more or less.'

'What was the logic of that?'

'I don't know. Everything was made so awkward that I decided against it at the end of the day. My daughter never came home. From the Trust's point of view, it was just that they didn't want too many people building their own houses.'

Chatting later over the workbenches, vices and buffing tools in Clare's neatly organised workshop in the south lighthouse buildings I was given a much more unsavoury example of the Trust's attempt to control the island. From Edinburgh and, latterly, Mull herself, Clare told me that she moved to the island in the 1980s with her husband, another crafts-man. At first they had only 'little battles' with the Trust about issues like the size of windows. Then her marriage broke up.

'Since then I've had quite a hard time from certain members in the National Trust,' she said. 'They want families on Fair Isle, not individu-als. Part of that is maybe based on practicalities, but part of it is based on what the Trust wants to have as an image.'

'Because you no longer fitted the Edinbourgeois stereotype of the happy crofter with a hairy-faced husband and barefoot bairns?'

'I think so.'

'That's an atrocious attitude.'

'It is really bad,' she said, giving me a steely look. 'I've had a huge battle to hold my ground here.'

Clare's pamphlet says her jewellery is 'inspired by a decorative style [in which] stacked patterns, parallel motifs and geometric forms have their origin in Norse influences'. The material is silver and the designs reminiscent of the Siberian patterns I saw in the museum. Her Diamond Range recently won the Scottish Gift of the Year Award. In addition she has won a small business award from Highlands and Islands Enterprise – which raised another issue.

'I think the National Trust should be supporting a business like mine,' she said. 'Other people than me think my jewellery is a good product and that the business has commercial potential. Almost everything is sold off the island. But marketing from here is difficult. The Trust has its network of shops I would like to use, but I've been led down the garden path by the people on the Trust's retailing side. They also said I could get into their mail-order catalogue, but when I followed that up I wasn't going to be able to get in there either. Eventually I was told that they have all their jewellery manufactured under licence by a company abroad who do a lot of heritage jewellery. I just think it is a total contradiction of what their remit is.'

'Why do you think they have taken that attitude?' I asked.

'I've gone through the thought that it is just because they don't want to support me as a single person and all that, but I actually think this problem has nothing to do with that. I think they have a remit to make money and I think they are running the retail side completely separately from the rest of the National Trust, and I don't agree with that. I think they should be understanding of what the whole Trust thing is all about. Rents are cheap on the island, so that's good. But travel off the island is horrendously expensive and you have limitations working here. Marketing for me is a nightmare. I spend a huge amount of money going off selling what I produce. The Trust have big clout and they could help me immeasurably by promoting my jewellery as a quality item. I really hoped that being given awards by other people that they would take that on board, but they haven't.'

Clare agreed with Anne that there are some positive sides to having a body like the National Trust owning the island.

'The old man, Jerry Stout, who assigned his croft to me,' she said by way of example, 'is 93 now and he can remember when the landowner for the south of Shetland made sure everyone on the island was always in debt to him. He owned the shop. All the fish that were caught and salted were sold to him. The locals were never out of debt. So when the National Trust took over, Jerry bought his house, which has given him a self-respect that was never there before. He's very pro the Trust because he feels that Fair Isle would not have succeeded if it had not become involved. But things are changing. He sees what is going on now and gives them a really good run for their money. He's very canny and thinks long and hard about all the things that the Trust are trying to do and he accepts no rubbish from them.'

When I asked what had changed, the main point Clare made was that the Trust was no longer the wealthy landowner it had once been. In 2000/1 the Trust made a loss of £2.7 million; currently it is appealing for £600,000 to cover the most recent deficit.[11]

'Worse than that,' Clare said, 'you see them spending massive amounts of money on Charlotte Square while you are thinking: all we need is £40,000 to get the next phase of housing completed here. Housing is always at a premium on the island. I understand about budgets and all that sort of thing but it is quite irritating.'

'Has this impacted on you in any way?' I asked.

'I had a major stumbling block in the division of the marital home,' Clare said. 'When we moved here we signed – totally stupidly I now see – a document saying that the National Trust would have first refusal on the house if a sale was to occur and it would be based on a sliding scale of the market value over a period of about twenty years. That very much inhibited what I could take out from my investment at the point

---

11 The 2000/1 loss appears to have occasioned the departure of the then director, Trevor Croft, a Yorkshireman whose training was in town planning. His
successor, Robin Pellew, is an ex-Tanzanian forester. When I wrote asking
for details of Pellew's career, I was sent a photocopy of his short entry in
Who's Who and told the information I sought could not be sent 'for reasons
of compliance with the Data Protection Act 1988'. (14 October 2002) I
was subsequently sent a short resumé which noted that his previous job had
been as Director of the Worldwide Fund for Nature and which ended by
saying, 'Robin is a scientist of international recognition [with] a substantial
publications record.' I wrote to ask for a copy of that record, but was told,
'There is no up to date list extant.' (20 December 2002) When I asked for
whatever was extant, I was first told Pellew was on holiday then, when I sent
a reminder, told that nothing would be sent because, 'as Dr Pellew has not
published as a research scientist for over twenty years, his list of publications
is not up to date and has little or no relevance to his current career'. (28
March 2003)

of separation and divorce. I went to the Trust and asked if they would relinquish that as my ex-husband and I were both staying on the island. Could they not see that it is very much against me? No, they said, they wouldn't let go of that right at all. I've suffered financially because of that.'

Clare gave me a final example of bureaucratic administration. 'I asked about extending the house that I am in, which has only two bedrooms. I wanted to put another bedroom on because I have a teenage boy and a teenage girl now, and the reply was that they would never allow the extension to happen because it would change the skyline. My need is for another bedroom, not to maintain a particular sight from the sea.'

'Is that final?'

'I will write and ask them again, but you can only ask so many times then you start being seen as a nuisance. It might be worth going back to them now because they have agreed for the museum to extend to give it storage.'

'But I've just come from there,' I said. 'That's *right* on the skyline.'

'Exactly. It's next door to me.'

It was now five o'clock, so we adjourned to Clare's house for a further chat over a dram. Her younger daughter was exercising the family gecko – a creature like a large chameleon – by allowing it to creep up and down her stomach and chest as she lay watching the television. Clare told me how much she likes living on Fair Isle, despite the 'political' problems. Apart from the landscape and the people, she said, 'I really enjoy working my sheep.' They earn no money and are a 'total hobby'. She told me that the island hill is worked as a common so that the whole community gets together for the annual gathering, which by chance was happening the next day. Despite the continuing rain, the forecast for tomorrow was good. Would I like to come and watch? Of course.

'Do you think your children will stay here when they grow up?' I asked.

'My elder daughter can't understand why we moved to somewhere where she had to be sent away to high school. She has accepted it now, but both my son and elder daughter have said they will never move back to Fair Isle again. They might well stay in Shetland, though they will probably go down to the mainland for higher education. My son would be quite happy on Shetland: he's talking about engineering. It's quite a male-orientated place, Shetland.'

'Why is that?'

'I think because everything is very much geared towards fishing, oil and so on. But, for all there's a lot of incomers, Shetland is very family-orientated. There's a lot of extended families.'

'Does that not make it a bit inward-looking?' I asked, thinking about Mull, which she had told me earlier they used to refer to as 'the Officer's Mess' on account of the number of 'expatriate Brits' living in retirement there.

'Not really,' Clare said. 'The oil has brought a lot of people and businesses to Shetland, and people are aware that we would never have developed and survived the way that we have if it had not been for oil, so there's a fairly happy acceptance that communities are stronger because of incomers. That's something that I like in the Northern Isles. My parents are still incomers on Mull, despite having lived there for thirty-odd years. There is a wee bit of that here, but you are not constantly aware of it.'

The next morning dawned fine and warm, as forecast. Brian and I breakfasted on deck in glorious sunshine. With a pint of tea steaming at my elbow, I was just tucking into my ham and eggs when I noticed a tousle-haired man in a blue shirt and white working trousers taking a seat on the quay-side above me.

'Just come down to collect £6.65 for the Shetland Islands Council, please.'

I glanced up to see a jovial, slightly tubby figure waving a receipt book. This was clearly the harbour master. Since Brian had finished his food, I asked him if he would mind getting out the ship's wallet and dealing with the matter.

'Where are you from?' he asked in a sing-song voice, filling in the berthing ticket. I thought I detected a South African accent.

'Islay,' I shouted up. 'Where are *you* from?'

'Port Elizabeth.'

'What on earth brought you here?' I said.

'My family comes from England. I had to get out of South Africa in 1995 so I came back.'

This was clearly a man I had to talk to. A chatty South African on the Fair Isle was not a chance to be missed. He seemed keen when I asked if I might come up later on and have a word with him about life in an 'English' museum.

At the gathering I found Clare and her younger daughter trotting about a large field with twenty or so other people and a slightly larger number of sheep. Others were already penned, but the total was not huge, considering the area of the island. All the shearing was done by hand. Clare seized one of hers from the pen and offered me a go with the clippers. I managed to avoid stabbing it, though I don't think I cut nearly as close as I should have done. After she had finished her flock we awarded ourselves an Ardbeg Moment, which is possibly why, looking at the remaining unsheared sheep leaping around in the fank to avoid capture, I asked about the most energetic of them: 'Is that a Fair Isle jumper?'

I spoke to the skipper of the *Good Shepherd IV*, Jimmy Stout, a tall, fit-looking man, whom I had been told was the man to ask if you wanted a Fair Isle lobster. He was going out to lift his pots that afternoon and he said if I was on the quay at 5 p.m. I could select one. I paid £10 for it then invited him and his son, Iain, aboard *Foggy Dew* for a dram. The Stout family has lived on the island since time immemorial, so I asked about the ratio of incomers 'versus' natives.

' "Versus" is a very bad word,' said Iain with mock seriousness.

We all laughed. 'OK,' I said, 'as opposed to, in comparison with, as a proportion of–'

'About half, I suppose.'

'So it's really quite strong.'

'Yes. You need the new people and you also need the indigenous people.'

'You are very lucky not to have a large population of retired people.'

'We have very few holiday homes,' Jimmy said. 'We don't own our own houses, we just rent them, which means that, if you leave, someone else comes in your place. You can't sell to someone who lives elsewhere. We've done this intentionally. You can't leave your house and sell it to the highest bidder, which might well be a holiday home owner. Once that happens, that's the end.'

'Are the National Trust reasonably good landowners?' Brian asked.

'They used to be good landlords, but now they're not so good,' Jimmy said. 'They are running on hard times and they don't have the money any longer. They used to be able to twist a lever and help Fair Isle, but now they can't twist any levers: they haven't the clout. They did a lot in the past, providing cheap housing and getting young folk back to live, but not now.'[12]

'Do they cause trouble, or are they just fading away?' I asked.

'The Trust have no influence here whatsoever – very little anyway,' Jimmy said.

'We hardly see them. Apart from signing a small cheque for the rent once every six months we don't have anything to do with them. We've seen the factor once in the last year perhaps.'

'So what's the purpose in them owning the place?'

'I would like to think they could help market the island. But they don't even seem able to do that. They're becoming very disappointing. Not bad landlords,' he said emphatically, 'no, not that. Just weak.'

I did not have a large enough pot on the boat to boil the lobster, so Jimmy offered to do it for me. We drove over to his house at the south end of the island where his wife, Florrie, put it in one of hers. Jimmy gave me advice about how to approach Foula from Fair Isle and I asked about the ferry. The crew are all based on Fair Isle, which provides four important jobs, plus two part-timer ones for the stand-ins. But European legislation zealously interpreted by British officialdom, in this case the Southampton-based Maritime and Coastguard Agency, is about to put this arrangement in jeopardy.

'We're struggling,' Jimmy said, 'because the legislation now is that you have to have sea-time before you can become a crew member. We have people on this island familiar with the sea, but now we are supposed to spend two years on super-tankers or something like that to get sea-time. That teaches you nothing about the sea, at least not the sea around here. Our people can become deckhands, but they can never improve themselves without going away and getting certificates. I am qualified to be skipper of the ferry, but not to teach people how to be skipper of the ferry. It's all become so paper-orientated. We need support from the people on the shore side if these islands are going to work, but the people who make these rules are maybe from England and they don't understand the situation. It's ridiculous.'

---

12 It is arguable whether lack of money is the main cause of this change. The Trust used to be run by members of the Scottish establishment, who were capable of pulling strings in all sorts of quarters. Today it is largely run by middle-class bureaucrats from England who, whatever their professional skills, do not have the range of contacts in Scotland that their predecessors had.

With my now-pink lobster in my bag, along with the only bottle of vodka we had aboard – I had been advised that the harbour master only drank vodka – I walked up the road from Jimmy's house to The Chalet, a prefabricated house standing in perhaps an eighth of an acre on the road back over to the harbour. I found my quarry, Brian Skinner, outside, dressed all in white and watering his garden. Inside the rather bare cottage I explained that I was writing a book and asked if he would care to help me understand about life on Fair Isle. He looked disappointed and said, 'Actually when I saw you walking up the road, I was hoping you were from the National Trust for Scotland.'

I pulled out the vodka and he brightened considerably.

'Help yourself,' he said gesturing toward a large bottle of Coca-Cola which was standing on the sitting room table with two glasses ready.

'And you help yourself,' I said putting my bottle on the table next to his.

He sat down and asked if I minded if he smoked. I sat down and asked if he minded my taking a record of the conversation. Those were all the preliminaries before he launched into a passionate denunciation of the contractors he was working for painting the north lighthouse.

'This painting firm's really schlapp,' he said, speaking quickly. 'They've arrived here with really ridiculous guys and they've been painting away and one of them injured his hand in the motor car and so they've all just gone and left the paintbrushes just, like, in the paint. Not even cleaned them. It's nothing to do with me, I'm just chipping paint off the wall because there's no-one else to do it. This is the thing that gets me about the UK: people don't give a shit. They're all union-orientated. Basically I've been involved in food, and plants and animals and the arts. That's my so-called career, if it's a career at all. In Africa people are conscientious about what they do. If they're paid from six to nine they'll work from six to nine and they will be there at five to six. But here they arrive at half past six and want to leave at ten to nine.'

'Cheers!' I said, raising my glass in the hope that I could stem the flow for long enough to phrase a question.

'Cheers! Well, here I am. I live on Fair Isle.'

'This must be a bit of a change from South Africa.'

'I lived for about ten years in Cape Town, in Seapoint. There I was involved in the arts. I worked at the National Art Gallery. I studied botany and horticulture and I worked for a Dutch family who were the

first people that had ever put up poly-tunnels in Africa. I went back
to Johannesburg and got involved in the film industry. But those were
the days of apartheid and I was involved in a lot of black organisations.
I wasn't really that politically-minded, but I had a lot of black people
working for me in black TV. In a way I broke barriers.'

'Coming from that, how did Fair Isle strike you?'

'I knew nothing about Fair Isle. I emigrated at the end of 1994. I
came to the UK. I had been back and forth all my life. I was adopted in
South Africa by English people and I went back to Harlech where I had
worked for three years in a Good Food Guide restaurant as a chef over
summer periods. To cut a long story short, that didn't work out so I went
back to Windsor, where I had been before, and opened a magazine called
The Lady and saw an advert for a job on the payroll as a head chef at the
bird observatory here and applied for it. At the same time I went to Eton
College and they took me immediately, so I got hold of the telephone
directory people on the phone and said, "Listen, can you tell me the
number of this bird observatory on Fair Isle?" and they gave me this
number and this woman answered and her name was Wendy and she
was Australian, so we had a good old yak. I said, "Are there any trees?"
And she said no. Anyway we became quite friendly on the telephone. I
said, "I've just been to this interview at Eton College and they've given
me this job," and I said I would much rather come to Fair Isle. I don't
know why, I knew nothing about Fair Isle. Someone had mentioned
Fair Isle jerseys and I pictured these toothless women sitting with their
home-made sheepskin slippers on, outside these mud huts, you know.
I didn't think they had television or cars. I thought they were knitting
jerseys, and gosh it sounded like a lovely, wild place to go. But she said,
"The directors make decisions on all that and I can't tell you anything
and the job is only from April and you should know at least by the end
of February." I said I was going to Eton College because I really liked this
family. I said I would never leave Eton College until they left and if they
did leave I'd pick up this phone and phone her. So then two years later
they took up a position in Montrose, so I gave in my notice, got rid of
all my furniture, put everything on my back and I came up to Inverness.
I had never been in Inverness before, but I came because of the monster,
because it's a famous place, a large town. I arrived in Inverness four days
before Christmas and opened the newspaper. I took the first telephone
number for accommodation, went there. Fabulous house, super room,

nice landlord, he saw that I wasn't just a rubbish so he said, "No, well I've got a better room for you with a bathroom, eksetra eksetra, nice view," and as soon as I booked I went straight down the road to the public telephone and phoned this number I had of the bird observatory all this time and I said, "Hello," I said, "Who's speaking?" She said, "Wendy." And I said, "Do you remember me? It's Brian Skinner." I said, "I phoned you two years ago and I said if ever I leave Eton College I am going to phone you." She said, "Yes, I remember you," blah blah blah. I said, "I've just left Eton College and I'd like to apply for the job if it's going again this year." She said, "Ja sure, I'll send you an application form," which she did. Then the form arrived back from there on Valentine's Day to say that I had the job. I was so excited. I still knew nothing about Fair Isle. I hadn't looked up anything about Fair Isle, but I'd heard people mention Fair Isle jumpers, Fair Isle jumpers, Fair Isle jumpers. I thought it was this place with the sheep. They dyed the wool. They were rough, raw, real islanders. I thought, this is going to be a change. I could only come up here at the end of April so I had two months to kill. So I worked in a Chinese restaurant in Inverness as a chef and as a chef in a little place called Invermoriston. The last two weeks I didn't work so I went to the Inverness library and read up everything I could on Fair Isle. I was actually shocked when I saw photographs of the bird observatory with a van next to it, you know, and the houses. I just had it in my mind that it was really remote and really wild and then I came here and I've been here ever since.'

There was a brief pause while he took a long swig of his drink, then he raced off again.

'I discovered Fair Isle is 99.9 per cent owned by the National Trust for Scotland. When I got here I heard an awful lot of bad, negative things about the National Trust for Scotland but I refused to listen because I've always been like that. Even under apartheid I always mixed with black people until I found that they were the way that people said. I refuse to be told. I've always been like that. So now I am not anti-National Trust for Scotland. I think that for who they are and what they stand for they are pretty good, but in actual fact most of the people who run the Islands and Highlands or whatever are absolute shits. There is only one chap who has any credibility as far as I am concerned, but the rest of them are just ridiculous. I've been made promises. You know it's a huge organisation and it's in debt, I think £2 million in debt. I feel like phoning them up and saying, "Why don't you just give me a job? I'll come down to Inverness and I'll work for you for £20 a week as long as I've got a roof over my head and I'll tell you some things about Fair Isle and who's who and what's what and how to run the place because I've been here five years. You've never even stayed here more than one night." They fly in, spend one night, there is not even enough time for the people to speak their grievances and they fly out again. And they've come in with this attitude as if they're lairds, as if they're lords, as if they're the Queen of England. I am a royalist, but a lot of them aren't; they're Scottish. Fine, you can have your attitude, but it's really poorly run. So the whole island is pretty much anti-National Trust for Scotland, which I think is a very, very sad thing. Since I've been here, they've never done anything. They're the biggest lot of snotty, little people. "Oh, we're from the National Trust for Scotland!" So I say, "So what? You're just appointed to some kind of body; you aren't the National Trust for Scotland. You're Joe or Jane or whoever you are." OK, so they're in debt, but they could do a bit of PR. They could come here and spend a week and they could hire that hall and hire local people to cook and prepare a meal and give a meal to the islanders to say thank you or something like that, but nothing, absolutely nothing. So ja, here I am. I am in a house that is probably the most expensive house on Fair Isle. I hardly have any work. I work for the Shetland Islands Council which this house belongs to. It is let to the National Trust for Scotland on a long-term basis and I rent it from them.'

Crikey! Just to give my ears a breather, so to speak, I got up and poured myself another vodka. He did the same. But it did not stop the flow. I tried to change the subject by saying, 'I spent thirteen years in Johannesburg when I was young. We both come from a blue-skies culture. You arrived in this foggy, windy, rainy environment. How did you react to it?'

'It does get me a bit in the winter but the thing that gets me most is that I am paying £100 plus for this building a month with this teeny garden. I dug the pond myself and made this garden. You can have a croft here, which is open to married people, which I am not. I went to agricultural college and farmed in Africa: angora goats and pigs and cattle blah blah blah, but yes, it is awfully sad that there is nowhere I can have (a) a larger house that I can do bed and breakfast in and have some kind of income which I can't do here, or (b) somewhere to have a restaurant or (c) to have a croft where I can keep some animals, sheep or pigs, even if they are just for myself to slaughter or to swap. I could do that. I could plough some land and grow some things. I was promised the south lighthouse two years ago, to be in there by January, and I am still waiting, so I still can't do anything.'

'Is that just the paralysis of bureaucracy?'

'Yes,' he said emphatically. 'But I am just so sick of phoning the National Trust for Scotland, phoning them and phoning them. Either they never phone me back or I get all these promises and nothing happens.'

'Getting back to the climate,' I said. 'The clear Highveld air–'

'The Highveld never really attracted me,' he said without missing a beat. 'I never really liked the Transvaal. The only time I ever spent in the Transvaal apart from in Johannesburg was in my army training in Middelburg. There was this vast area and I had gone there as a corporal chef to cater for all these people in the middle of nowhere. It was wild and beautiful and stunningly different. I studied botany, did horticulture – my mother's a famous botanist – but I still felt most of all for the Cape. But I just wasn't prepared to settle down. This is the first place I've ever stayed apart from Eton College. I spent two years there. Everywhere else I'd stay two or three months, then I'd move. I always felt unsettled. I also think that was to do with the culture of apartheid. You couldn't mix. In the latter part of apartheid I was casting for films, I was working a lot with black people, doing Zulu soaps and Xhosa soaps. I speak Zulu and Xhosa to a degree, not as well as I speak Afrikaans, but my schooling was at a private English school and agricultural college was in Afrikaans. I grew up in Port Elizabeth, which is a Xhosa area. I was mixing with black people. They were a super crowd, but you still weren't really allowed to walk on the street together. Maybe that was upsetting me inwardly. I sort of accepted it. I was never so rebellious that I chained myself to government gates, you know what I mean?'

I hardly had time to nod before he went on.

'I had been back and forward to England pretty much all my life. There was this something about Fair Isle, I can't explain that. I often like to think there is some Norwegian blood in me and maybe that is why I feel at home here, but even before I got here it was a gut, visceral feeling that I was going to this place and it was the ultimate place. So I flew up from Inverness and I can remember the pilot saying, "If you look out to your right you can see Fair Isle and we will be landing in Sumburgh in twenty minutes," or whatever it was, and I remember looking out and all I saw was grey cloud and about five minutes later I looked out and I saw Fair Isle. He had misjudged. I saw Sheep Rock as we flew over. I just saw it and it was this fantastic place to me, it was like gravitational pull, wonderful. And when I actually got here, I thought, God, I've finally come home. This is my clan and yes, I am introduced, I am from down south, but all of them are introduced. Some have been here longer than others, but they're all introductions. After you have stayed here a while you become part of it. You see people are relating to you differently because they know you, but at the same time there are these divisions, this whole hierarchy. It is wonderful place. I love it with a passion. It is only work-wise and financially that it's a problem. I live in this little box house which was built for the men who were dismantling the residential buildings at the north lighthouse. After that job was finished this house was to be dismantled. When they finished pulling down the buildings at the north lighthouse, which was the first one to become automatic, they then decided it would be useful as alternative accommodation for people waiting for crofts or if people were having their house renovated. The garden has been de-crofted. The people from the shop have lived here; Clare lived here for five years – one of the kindest, most genuine people on the island. My second year was when Princess Anne came to close the south lighthouse, in other words to make it automatic. The last of the lighthouse men left. It was a very sad occasion; they had been here for years. She came to close it and make it all official. The end of the first winter I went and worked in Yell, an island north of here. I told the owners I am only coming for the Christmas period because I am definitely going back to Fair Isle; my heart lies in Fair Isle. So the agreement was that I'd work from the end of October until February. Because of Princess Anne coming here in February I came back early, whereas normally I would have come back towards the end of April.'

'Where did you work?' I asked, as Yell was to be our first stop on Shetland proper.

'The Hilltop Bar. It's a box like this in the middle of nowhere and everyone gets pissed out of their minds and they smash the billiard table and rob the public telephone box. It's a wild place. When I first got there I thought these people are just so awful. The majority of them are what do you say in Scottish – dour? They say dour here. Dour people, you know the women with this jaw, very plain, and the men the same, drinking like mad. I mean, I drink too, but they really got pissed out of their minds. I was working in the kitchen and suddenly I'd find these arms around me and somebody would be calling me James, and I'd say, "I'm not James, I'm Brian. Who's James?" That was how Yell was. But after I'd been there for about three weeks suddenly all this sort of icy feeling – the way that people looked at me as a foreigner, as an outsider – it melted and suddenly people were stopping me on the road and offering me lifts when I went down to the local shop. I met some who were really, really nice people. They are friends. I can phone them up and say, "Listen here, can you send me this or can you do that?" and they'll do it. People who do smoked salmon: I say, "Won't you send me a parcel, I'll pay you when I can?" They know that I'm not a bullshitter. I met really super people. You've got to go through this period of isolation and they look at you and you've got to look at them and when they accept you, they absolutely love you. They are super people. So then I came back and stayed the following winter in the Puffin, which is right down by the south lighthouse which used to be an old smoke house there. So the National Trust for Scotland said, "Fine, Brian, you can stay in this building as long as you pay for your gas and electricity. We don't want any rent." The couple who had run the bird observatory that year were absolutely appalling. It is seldom that I dislike anyone, but this couple were the most disgusting, obnoxious couple you have ever met. They were that real sort of working-class English; English working-class vulgarity, take, take, gimme, gimme. They were just awful. Their contract was not renewed after that year. Later on Hollie and Deryk, who are the couple there just now, came and so the National Trust for Scotland phoned me and said, "Clare is leaving this place, would you like to apply for it?" I said, "Ja sure." But at the same time I was phoning up the directors at the observatory every night, saying, "Have I got my job at the bird observatory?" "Yes, I am sure you have." So I signed the lease in good faith that I would be working and as soon as I signed the lease, two weeks later, one of the directors rang saying, "Sorry, Brian, bad news, we are not taking you on this year, we are taking on this woman who worked there years ago. She'll be able to help the new couple who have young children probably more than you will," yeah yeah yeah – all this jazz. People said to me, "It's because you have become an islander, Brian, that they are not going to employ you." They'll always employ outsiders. They won't employ anybody from the island, except when they're very busy then they'll take on somebody part-time." I was devastated. What the hell am I to do? I've signed this lease. At the same time if you'd told me before that I wouldn't have the job I would not have signed the lease and I wouldn't be here now. I would have gone off somewhere else. Initially I was worried, but I'm glad it worked out that way.'

At that point somebody came in and collected a cake. A few words were exchanged in friendly but not particularly warm tones.

'I bake for people on the weekends,' Brian explained after his visitor left. 'So there we are. Here I am.'

Before sitting down again, he walked over to the table and helped himself to another vodka. I did the same.

'I've been told that you have been going round the island planting gladioli to brighten the place up,' I said. 'Is that true?'

'I planted some gladioli, which are a hardy species, non-toxic and sterile in the sense that they don't make seed. I planted some in front of the shop and they're flowering now, red ones. That was purely to see if they would grow or would not grow and to make it more attractive.'

'And how did people react?'

Brian made a despairing gesture, striking his forehead with the palm of his hand. 'I had a letter from Kew Gardens saying were these plants toxic and what were their origins and was there any chance of them being invasive? I wrote a letter back saying they were not invasive, that they could not set seed because they are sterile. Yes, I planted them and some of them have grown and they're very attractive.'

'I thought all plants set seed.'

'No they don't for instance we have a plant here, see that white daisy on the other side of the pond?'

'Yes.'

'That is called Magellan's Ragwort, *Senecio snipiae*, and it comes from the most southern part of Chile. It is a daisy, a member of the compositae family. There is one real arsehole on this island, *the* conservationist, you know, he is the only one who knows about conservation. But conservation is a communal thing. I took one lesson from the black servants in South Africa: "Always pretend you don't know, Brian, and let someone speak first and you can find out what they do know." I have had so many bullshit stories from this guy. It was he who reported me to Kew. Anyway, this white daisy: there is a clump of it in front of the shop. This plant is indigenous to the most southern bit of south America – it comes from Tierra del Fuego – and any of the plants that do well here come from really wild, cold environments. They either come from the Aleutian islands or they come from Tierra del Fuego or the Chatham islands and the islands that reach south from New Zealand which are uninhabited. Of course a lot of plants have never been tried here, but any that will grow here need shelter initially. Anyway, someone brought a plant from Chile and it was divided and divided and at one time it was quite plentiful in Shetland, then they found that it is infertile. It was prolific only because it was attractive and people divided it. When I came here there was only the one plant, in front of the shop. People said, "You mustn't touch it." But I've done propagation. I took a piece of root, planted it at the bird observatory and at the end of the first year I had three plants and the following year I divided them and planted some here. I gave them lots of manure – I found it loves cow manure – and kept dividing it, dividing it, and you can't see it now but my garden is absolutely full of it. Last week the whole pond area was absolutely covered with those white daisies. That's one thing I am awfully glad I've done on Fair Isle, I've multiplied that plant.'

'Is Fair Isle not a bit sterile, as a society, like your daisy?' I asked. 'The whole island is owned by the National Trust, and seems to me a bit of a museum, especially if you cannot even plant colourful flowers without some pharisee from the conservation bureaucracy reporting you to Sir. Is there any freedom to grow?'

For the first time, Brian thought before answering. 'This is a place where people want grants. And they want grants, and they want grants,' he said slowly. 'They look after themselves and their own kind. There is a lot of nepotism on Fair Isle. Also it's a place where people become actors in the sense that they play to the tourists, to how they feel the tourists should see them. But they are talented. There is talent here. I wonder if I am not being negative. It is a great place, but at the same time they will hold you back if you are not one of them.'

'Surely all small societies are like that?'

'It's very much like being in Africa with a lot of black people. I had an insight into that because of the fact that they were black and because of apartheid they became natural actors. They would be what the white man wanted them to be up front, but behind that there would be something completely different. They had the most amazing insight into people. They could just look at you and could tell you straight, "He's like this, he's like that." It's a bit like that here. People are being the friendly islander. The talented islanders are the ones who say, yes, our arms are open to you. I am cynical now, to a degree, but I am also very realistic.'

We were interrupted again by the phone ringing. Then someone came in to arrange work for tomorrow. Once again I was stuck by the coolness between him and the visitor. Brian seemed as out of place as his colourful flowers.

'What's the party scene like on Fair Isle?' I asked once he had put the phone down. 'Don't you get a bit lost for entertainment? What's the social life like here?'

'There isn't any, unless I ask someone to dinner, or unless there is a dance on in the hall. But it's not really a dinner party culture. Cape Town is dinner party culture. South Africa is, as you know. Sunday lunch is a big thing in Cape Town but not here.'

'Do you think you could spend the rest of your life living like this?'

'This is something I am going through right now, about my future and what am I doing here. That is a crisis I am going through right now. I work for the Shetland Island Council going to the harbour every day for £26 a month–'

For once it was I who interrupted: '£26 a *month*?'

'£26 a month. The irony about living on an island is that people think that because it is remote it is therefore cheap. They don't think that because it is remote it's expensive, and you can't earn any money. I tried to do bed and breakfast here but even though I joined the Shetland Islands Tourism Board, the only people that I have ever had was when Hollie sent me this couple of birdwatchers from the observatory. We have overbooked and could they stay with you, Brian, for one night? I said, fine. They came here booked for bed and breakfast, and when they got here they said, we don't want breakfast, we'll go and have breakfast at the observatory. I thought, fine, but I had bought all the bacon and eggs, bought everything, tomatoes, mushrooms. They came here and when they left in the morning they had tea, I had made up the bed cleaned the room and gave them a hot bath, and they said, here's £10. I couldn't believe it. When you live on an isolated island like this all the bacon comes packed, the eggs come in from Shetland. I used to have chickens but, even if I still had, legally I am not allowed to go outside and pick that chicken's egg and crack it and fry it for you. I am not allowed to give you home-slaughtered lamb if I charge you for it. I can eat it myself, but by law I am not allowed to sell it unless that animal has gone to Shetland and been slaughtered in an abattoir and come back here on the boat. It's an absolutely ridiculous situation. I don't know where these tourists think the food comes from, but it all is imported and it comes in on the boat; it is fetched by Jimmy Stout. I absolutely adore Jimmy and Florrie. Of all the people on the island they are probably the most sane and the most sensible and the nicest. I have always respected people who have been nice to me and kind to me but who have never said, "Oh yes, come in, come in" – been all over me from the word go.'

'These people who gave you ten quid–'

'They offered me £10 and I kind of gave them this look and, OK give him £15, but they had booked me through–'

'I'm on a slightly different tack,' I said. 'It's well known in the tourist industry that bird-watchers are financially retentive. Is this an example of that, or were these folk just odd?'

'I came to the bird observatory as head chef, I didn't know what it was like, it was bit schlapp. I mean schlapp in the good old-fashioned English way, but er, er I came here and, er, what was it you asked now?'

'About your £10 customers here.'

There was an even longer pause, then Brian started telling me about the disorganisation in the observatory in the years when he was there, so I asked, 'How would you run it?'

'I would certainly have had it that the kitchen staff are under control. I am sure it is different now, but for instance the first year I was there – this was a while ago now – there was one chap, a very nice guy, I liked him, I was not anti-him, he was into cetaceans, whales and all that stuff and starlings, but there are flies that you get on birds that are parasitic, they live under their feathers and suck the blood vessels of the birds. Well, he had them in his hair. He would go out and he would start ringing these starlings and take blood samples from them and because he is in some way affiliated with the place, kind of like a director, I don't know exactly, he would put these blood samples in the fridge, the one and only fridge, where I keep my milk, my butter. I would say, "Why the fuck don't you use the fucking fridge down the road there in the ornithological section?" You know, it's that kind of attitude. It's schlapp. I do believe in a certain amount of hygiene. When it comes to food hygiene, the kitchen is the kitchen. It is just the kitchen staff that work in there, and I don't give a shit who you are. But they were also disruptive. They would come in and start asking questions, "Could we have this, could we have that?" People don't realise that when you're cooking your mind is focused on one o'clock because it's lunchtime and we've got three vegans, and we've got two Moslems and five Jews and another twelve vegetarians. You're thinking of all that and they say, "Could we have jelly and custard?" There was a lack of organisation then, though I am sure it is quite different now.'

Once again, he got up and helped himself to another vodka. I said that I thought I really ought to go as we had to leave the harbour at 2.30 a.m. the next morning to catch the tide for Foula.

'No, stay awhile,' he said. 'Why are you going?'

'Ons moet vroeg opstaan, om half drie,' I said, meaning we have to get up early, at half past two.

'Jy praat Afrikaans?'

'Not very well at the best of times, and extremely badly when I've a few drinks.'

'Ja,' he said with a deep sigh. For the first time there was short silence. The rain had stopped and a few pale pink streaks could be seen in the layers of blue cloud outside. The ghost of a breeze wandered in through the open door and windows, easily lifting the flimsy, cheap-looking curtains.

'Do you *really* like living on Fair Isle?' I asked.

'I can't explain to you what I feel,' he said in a low voice, with a pained look on his face. 'In a way I don't know what I feel. It's a deep, deep feeling that whatever I do it is somehow right if it's got to do with Fair Isle. I can't quite break this bond. I can't quite say, "Fuck you, I'm going," because I don't want to say that. It's an awfully difficult thing to explain because I have never lived anywhere for such a length of time, ever. I've never felt so at home. I know these people. They are rough, and they are wild, and they are wicked, and they are beautiful, and I love them. I love all of them. There are disgusting people here: they have come here with no job, their wife has had a job and they've come here and made themselves the this and they've made themselves the that, they've got onto the housing board and they've got onto this and they think they're Christian. They are not Christian, they are fuck all. But you tolerate them, you understand them. "We're this, we're that," brag, brag, brag. It's pathetic. Yet in their juvenileness, I can't say I dislike them. You'll get

another insight when you have been here five years. You'll get another
insight which you never, ever thought that you would have when you
first came here. Totally different. They're pretentious, aargh! They are just
so totally ridiculous. I see them for what they are and I can see the good
and the bad in them and yet I still love them. It's a whole big mafia, but
you won't see that until you've been here. Some of them are so awful, so
unkind, so unChristian, yet they go to the church every Sunday. These
are definitely not Christians. I am very grateful for my upbringing in
South Africa in the sense that I questioned my birth; I questioned my
religion; I went and joined Indian people in worship; I went and joined
Moslem people; I thought if I wasn't born this I would have been born
that. What I am trying to say is that I am open to many things, but on
Fair Isle they are vicious, vicious.'

Then he relaxed, as if he had got what he wanted to say off his chest
and there was nothing left but to accept the ineluctable dilemma: to live
here as a loner for life, forever frustrated by bureaucracy, or to leave his
beloved Fair Isle.

Brightening just a little, he looked at me almost coyly and said,
'Obviously you can't listen to me and think, gosh, what he says is the
truth.'

'I really must go,' I said as firmly as I could manage, given the emotion
of the moment. The vodka bottle was almost empty.

'I've got one cigarette left,' he said as I stood up. 'Please let me smoke
it.'

5
FOULA

AT 3.30 A.M. NEXT morning there was hardly a breath of wind as Brian clambered up onto the quayside to slip the lines. I had raised the mainsail, but more in hope than in expectation. In almost complete darkness we nosed our way out into the apparently empty seascape. Outside, we encountered a long swell coming in from the north-west. This, I have been told, seldom varies and was what the nineteenth-century fishermen in their sixareens watched when navigating without a compass. They could 'read the swell', even when a cross sea was running, and so maintain a steady course over long distances, as the Vikings had done before them.

Once we had the north lighthouse astern, a lazy slop came in from the south-west, the effect of yesterday's wind. The two wave patterns gave the boat a most uncomfortable motion. The slatting of the sail was such that it was impossible to sleep down below. Eventually I took it down, which made the motion even worse. Motoring, we made a good 5 knots, tide assisted, so that by 8 a.m. we had a clear view of Foula, dead ahead through the overcast. At one point a pod of perhaps six dolphins gambolled about the boat for ten minutes. Then a dead mist began to descend. By 9 a.m. visibility was down to half a mile or so. Approaching the island this decreased to no more than two hundred yards. We were alarmingly close inshore before we saw surf on the rocks ahead. With the GPS there was no question of any uncertainty about our position, so we were able to turn confidently to starboard and follow the coast as Jimmy Stout had recommended.

The reason for hugging the shore is the presence of the infamous Hoevdi Grund, a huge reef a mile long with a rock in the middle which breaks in a swell. That was where the SS *Oceanic* foundered on 8 September 1914, in flat calm weather. The *Oceanic* had been built in the same yard as the *Titanic*, though ten years before. She was an equally luxurious, though smaller, vessel designed for the north Atlantic run. Converted at the beginning of the First World War to an armed merchant cruiser, she was despatched to the Northern Isles to patrol the shipping lanes with a view to intercepting vessels trading with the enemy. In thick mist on her first patrol, while zig-zagging to avoid submarines, the navigator became confused with his dead reckoning calculations. When Foula was finally sighted it was not on the expected bearing. The captain ordered a sharp turn and the ship was borne, by immensely powerful currents running over the Hoevdi shallows, onto the reef where she stuck fast. Everyone was taken off alive, but efforts to refloat the vessel were unavailing. As autumn came on, the great liner was buffeted by storms. Though she appeared intact when seen from the shore, in fact she was disintegrating internally. On 29 September a north-westerly gale of exceptional ferocity blew up. When dawn broke on the 30th, there was nothing to be seen of the 700-foot liner. The whole immense structure had been pushed off the reef during the night and had collapsed in a mass of tangled steel into slightly deeper water. There she lay undisturbed until the first divers prepared to brave the fierce currents on the reef went down to her in the early 1970s to start salvaging the non-ferrous metals, an operation that eventually lasted five years.[1]

The danger of the Hoevdi Grund is not just the underwater obstructions but the strength of the tides which carried the *Oceanic* onto them. They run at up to 6 knots, which is faster than *Foggy Dew* is capable of motoring. It was therefore imperative that we kept well clear as we groped up the mist-obscured coast. Too far out and we might get caught in the stream; too far in and we could be in more obvious danger. Added to that was the fact that the 'harbour' we were making for, Ham Voe, is so small – just an inlet, really, that we might motor past it unless we had the coast in constant view. But to have the coast clearly in view, we would have had to be uncomfortably close to the rocks. Without the GPS we would have had to stand off in the fog until visibility improved.

Ham Voe is about half way up the east coast of Foula, which runs nearly due north. I therefore noted the exact latitude of the inlet, and we steered on a fixed longitude until the GPS showed us to be on the exact latitude of the Voe. Still seeing nothing, we turned hard to port,

---

1 See *The Other Titanic*, Simon Martin, Newton Abbot 1980.

motored for no more than a couple of minutes and, to my intense relief, there it was, dead ahead. We crept in at less than a knot, Brian at the bow conning for rocks or any other uncharted obstructions, while I tried to make out the harbour entrance through the mist. As we approached I saw a strange, dark-looking structure inside it, rising 40 or 50 feet above the sea. What on earth was that? At first it looked like a rocket waiting to be launched. Gradually I was able to discern the shape: I saw a lifeboat-like vessel sitting on top of a high concrete quay, behind high walls and supported by two massive davits. That, we learned later, was the Foula ferry, the *New Advance*. So wild can the weather be here that even in summer the boat has to be hauled nearly twenty feet above the sea onto a specially-constructed hard-standing for safety.

By 11.30 we were tied up alongside an older-style lifeboat at the harbour wall. There had barely been enough room to manoeuvre the boat between the ferry quay to the north and the rocks to the south. Visibility went no further than the head of the voe, 60 or 70 yards away. We could just make out a tiny expanse of sand, possibly 10 yards wide. This, I learned later, is the only beach on Foula. The rest is rock.

We snugged the boat down and had an early lunch, after which I slept for an hour while Brian went for a wander. By the time I woke, the whole aspect of the day had changed. I came up on deck to see brilliant blue sky above us and a strong sun illuminating the green lower slopes of a hill that reared up into clouds that still obscured its higher reaches. This was the Sneug: 1,350 feet high and the summit of the island. While admiring the view I saw a jovial-looking figure adjusting the lines on the boat next to us. This turned out to be Brian Taylor, an emigré from Edinburgh who was skipper of the *New Advance*, though temporarily suspended, as he explained, for having struck an uncharted rock with the keel of his ship a few weeks before. The boat we were tied alongside was the previous ferry. On it he takes tourists round the island in summer, to view the seabirds and the cliffs on the west side. At 1,220 feet, they are almost as high as those on St Kilda, the highest in Britain, and nearly twice as high as those on Mingulay.

At length the island's owner, Magnus ('Magnie') Holbourn, a casually dressed, bearded man in his thirties, sauntered down to inspect the new arrivals. He looked at *Foggy Dew* and remarked, 'The bowhead looks a little tired.' Apparently he is a keen sailor himself. Up on the hard he had a Folkboat in which he is planning to sail round the world. Then the new district nurse and her partner came and 'strolled' for a bit. Finally, the ex-teacher from the island's school arrived with all her household belongings to be flitted on the temporary ferry – a busy spot.

Above the harbour lay immense heaps of rubbish, and above those a lightly castellated cottage known by the Norse word, The Haa (Hall). This is where the laird resides. Adjoining it is another house, now empty, which was a shop when the island had one. Elsewhere round the Voe I could see other houses, ranging from ruins to a smart, modern bungalow, with almost all levels of dilapidation and modernity in between. The same was true of the range of vehicles which were either parked or abandoned: cars, diggers, tractors and a minibus. The whole scene conveyed the comfortable untidiness which any large city displays but which the National Trust will not permit on Fair Isle.

Later that afternoon, Brian Taylor drove us out through the amazingly disorganised landscape to see a New Zealander friend of his who has lived on the island for many years, Dal Prytherch. Dal is a tall, slim, upright man in his seventies who inhabits the stone house which he built for himself and his late wife – an ex-district nurse for the island – on the road south of Ham. We found him sitting in front of a large-screen television watching England batting against India at Lord's. He was dressed in corduroys, cardigan, cravat and flat cap. He offered us bottles of beer then sat down to relight a pipe the colour of his peat-stack. In a fug of smoke and dog-odour, we chatted lazily about the cricket, the Cumbrian archaeologists who were on the island studying the ruins of Viking long-houses, the length of the Foula summer (fourteen weeks or sixteen?), the complexity of social relations on an island with a population of twenty-seven and the irritation of having to delay fencing work because of nesting bonxies. The birds are not under any sort of threat, Dal said, so why should he be prevented from doing his outdoor work in the few weeks of good weather.[2]

---

2 Fifty years ago human persecution had reduced the British bonxie population to final refuge on Foula and Unst. (They still bred in large numbers in Iceland.) The birds were given statutory protection in the 1950s. Numbers rose from perhaps fifty pairs to a current total of about 8,000. However, in recent years, the Foula population has declined slightly. Over-fishing is the explanation professional ornithologists give, even though there is no more fishing off Foula than nearby Shetland, where numbers are still increasing strongly. There is, however, a possible connection with disturbance. Foula is the only site showing decline and also the only one where research is carried

I asked Dal how he took to Foula when he first came to this wind-swept island from the lush climes of New Zealand.

'It was Shangri-la,' he said. 'There was no running water, no electricity, no proper road, no fences.'

'And now?'

'We've got nineteen crofts, twenty-seven people, two thousand sheep and four thousand bonxies. It's great.'

'And, it seems to me, a real feeling of freedom,' I said. 'More than the Fair Isle, anyway.'

'Yeah, that's Walt Disney-land, Noddy-land. They have a lot of rules set down by the Trust. You are living basically a regimented life. You can't do this, you can't do that.'

'What sort of things?'

'Your house has to be painted every year, pristine white,' Brian Taylor said with disgust. 'You can't have any rubbish lying about the place. They get a cruise ship at least every fortnight. They get hundreds of visitors. They're geared up for it, selling them knitwear and so on. I really don't think they can possibly be enjoying their lives.'

Foula was ruled by the Vikings and owned by their successors under udal law, which meant there was no single landowner, until a descendant of one of the Scottish immigrants into Shetland, John Scott of Melby, managed to trick them out of their title in the eighteenth century by persuading them that they needed his help in taking the documents to Edinburgh to be endorsed due to a change in the law. From then onwards a society of independent fishermen and farmers was, like their counterparts throughout Shetland, gradually reduced to almost total dependence on the laird. Shetlanders in general have been described in the period from the early eighteenth to the late nineteenth centuries as living in conditions not far removed from slavery. The tenure of crofts was conditional on surrender of the whole fishing catch to the land-owner, at a price dictated by him, and paid for in credit at a shop owned by him. This was known as the 'truck system' and was, despite laws

---

out. Every year scientists from Glasgow University come to 'monitor' the bonxies, which have been extensively ringed: 494 rings from 1988 to 1990, and more since. See Non-breeders as a Buffer against Environmental Stress: Declines in Numbers of Great Skuas on Foula, Shetland, and Prediction of Future Recruitment, N. Klomp and R. Furness, *Journal of Applied Ecology* 1992, p. 341.

dating from the early eighteenth century, common practice in industrial Britain until it was outlawed by the Truck Act of 1831. This made it illegal to impose any conditions of employment which, directly or indirectly, dictated where, how or on what wages might be spent. But that covered employees only, not tenants. It was not until the early 1880s that the crofters, fishermen and knitters of Shetland were freed from the truck system. A few years later the Crofters Act gave them security of tenure, finally destroying the economic hold of the landowners.

Soon after being freed from oppression based on the ownership of land, the people of Foula were subjected to a new form of oppression based on the narrow ownership of capital. In 1881 the island had a population of 267. Fifty years later this had dropped to 118 and fifty years after that to 39. The reason was the destruction of the 'haaf' fishing – *hav* is Norwegian for 'ocean'. The island has just over 3,000 acres of ground, most of which is hill, moorland or bog. Only a small part of the south-east is fertile, round Hametoun. That was not a problem so long as there were rich pickings to be had from the sea. Sheila Gear, whom I spoke to a couple of days later, wrote in her book, *Foula: Island West of the Sun*, that on the Far Haaf, 50 miles north-west of Foula (the edge of the continental shelf where the depth changes from less than 300 feet to over 2,000 feet), island fishermen used to catch adult ling which were as much as nine feet long – unheard of today. They rowed out in their 30-foot, six-oared open boats of Viking-derived design, called sixareens, and spent several days catching fish which they would later split, salt and sell to merchants in Shetland.

Despite the superb seamanship of the fishermen, this was still a very dangerous occupation, as was shown by the disaster which overtook the little fleet on the night of 13–14 July 1881. In the worst storm on record over a hundred lives were lost. But one survivor, Charles Johnson, from North Roe in Shetland, wrote about his experience.[3] After rowing for nine hours, the four men and three boys in his boat started fishing 30

3 I am grateful to the Shetland Archivist, Brian Smith, for locating Johnson's (unsigned) text in *Mansons' Shetland Almanac Companion*, 1932, pp. 189–196. Extracts with commentary can be found in the *Journal of Northern Studies*, vol 18 (1981), pp. 20–39, in an article by Ian A. Morrison entitled: Maritime Catastrophes, Their Archaeological and Documentary Legacies: with Reflections on the Centenary of the Shetland Fisheries Disaster of 1881. See also, for fuller details of the boats involved, *The Sixareen and Her Descendants,* Charles Sandison, Lerwick 1994 (1954).

miles off-shore on the edge of the Continental self. By mid-evening they
had 180 'very large' ling aboard when, on a smooth sea, they 'heard
and saw the weather coming'. Soon huge seas were breaking over them.
They put up the mast and raised the square sail close-reefed to 'give the
boat a fair chance'. Two men controlled the halyards, while the helmsman crouched under the tiller and the other four members of the crew
'kept quiet and still; no-one spoke for the men at the halyards knew
what to do'. The helmsman took note of the wind direction as they 'did
not expect the wind to shift after the first bat' and 'there would be wild
steering when the water was going over the boat and flooding the glass
of the compass . . . They pressed her with the sail when the surge came
around her, and although the sail was laid down she ran in it for a bit
(like a field of snow) and took water over both sides. It was not good to
look at . . . The three men who were managing the boat did not pass any
remarks to us nor to one another; they appeared quite contented and
fairly understood what they were doing. I had been brought up with
boating since I was a child, but this of course was a bit extra.' Four hours
later they came to shelter in Ronas Voe on the north-west of Shetland.
But ten other boats failed to find a gap in the otherwise implacable rocks
in the darkness and were dashed to pieces on the cliffs; others foundered
after being swamped.

Despite the courage and seamanship of the long-liners, their trade was
doomed. Deep-sea trawling destroyed it just as surely as inshore trawling
destroyed the local fishery on Fair Isle. Foula had no harbour at all in
those days. Despite repeated requests from the islanders, the first breakwater in Ham Voe was built only at the beginning of the First World
War. Sixareens had been dragged up above the high water mark on the
little beach but larger boats had nowhere to lie alongside. Consequently,
island fishermen could not join the trawler trade unless they migrated
to Shetland. Many did, which is why the population dropped. As the
population declined, so the island became ever less useful an asset. The
Scotts ran out of money and were forced to sell the island. In 1899 it was
sighted from a boat sailing to Iceland by an Oxford classics student who
determined then and there that he would try to buy it. The following
year he succeeded. His descendants own it to this day.

Though subsequently an academic who was hard-headed enough to
make a lot of money lecturing in America, the new laird, Ian Holbourn,
was also a romantic. In 1938 his recently widowed wife published a

book of his writings on Foula, which makes interesting reading for anyone curious about the way in which incomers a century ago viewed places such as this.[4] Today, I discovered, the book causes embarrassment. Most islanders think it an inaccurate, and in some respects an absurd, portrait.

Holbourn was a home-counties Englishman who claimed distant Scottish ancestry and wandered about Merton, his college in Oxford, in a kilt woven in a tartan of his own design. The fact that neither Foula nor any of the Northern Isles have ever had either kilts or tartans did not seem to bother him. He was not a 'Celtic twilight' fanatic of the sort which was common in the first few decades of the twentieth century. On the contrary, he was a fierce defender of what he saw as pure Nordic culture, including udal law. He noted that one of the conditions of the impignoration of Shetland and Orkney in 1469 had been that the laws and customs of the kingdom of Denmark should continue to apply. 'My belief', he wrote in his essay, Udal Property and the Kings of Foula, 'is that the Crofters' Acts of 1886 and subsequently were all of them *ultra vires*.' Holbourn referred to himself as 'the Udaller':

> The Scotts [of Melby] settled in the island of Vaila . . . and as Vaila lies just opposite Ham Voe they changed their landing place and abandoned the south landing, which the Danes had always used. Thus Hametoun in the south end, which was the original hame or home of the people with its Haa, school, temple-site, and later its Established kirk, ceased to be so to speak the capital of the isle as it had been in the days of the Danish rulers. It is still the centre of population, with its seventeen crofts surrounded by a stone dyke, but Ham (meaning harbour in Norse), has been the capital and seat of government since the Scott dynasty was established. The Hametoun is Glasgow or New York, but the Tun o' Ham, although it has only ten crofts, is the Edinburgh or Washington of the isle. Here is the laird's house, the school, the post office and the shop – the centre of news and discussion. This, too, is the headquarters of the fleet – the fishing boats, the mail-boat and the Udaller's yacht.[5]

---

4 It has recently been re-published as *The Isle of Foula*, Ian B. Stoughton Holbourn, Edinburgh 2001.

5 *Ibid.*, p. 80.

In later years, Professor Holbourn worked hard representing Foula on the Zetland County Council while at the same time advocating restrictions to the franchise so as to exclude what he called 'cabbage heads'. He thought a programme of selective breeding would 'improve the population'. Two other preoccupations of his were dress reform – the professor preferred that women should go naked rather than be clothed in newly fashionable masculine attire – and pronunciation reform. He believed that the slovenliness of modern speech was 'one of the main causes of the failure of our civilisation'.

His descendants are all now technically crofters on the estate of the Trust which owns the island, and they live as ordinary members of the island's small community.

'They're all good, hard workers, the Holbourns,' Dal said as he went to get us a second bottle of beer. 'But they've all got a disease. It's bred into their genes.'

'What is it?' I asked.

'Money. There's nothing they can do about it.'

'He's not joking,' Brian Taylor said. 'They're physically sick if they have to part with money.'

'I remember one who had to get a tyre from me for his trailer,' Dal said. 'I had just bought some; they were second-hand but they were wheels. They didn't cost much and he came up and said, could he borrow one? I said, no way, son. So he had to buy one, for £39. It nearly broke his heart.'

'But Magnie's all right,' Brian said. 'He's my deckhand on the ferry. The whole crew lives on the island. We all have to do different jobs. It's no problem. He can tell me what to do on the land and I can tell him what to do on the sea. It levels out quite nicely.'

'That's a nice wee twist,' said Glasgow Brian. 'The laird's the deck hand!'

'He's also the dustman.'

'The laird's the dustman?'

'Aye, he is!'

At this point the Glaswegian dissolved in fits of laughter. It is definitely not the Central Belt image of the status of lairds on remote islands. But then Foula is not an ordinary sort of island.

Later that evening, Brian Taylor drove us up to see another friend of his, Eric Isbister, in his cottage on the family croft at the Hametoun.

Without electricity, Eric plays his large collection of records and CDs on battery-driven equipment. His television works off a 12-volt car battery. Foula is not connected to the national grid, but the residents were offered windpower in the 1980s at three times the then current price of domestic power elsewhere in Britain. Eric declined to take it. His house is heated by a stove which, he told us, his father built in the 1920s. It is fired by peat, of which the island has a supply almost as inexhaustible as the wind. The weather had worsened and it was very snug settled round the stove, with a Tilly lamp hissing over the table – much cheerier than an electric fire and light-bulb would have been.

An expert musician, Eric picked out flamenco tunes on his guitar. These were interspersed with stories, like the one about the German three-master which, in the 1930s, drove onto the rocks at the south of the island, near Eric's croft, in a dense fog. After seeing the crew safely ashore and collecting as much timber as he could from the remains of the cargo, Eric's father asked the mate, who was the only one who spoke English, what had happened: 'Ve haff plenty off good Scotch viskey, and zen ve go BANG!'

Due to streaming rain and malfunctioning headlights in Brian's car, we drove all the way back to the Voe in first gear. Given the narrow road and unguarded bridges, as well as the generosity of the hospitality, it was lucky that we experienced no unexpected bangs ourselves.

Next morning I treated myself to the tail of the Fair Isle lobster, with mayonnaise and tomatoes, plus a fry-up of garlic, onions and potatoes. By mid-afternoon the weather had lifted slightly. I set off up the hill to what, if this part of the island is 'Edinburgh', must be the New Town, namely the house of Sheila and Jim Gear. This is also the literary quarter as Sheila Gear is the only resident to have written a book about Foula since her grandfather, Professor Holbourn. Her immensely tall husband, Jim, is the grandson of a minister who came to the island in the nineteenth century. Jim had represented the parish, which includes part of western Shetland, on the Shetland Islands Council from 1995 to 1999. It being Sunday, they were off to church – held in the smart new community school – just before 6 p.m., so I had to be brief. This was a shame because, though a small island, Foula is a big subject.

My main question concerned the cost of all the recent infrastructure improvement, namely the harbour, the ferry, the school and power provision. Jim gave me a figure of about £2.5 million.[6]

'That is an awful lot of money for a community of twenty-seven people,' I said.

'The reason why so many things have had to be done recently is that the island was starved of any investment for decades, by all the agencies. There was no investment at all for seventy years. The previous pier dated from 1914 when the government wanted a firing position on the island. That was the last major investment.'

'They were expecting a German occupation of Foula?' I asked.

'Only in that they were seeking to defend all parts of the British Isles against possible German invasion. I think that was true of Britain as a whole. This would simply have been one of the parts of it. They put in a telephone cable at the same time, running a line up to the top of the Sneug where they had a lookout post.[7] The first written record we have of people requesting that a harbour be built on Foula was the evidence given to the Napier Commission on crofting in 1884.'

'So the government ignored their own crofter-fishermen but responded to the Kaiser's navy?'

'Yes,' Jim said. 'And after decades, arguably centuries, of neglect, the cost of putting things right is going to be very high.'

I did a quick computation. If the investment was £2.35 million and the period of neglect was, say, 120 years, then that made an infrastructure investment rate on a non-compound basis for the present population of twenty-seven, £725 per person per annum. That is not a lot. The United Kingdom has, in round figures a population of 58 million and a Gross National Product of £1,000 billion. About 40 per cent of that is government expenditure and of that at least a tenth is for infrastructure investment of the sort that has recently been made on Foula: transport,

---

6 The exact figure was £2.35 million: harbour £1 million; ferry £350,000; school £500,000; electricity (wind, water, diesel) £500,000. Total: £2.35 million. This was financed as follows: Scottish Office: £400,000; Shetland Islands Council £1,215,000; European Union £570,000; Highlands and Islands Development Board £165,000.

7 This is the general island experience in Scotland. Electricity came to Islay, for example, purely as a result of the anti-submarine patrolling base which was established in 1940.

education, power and so on. That is £40 billion, or nearly £700 per person per annum. Though this is far from an exact comparison, it would be fair to say that Foula has not been over-generously treated, especially when it is considered that the British total will continue year after year, while it is highly unlikely that Foula will receive around £200,000 of further infrastructure investment every year in future.

By contrast, the income side of the equation looks less healthy. Trying to get a vague idea of the island's Gross Domestic Product, I asked Jim about the sheep. He said there were 1,500 breeding ewes and that 800 lambs were sent off the island in a typical year. At a pre-BSE price of £20 per lamb, that made £16,000 per annum. Add in gimmers and others livestock sales and you get, he said, about £20,000 as the total agricultural output of the island. If you add in tourism and those parts of the island's management which are carried out by islanders, like running the ferry, the school, the airport and the nursing service, the total rises. But it is still very small, almost certainly no more than £100,000 per annum. What justification can there be in the long run for public investment of £200,000 per annum in an island which earns no more than half of that from all sources?

'The island's balance of payment is in substantial deficit,' I said. 'In pre-industrial days, when people were self-sufficient, the island would have been a net generator of income, in the form of rent paid to the landowner, who gave little or nothing in return. But not today. The situation is reversed. With televisions, vehicles, schools, nurses, ferries and so on, you will be in permanent and considerable deficit. Is that something that causes questions to be raised in the council?'

'The council has a duty of care to the people they are providing government for,' Jim replied. 'There was a time, when the council proposed to run the ferry from the mainland, that it appeared to be turning its back on Foula. So we said, if the council turns its back on Foula, we will petition the Faeroes to see if they will take us on.'

'Seriously?'

'Fortunately it didn't come to that, but some of the councillors said, they wouldn't have you. I said they jolly well would. I said, the first thing they would do is to build a large harbour for their fishing vessels, and indeed for the oil vessels. With Foula, if the international boundary ran between Shetland and Foula there would be very significant gains for the Faeroese. They would probably be several hundred millions better off each year.'

Jim also pointed out that Foula is a part of Shetland and the Shetland economy as a whole, even omitting the taxes raised by oil, contributes a nett £100 million to the British exchequer. Many parts of Shetland are unprofitable, but taken overall, the area is in substantial surplus. There would be areas of Glasgow, or the north of England which would probably be in substantial nett deficit in the way Foula is, not to mention many farming communities throughout Britain. But no-one argues for them to be evacuated. Why should small islands be singled out for cost-benefit scrutiny?

I asked Jim how he thought Foula might expand its domestic economy. He said he thought there were possibilities in tele-commuting, though not until the phone link has been improved (more infrastructure investment). He thought there are people 'who for reasons of their own want to live in very remote parts of the world'. Unlike most islands in Scotland, it would not be a problem obtaining planning permission to build a new house on Foula. In general, the planning system is the highest hurdle for all rural development in Britain. Working against the grain of central government policy, the Shetland Islands Council has done what it can in the face of central government obstruction to allow development within its area. The Shetland Local Plan zones almost all the low ground on Foula as either Zone 1, in which housing development is actively encouraged, or Zone 2 in which it is 'favourably considered where it reflects existing settlement patterns'.

The other problem which besets housing development in the Highlands is landowners who either refuse to sell ground or expect a premium for 'planning gain'. Foula escapes this difficulty because all the islanders, including those who own the land, see that survival depends on increasing the population and would therefore not make difficulties about selling land for development. In short, Foula was the first island I have come across in Scotland where it was clear that new arrivals would be made welcome, both by their neighbours *and by the bureaucrats*.

Throughout this discussion, Sheila had kept almost completely quiet. She has very clear blue eyes and exceptionally smooth skin for one who has spent so much of her life outside in the wet and cold. There was a serenity about her which was reflected in her book:

[Foula is] the loveliest of all islands . . . The essence of Foula is her hills. These hills are the background to our life. Golden and ethereal in the early morning sun, dark blue and lowering in a storm, russet-red and far away in the pink autumn haze, white with snow they rise high and sheer into the sky, grey and bitter in the cold of winter. Always our hills are changing, always our eyes are drawn to them and always we are refreshed by them.[8]

Foula is an evocative description of a year of island life, interspersed with reflections on wider issues and local anecdotes which give them point and emphasis. I particularly liked her account of the round-up:

The first signs that the men are coming up from the back of the Kame are shown by our Shetland ponies as they pause in a bunch then gallop full tilt down the steep grassy face right along the very edge of the cliff, manes and tails flying, hooves pounding, mares whinnying to their foals. I can hardly bear to watch, expecting any minute to see one skid and plunge over the thousand-foot drop. Twenty-one, twenty-two, twenty-three – one missing! No, here she comes now, over the top, lazy old Flossie, last as usual. (p. 36)

But nature is not always benign:

Over the tail of Soberlie I spotted two bonxies sitting working with something down at the back of the Bloburn dyke, so I plodded down to investigate. The birds rose up as I approached and sat down on a broo [small bank] watching me. It was my dear little Funny Face. She lay in the middle of a small boggy hole, all four legs had gone through the surface and her head lay stretched out in front of her. Instead of her friendly golden eyes were two red gaping holes from which the blood had run down the sides of her cheeks and formed two large pools, crimson on the green sphagnum moss. I stretched out my hand and touched her – dead but still warm. The blood had not congealed . . .

Further down the burn I found the corpse of Rat Tail, lying half-submerged in a bog which she had foolishly tried to cross. The birds had already eaten her eyes and tongue and had pulled out long strips of her intestine which were tangled up on a tuft of crowberry. So,

8 *Foula: Island West of the Sun*, Sheila Gear, London 1983, pp. 11–12.

poor auld ewe, did they get you after all? The wind was whipping up
the loch into steep brown waves . . . A host of bonxies rose up and
circled round my head in the swirling grey mist, calling their harsh
'kak kak'. (pp. 146–8)

Sheila says that bonxies have been responsible for reducing numbers
of kittiwakes and Arctic skuas, as well as for innumerable attacks on
sheep and lambs. In her view the counts by visiting ornithologists under-
estimate the population, which is too high and ought to be reduced.
Islanders, she writes, 'are fond of their birds and will always be in a way
that outsiders often find hard to understand'. That is why they resent
the interference of people who cannot see the local picture in the round.
'The bonxie situation is a reminder that our island is no longer our own
– we have lost control over our environment. Foula has now the largest
colony of breeding bonxies in the northern hemisphere, but no-one ever
asked if that was what the people wanted.'[9]

The most interesting reflection provoked by Sheila's text is the whole
question of what I think of as 'islophilia' – the exaggerated veneration
for small islands. A bit of history is important. Until the late nineteenth
century islands were not considered special. The spate of books which
was published from the 1870s about St Kilda inaugurated a period
when islands in Scotland were no longer considered much the same as
anywhere else. Until the arrival of, first, the railways and then motor
cars, islands were no harder to get to than remote parts of the country.
Indeed in the Middle Ages when there were no roads of any sort in the
Highlands, islands were far *more* accessible than most non-coastal parts
of the mainland. That is why the McCormick Isles, a tiny uninhabited archipelago in the middle of the Sound of Jura, once contained a
hostel for travellers. It was rapid overland transport that made islands
seem comparatively remote and therefore romantic. In the nineteenth

---

9 Beyond control of islands, there is also the issue of information. When I
  contacted the Joint Nature Conservation Committee in Aberdeen, which
  keeps the government's official British Seabird Register, asking for simple,
  overall figures for the bonxie population in the Hebrides, I was refused unless
  I (a) agreed to pay for the information, (b) signed a declaration 'agreeing to
  conditions [unspecified] for use of the data', and (c) gave a written explanation of 'exactly what the data will be used for, giving details of any publications proposed'. (email 18 July 2003)

century Scotland, the Highlands came into fashion; in the twentieth, the islands.

The shift in public attitudes coincided with the traumatic experience of the First World War. At the same time as Britain lost the appetite for empire, it started to find life 'away from it all' appealing. Between the evacuations of Mingulay in 1909 and St Kilda in 1930, a world had changed. By the end of the 1930s people like Fraser Darling and Robert Atkinson were popularising 'island going'. Compton Mackenzie had gone to live on Capri at the end of the war, then bought one of the Channel islands, which he soon afterwards exchanged for the Shiant Isles, before moving to Barra in 1932.

After the Second World War, the 'new Jerusalem' mood gave many people island fever. The most literate expression of that craze is to be found in Gavin Maxwell's book *Harpoon at a Venture*, which begins with an incident which took place in a military depot at Deptford and which has strong echoes of George Waterston's approach to Fair Isle:

> This story begins in 1940 . . . It was the third week of the Battle of Britain blitz, and we were tired and nostalgic. [After nearly being hit by an unexploded bomb] I said, 'I've made a resolution. If I'm alive when this war is over I'm going to buy an island in the Hebrides and retire there for life; no aeroplanes, no bombs, no Commanding Officer.'
>
> Deep in the spirit of nursery make-believe, we spread a map of Scotland on the floor, and like children lay full length before it, propped on our elbows . . . We spoke of Hyskeir, Rona, Canna, Staffa; in my mind were high-pluming seas bursting upon Atlantic cliffs and booming thunderously into tunnelled caverns; eider ducks among the surf; gannets fishing in deep blue water; and, landward, the scent of turf smoke.
>
> After an hour there were rings drawn round several islands. I had drawn an extra ring round Soay, below the Cuillin. We were still playing at make-believe; Soay was my Island Valley of Avalon, and Avalon was all the world away.
>
> Presently the sirens sounded, and down the river the guns began again.[10]

---

10 London, 1952 (1998), p. 17.

The most extreme example of this trend was James Fisher's book, *Rockall*.[11] Like the moon, the only possible romance about an uninhabitable lump of rock can be the process of getting there and the sense of achievement on returning to normal society.

By the 1970s, island going was so common that the islands themselves began to change. Helped also by the influence of television and, more recently, European bureaucracy, they have increasingly lost those differences from the mainland which made them seem exotic. But it is easy to forget that there was a time when the future of many Scottish islands hung in the balance. In 1939 Michael Powell made a film on the theme of the St Kilda evacuation. The title sequence contained this introductory comment: 'The slow shadow of Death is falling upon the Outer Isles of Scotland. This is the story of one of them – of all of them.' The credits end with the mention of 'All the people of the lonely island of Foula, where this film was made.'

The reason Powell took his film crew to Foula was that St Kilda's then owner, the Earl of Dumfries, refused to let the birds be disturbed. Powell wrote a book about the adventures he had making the film, an account which ranks with Maxwell's shark-hunting story as a classic of Scottish island experience: *Edge of the World*.[12] Apart from the islanders who helped with the filming, Powell also wrote about two of the most powerful influences on island life: the bonxies and the Holbourns. 'The bonxie is a big bruiser. He ought to wear a check cap. He already has a striped sweater. He is a cannibal and a racketeer, who lives by hi-jacking his friends. He is Public Enemy No 1 on Foula.' (p. 263) About the latter, he echoes Dal, noting that, 'a Holbourn never lets go; it is a point of honour, as with lobsters'. (p. 279)

After leaving the Gears I walked to the north end of the island, hoping to find Isobel Holbourn, the daughter of a Shetland schoolmaster who

---

11 London, 1956. When Fisher was winched ashore with the Naval party claiming the seventy-foot high rock for Britain, on 18 September 1955, he asked the accompanying Marine sergeant for permission to kiss it. That granted, he then took a geologist's hammer and smashed off lumps of the 'unique' granite to take home with him. (pp. 160–1)

12 Originally published as *200,000 Feet on Foula*, Michael Powell, London 1938; republished under the new title, with a new introduction, London 1990. It is interesting that the books written about wild and chaotic Foula, including *The Other Titanic*, are so much better, simply as books, than those written about genteel, orderly Fair Isle.

moved to the island when she was a young girl and later married into the owning family. Though now divorced, Isobel is still one of the prime movers of island life. I caught up with her as she returned from church to her neat bungalow which sits close to the shore on one of the few areas of fertile-looking grazing, under the looming mass of the Sneug.

Having been for five years the Shetland islands' representative on the North Areas Board of SNH, and also having heard my interview on Radio Orkney a fortnight before, Isobel was initially guarded. But good nature soon overcame her professional caution. We sat in her kitchen, where she insisted on making me tea and sandwiches. Since she seemed so personable, I asked her about the impersonal world of SNH.

'One of my specialist areas is community interaction with the natural heritage,' she said.

'Which is?'

'It involves trying to get closer to people. I thought more could be done and that SNH had to adapt its processes in the way it dealt with people on the ground.'

'How?'

'Just not being so bureaucratic and dogmatic, and including people in their calculations, accepting that people had to live in these areas, that they owned the natural environment.'

'Was that a new thing?'

'Yes. But no-one was interested. It took me a long time to be listened to. Eventually I helped to restructure the meetings that SNH held in conjunction with their board meetings. The evening before each meeting we have an open meeting. To start with it was just like a school assembly with the heid yins up here and the populus in rows. It wasn't productive or useful at all. I redesigned it to put one or two SNH people in the middle of the public where they could have a really horizontal discussion. That was then copied by the rest of SNH. That's the one little thing I can pride myself on!'

'Well done!' I said. 'I'm all in favour of horizontal discussions.'

Isobel told me that when she was young she remembered there being much more birdlife on the island before bonxie numbers exploded.

'There were more shore birds and more moorland birds,' she said, 'because the people harvested the bonxie eggs in the spring. Later the number of people dropped. And also they weren't so hard up, so they didn't need the eggs. The result is that we have sacrificed moorland and shore birds.'

'A bonxie egg is edible then?' I asked.

'Yes. I didn't like them. But the old islanders all did. I remember my mother-in-law, she'd be way among the sheep on a May evening and she'd come back with a whole lot of bonxie eggs and they'd float them in a bucket to see if they'd been incubated. In the spring, when salt beef and the salt fish was done, it was good fresh food.'

'Did folk eat the birds as well?'

'People did eat the chicks. I've never eaten a bonxie, but I've eaten puffins.'

'What does a puffin taste like?'

'It's brilliant, especially the young ones. They are very fat, and we used to cook them on an open fire. Nowadays folk'd rather send to the Co-op for a box of food.'

'So it'd make very little difference to the puffin population if it were legal to eat them, because very few people would.'

'That's right.'

'So why should that not be de-criminalised?'

'Ah, yes, yes,' she said, hesitating. 'Fulmars are another thing that should be de-criminalised. Fulmars are just horrendous. There are a lot of old buildings in this area and they nest in them because all the cliff sites are full up. The ones nesting in the buildings spit on the lambs and that spoils the coats, which decreases their value for market.'

'Fulmar oil doesn't clean off?'

'No, it's disgusting stuff. Don't get near it. The smell never leaves you. What I used to do before I realised there was a big fine was to take the eggs. It's a big white egg, very bland, but makes a lovely omelette when they're newly laid. When I had a family of kids, with no freezer and very few boats, I had to.'

'Once again,' I said, 'as few people would eat them now, what would be wrong with de-criminalising egg taking?'

'With most ordinary people it would work, but there is an element who would exploit a loophole like that.'

'What collect millions of them?'

'Yes, egg collectors and stuff.'

'But surely there is a limit to how many eggs even the looniest egg-collector is going to want? You could still have it illegal to trade in them so that collections would have no monetary value.'

'Possibly. I do not have a legal mind. But,' she said, breezily changing the subject, 'I know that you can take out a rogue pair of bonxies if they develop a habit of getting amongst your livestock. I got a licence one year because we used to lamb our sheep in a field which has got a hollow in it that gave shelter from all the winds but was also a very popular nesting place for the bonxies. They are very clever birds and it was horrendous trying to lamb sheep there. Bonxies are like golden eagles, they go for anything. They'll take a living lamb, have its eye out, its belly out, in no time. And they're not afraid, you can't scare them away, only kill the rogue ones.'

The big question I wanted to ask Isobel was, why is anyone still living on Foula? In 1965 Eric Linklater described the island as 'an old folks' home remote in the pitiless Atlantic' and said that it 'will not survive much longer as a human habitation . . . [The people] are waiting until their surviving boatmen are too old to face the hazardous little voyage to Walls. And when their boatmen retire, the island will be evacuated and left as a sanctuary for the myriad sea-birds that first gave it the name of Fowl Isle.'[13]

Isobel described the situation on the island in the period of which Linklater wrote. 'When I came in the 1950s, a big chunk of the population was between fifty and seventy, often unmarried brothers and sisters living in one house.'

'Why was that?'

'Because there is not a lot of croft land so there was land-hunger, also the Depression of the '30s was a time when people didn't marry. People courted and became sweethearts, but they didn't marry. There wasn't land for them to go on. It was subsistence crofting. The only other way of earning a living was going to the herring or going to the mainland. I was the first one of my generation to marry and have a family. The generation ahead of me didn't have children.'

'So why was the island not evacuated?' I asked. 'Why did it not suffer the same fate as St Kilda?'

'It's different attitudes, different cultures,' she said. 'St Kildans were fatalists. They huddled together and made decisions jointly so that if a wrong decision was made the whole island suffered. Foula people are fiercely independent, though cohesive when it is needed. And also

---

13 *Orkney and Shetland*, London 1965 (5th edition 1990), pp. 163, 207.

they're bloody stubborn. Somebody called it a "limpet-like population".
But the one thing I think is different is that everybody who lives on
Foula is passionate about the place. And that applies to those who move
here as much as the native islanders. A lot of people married in, so it
made the families half-breeds, if you like. But that was great because it
brought in new blood and ideas. That was a good evolution, it happened
in the 1950s and '60s.'

This is one important difference between Fair Isle and Foula. On both
islands about half the population is incomers and half natives, but the
distribution is not identical. On Fair Isle there are many families which
have moved to the island – social refugees, if you like – and many who
are native. On Foula, incomers have tended to marry into local families, bringing community integration a generation earlier. Isobel's view
was that exogamy gave energy to Foula which helped to save it from St
Kilda's fate.

For an island to be part of wider society, communications of all sorts
are fundamental. Foula was disgracefully treated in most respects. The
telephone link which was established during the First World War was
allowed, once peace had come, to disintegrate. It was not until 1954 that
a phone box gave ready contact with the outside world. Likewise the
Post Office made difficulties over the expense of mail delivery, the policy
of a national flat rate for deliveries notwithstanding. Worst of all was the
ferry, which was a hopelessly inadequate 30-foot boat which the authorities would not replace because they predicted that the island would be
evacuated within ten years. Ten years later, when Isobel arrived, they
said they would not invest in a proper school building, a water supply
or an improved harbour or ferry because, they said, the island could not
guarantee the size of the population in ten years' time. The same thing
happened ten years after that, in the early 1970s.

In the meantime, the island would go for up to two and a half months
without the ferry being able to make the run from the mainland. Tobacco,
paraffin, even soap would run out. These, remember, were the years of
Harold Wilson's 'white-hot technological revolution'. While Concorde
was being designed in Bristol, food was often so scarce on Foula that
Isobel remembers a whist drive at which the very valuable prize was half
a pound of Echo margarine. The response of the Foula people to inadequate transport provision was very different from that of the St Kildans.

*   *   *

In 1968 Foula was left with a population of 27 men, women and children. When St Kilda's population fell to that level they felt their way of life couldn't be maintained. The request for evacuation in 1930 was the result. Foula folk are an independent and tenacious lot, and we all love the island passionately and were determined to stay, whatever it took. In 1969 with the coming of Loganair to Shetland, the Foula community saw their opportunity and built an airstrip, starting in 1969 and finishing it in 1972. No mean feat for 27 men, women and children, 2 grey Fergie tractors, one trailer and a back-actor. Every single person, young and old, contributed in whatever way they could. The only suitable site on the common grazings had to be de-crofted, tons of peat had to be carted off an area 500 yards long by 25 yards wide, the underlying clay coated with hardcore from the local quarry, then top-surfaced and rolled. The younger physically able folk did the harder work, the pensioners looked after the youngest bairns, the primary school boys broke stones after school, women folk kept the croft work going and did the paper-work. We carefully recorded every hour of voluntary labour at £1 an hour, which the Highlands and Island Development Board matched pound for pound. This grant money kept the vehicles fuelled and repaired. No-one was paid a penny for their labour.[14]

What was the reason for this heroic response – more like something in the early Soviet Union than modern Britain – when St Kilda society so meekly folded? Isobel thinks there were two main factors: the in-migration already mentioned and, more controversially, the 'very significant' fact that 'St Kildans were Gaelic speakers, Celts, with I assume a good measure of Celtic fatalism'. She explains this view by saying that St Kildans built their houses 'close together for mutual support, and decisions about daily and seasonal work were taken communally . . . In the three crofting townships, Foula crofters built their houses round the edge of the arable land, at a distance from each other, and each made their own decisions about how the work was to be done . . . Daily independence of decision spread any risk, and allowed folk to try their own ideas and improve their lot in their own way by their own efforts, and gradually good practice was copied and the whole community benefited.'[15]

Sheila Gear in her book made a similar point:

14 From Isobel Holbourn's essay, Foula and St Kilda, Island Book Trust, Stornoway 2002, p 8.
15 *Ibid.*, pp. 10–11.

Like all other sea-faring people the Foula folk have always been strong individualists. This is the greatest difference between them and the islanders of St Kilda with whom they are sometimes compared. The St Kildans were landlubbers with a close-knit co-operative society based on fowling, living side by side in a crowded little street – an extraordinary idea to anyone here, where houses tend to be on the outer edges of the crofts as far apart as possible. Excessive dependence on one another is a bad thing and makes an island very vulnerable. (p. 14)

My own thought when Isobel explained all this to me was that it sat uneasily with her role within SNH. That is an organisation which believes in 'partnership politics', which is another term for communal action. Likewise, most of the modern initiatives in rural Scotland, which SNH is usually at the heart of, are based on 'community' ideas and practice. Community buy-outs of land are permitted under the land reform legislation, for example, but buy-outs which could transfer ground to individuals, Foula-style, are not supported. It is highly arguable whether it is healthy to impose a Hebridean model all over the Highlands and islands, where not everybody is any longer 'Celtic' (if ever they were). But it is unarguably oppressive to foist an alien model such as that on the Northern Isles with their quite different social and cultural traditions deriving from Nordic maritime individualism and self-reliance.

I tried to put this apparent contradiction to Isobel but was deftly deflected onto the story of how the Foula air service actually works. Not being licensed by the Civil Aviation Authority (CAA), it is blissfully flexible. The airstrip is private and so can be operated by part-time islanders. The service is, formally, a series of charters, which were originally laid on when the vet, teaming up with the doctor, needed to travel to the island. In the early 1980s, a timetable was introduced. Today there are seven flights a week in the tourist season and three in the winter. Tickets are £42 return, or £30 for islanders, for the 15-minute hop to Tingwall, near Lerwick. In the summer the flights are full and more than pay for themselves. Taken over the whole year the deficit is tiny. So economical a service is only possible because of freedom from the bureaucracy of the CAA.

I asked Isobel what happens in a medical emergency.

'The nurse phones Lerwick and says she needs an air ambulance flight. She then phones the chief fireman on the island and asks for people at the airstrip, and it just happens. If the weather is exceptionally bad then a helicopter comes. Cross winds and poor visibility are the main problems. Visibility is not a problem for the helicopter, as it comes in on heat signals.'

'What, you switch on the microwave?'

'Nothing as sophisticated as that,' she said with a laugh. 'What happened three winters ago was that a woman went into premature labour on a snowy, winter night. At Sumburgh they said to light four flares in a square. We went down to the airstrip and put sand in biscuit tins. We soaked them with petrol and lit them. They were only about half a mile out of Sumburgh – 30 miles from here – when they picked up these flares on their heat-seeking equipment and were able to home in on that, which made us feel a lot less vulnerable.'

With almost the air of a saleswoman, Isobel went on to tell me about the way in which Foula people help each other in times of need. Not everyone is fit enough to lift their own peats.

'So someone going for a walk by the bank of one of the older people will raise some peats as they pass,' she said. 'Over the summer they are all raised. We have a communal peat casting service. It doesn't cost anything for a household that doesn't have a man. It is different on Fair Isle. I have a lot of very good friends on Fair Isle that I was at school with. Fair Isle is very highly organised. Foula is the black sheep of Shetland. But the people here are generous to a fault, to an extreme fault.'

I asked about Papa Stour, where Brian and I were going to sail in the morning.

'Papa Stour is a sad island,' she said, echoing what people on Fair Isle had said of Foula. 'Its population went down the same as Foula's did, but they made a big mistake trying to counteract it by running an advertising campaign. We've never done that. All sorts of strange people arrived there.'

By 11.30 it was time to go. Isobel had given me more time than I thought I deserved. But she would not hear of my walking back down to the boat, even though there was still some light in the sky, so she drove me. But so full of talk was she that it was 1.15 before I was back aboard.

*   *   *

We awoke next morning to a cloudless blue sky, without a breath of wind. We devoted a couple more wasted hours to fiddling with the boat's charging circuit, which had stopped working again. To no avail. After hand-cranking the engine, we cast off at 11 a.m.

Outside, there was a great heave to the sea, a swell so long that it was more like an exceptionally slow pulse. We motored round the island to see the cliffs of the west, which were spectacular, towering above a small creel-boat we saw working right under the Kame. The rock looked much harder than either the green cliffs of Mingulay or the sandstone of Hoy. Under one of the cliffs there was a huge arch and, further round, just off Isobel's house, a sort of rock tripod: three irregular pillars joined at the top, nearly 200 feet above the sea.

By the time Brian went below to brew up a bit of lunch, Foula was beginning to recede into a blue-grey haze that was slowly softening the day. The glass was now up to 1052, which is extraordinarily high. There was hardly a ripple on the water as Papa Stour came up, flat, low and undistinguished-looking compared to majestic Foula.

The Sound of Papa, which has the township of Melby on the mainland side, is studded with rocks, so we had to make our way through and into Mousa Voe, the anchorage, very carefully. We did so without mishap, tying up alongside a rather primitive ferry pier at 5 p.m., by which time a chilly wind from the east had got up. The sea was restless all night. Unusually for an island, there was no house above the landing point. There was an unwelcoming sign on the unfenced grazing above the pier: 'No Access Vehicles Prohibited Don't Enter Croftland'.

I had been told about the feud between two English families who moved to Papa Stour to escape from the world. One arrived thirty years ago, while the others were more recent arrivals. The former were ostentatious Christians who had tried various ways of making money on the island, the most recent of which was to open a bitterly-opposed drug-rehabilitation clinic. The other family included a minister with the Apostolic Faith Church who had alleged, in an article in the *Sunday Telegraph* in 1997 – written, incidentally, by Andrew Gilligan – that he had had the tyres on his Land Rover slashed, his 'drive' decorated with sheep skulls, a cat doused with petrol and his children assaulted. While Brian cooked the dinner, I picked up Alain Gerbault's beautiful book *In Quest of the Sun*, which I had found in a second-hand bookshop in

Kirkwall, and which has some reflections on people who wish to escape from 'civilisation' by retiring to remote islands.

Gerbault had been a French international tennis player around the time of the First World War, a flying ace during it, and afterwards a lone yachtsman who tried to escape the ugliness of early twentieth-century society, as he saw it, by taking to the sea in his 39-foot yacht, the *Firecrest*. While a song called 'Donald in the Bushes with a Bag of Glue' blasted gruesomely from Radio Scotland, which Brian had on in the galley, I read about Gerbault's reception at the residence of the governor of the Galapagos islands, where 'dancing went on until the late afternoon', and after which he set sail 'for a distant goal, the mysterious coral islands three thousand miles away'. Gerbault was a resourceful sailor and a man who loved the simplicity and grace of life amongst the unsophisticated peoples of the Pacific and Indian Ocean islands. At the end of his six-year trip, he found it hard to re-adjust to life in France. As the shades of fascism fell across Europe, he decided he would escape for good. He built a new boat and set sail for the Pacific, searching for his ideal island. No sooner had he found it than the Japanese army found him. He died of disease in prisoner-of-war camp in East Timor. There was – and is – no escape from the world.

The next day dawned cool and grey, and I set off for a quick look round the 'sad' island. The first person I met was a Mr Holt-Brooke, who, while loading stones into the back of a Range Rover, morosely said, 'You're a journalist, aren't you?'

'Sort of,' I answered.

'No-one on this island will talk to you.'

He was largely right, except that I met Anne Glover, a friendly woman who had come to live here with her large family from Bournemouth six years previously. She described the feud and explained to me that phone calls would have been made around the island when it was learned that there was a journalist about – very different from hospitable Fair Isle and Foula.

'When I was on Fair Isle,' I said, 'and asked what they thought of the people of Foula I was told they're very sad. When I was on Foula and asked about Papa Stour, I was told it was a very sad island. Now I'm here on Papa Stour, who do you think the sad people are?'

'Us,' she said laughing gaily. 'We're sad!'

Clearly there was hope for some of them.

*   *   *

At 1.20 p.m. we cast off, bound for Yell where a friend, Robert Cunyngham-Brown, had offered us 'r & r' at his large house on Yell Sound, more or less opposite Sullom Voe. The glass had dropped slightly, to 1046. The wind was easterly 4, ideal for a passage north past Esha Ness and then round the jagged Ramna Stacks and south into the Sound.

The sailing conditions at first were lovely, with low but broken cloud behind which brilliant patches of sunlight glowed from time to time. For a couple of hours we kept up a steady 5½ knots, then the wind began to die, and also to back north-east, which forced us out to sea. At six o'clock we tacked ship and were almost able to make a heading due east. But by now we had full tide against us and had to put in a couple more tacks before we rounded the Isle of Fethaland, inside the Stacks, in near darkness, with showers of rain driving whichever one of us was not on watch down below.

With the tide now strongly against us, time ran on. It was after 10 p.m. when we rounded up into Southladie Voe and motored gingerly up past the Urabug, a stony spit of land which projects half way across the bay from the east side, grounding lightly as we slid inside. In pitch darkness, we dropped anchor just beneath the stone pier that leads directly up to the North Haa, where Robert lives. We inflated the dinghy and rowed ashore to be met by the tall, erect figure of our host, a mane of grey hair flying in the wind. He was attired in a light blue dressing gown and green wellies. He greeted us as if we had just returned from the North Pole.

'Come on up,' he said with gusto, 'you must be famished. I've got a couple of steaks ready, but you'll need a drink first!'

6

SHETLAND

AFTER THE BLEAK DAMPNESS and darkness of Yell Sound, the kitchen at the North Haa was wonderfully warm and cosy. Robert poured us each an enormous dram, then opened the top of his stove and slapped two steaks into a frying pan – simple food, but delicious. Later he showed us to separate suites of rooms, each with a bedroom, bathroom and sitting room looking south over the Voe.

Next morning we slept late, foregathering in the kitchen at lunchtime. Robert kindly offered to lend me his Land Rover while we were in Shetland. He also referred me to a man who was knowledgeable about diesel engines. So while Brian went down to the boat after lunch to unload laundry, bedding and so on, I took advice to the effect that we almost certainly had a faulty alternator. I was told where in Lerwick it could be exchanged – which gave Brian another job removing it. After doing that, and replenishing fuel and water, he was largely free for the next ten days, during which time Robert showed him how things worked on Yell and the farm. Slightly to their mutual surprise, I thought, since they are such different characters, they got on well together. We had been there only a couple of days when Robert leaned over the table towards me and said with a resolute jut of the chin, 'Brian's all right!' Likewise, I remember Brian saying to me soon afterward, 'Robert's a great guy.'

I had stayed with Robert once before, a year previously, when I had helped him fight SNH over a designation they wanted to impose on part of his ground on Yell. He takes an old-fashioned, anti-bureaucratic position on most issues, and also has little time for many of the more obtuse apparatchiki, as he thinks of them. One had 'manicured eyebrows' and 'looks as if he spends thirty or forty quid a week on his suntan', while another was 'as thick as a Gurkha's foreskin'. Most of all, he dislikes their combination of local power with lack of local knowledge. Despite his 'establishment' appearance – Winchester, Cambridge, Royal Institute of Chartered Surveyors – Robert is a hands-on farmer on land his family has owned for centuries, which is almost unique in Shetland, since most land is crofted.

The next morning Brian and I drove into Lerwick to make the alternator exchange and indulge ourselves with lunch at the excellent curry house which I remembered from my previous visit. Back at Westsandwick, the little township below Robert's house, beside Southladie Voe, I went straight out to the boat and fitted the new alternator. Hey presto! the batteries charged beautifully.

Next morning, I motored down to see Magnie Burgess, who farms at the southern end of Shetland and who had heard my interview on Radio Orkney. I drove the 70 miles down from Robert's under an almost cloudless sky with the wind blowing near gale force from the north-east. Shetland has pockets of cultivable ground and much of the coastal scenery – nowhere is more than 3 miles from the sea – is coldly impressive. But very few places look cosy, in the way that parts of Orkney do. Eric Linklater made this comparison between the two communities:

> Shetland does not enjoy the self-satisfaction which allows many people in Orkney to find in the compass of island life an absorbing mental occupation as well as a sufficient livelihood. A wholesome insularity still characterises Orkney . . . but Shetland is open to the winds of anxiety and discontent.[1]

The basic fact is that Shetland is open to the sea. It dominates the view almost everywhere and the port of Lerwick is on a wholly different scale from Kirkwall or Stromness. The huge pelagic boats, many of them locally-owned, disgorge their cargoes at the fish quay under a cloud of swooping, screaming gulls while a host of other ships are tied up elsewhere along the extensive waterfront, sheltered by the island of Bressay. It is immediately apparent why the popular saying is that an Orcadian is a farmer with a boat, whereas a Shetlander is a fisherman with a croft. They are two very different communities. And quite distant ones too: as the crow flies, Muckle Flugga is further from the Old Man of Hoy than Hoy is from Dundee.

---

1 *Orkney and Shetland, op. cit.,* p. 161.

A similar point can be made about the northern isles generally. Lerwick, which is on the same latitude as Cape Farewell in Greenland, is closer to Bergen than it is to Aberdeen, much less Edinburgh. Once again, Eric Linklater observes with justice:

> In both archipelagoes the people have a lively awareness of their Norse background, and a staunch belief, not merely in their inheritance of Norse blood, but of its dominance in their constitution. There is no enmity to Scotland, but no inclination to accept more than a political relation with it, and no sense whatever of any kinship with the Hebrides.[2]

Part of the reason for the coolness towards Scotland derives from the exploitation of the islands by the Scottish ascendancy which was foisted on Shetland by James VI and which decayed over the next two and a half centuries into the petty oppression of the truck system which I described in relation to Foula. Part of it comes from the more positive sense of kinship with the wider North Sea/North Atlantic community, especially Norway and the Faeroes.

Magnie, presumably originally Magnus, but Mansie to his friends, is a burly, bearded man whose spacious kitchen was full of boots, dogs, strimmer components, teenage daughters and copies of the *Scottish Farmer*. Though almost all of the poor ground in Shetland is crofted – Robert has only about a tenth of his own ground in hand – some of the tiny fertile areas are owner-occupied. Magnie's farm is one of those. It looks south over the Loch of Hillwell – a magnet for both nesting and migrating birds – to the dunes and wide sandy beach of the Bay of Quendale. He is less than 2 miles from where the oil-tanker *Braer* went aground, at Garth's Ness, just south of Fitful Head. One of his pre-occupations is the danger to his rights of ownership posed by the conservationists' assumption that wildlife is a communal resource which must be managed by a rule-bound bureaucracy.

'Shetland has always had wildlife,' Magnie said almost as soon as I had got myself seated. 'What RSPB, SNH and all these people do is claim, "Look what we've done by imposing all these rules!" But we were brought up to respect wildlife. Wildlife needs three things: a courtship period for

2 *Ibid.*

establishing safe territory before nesting; an incubation period; and a
short period thereafter for fledging. That's all they ask for, and they need
it at a certain time of year. Shetlanders do not go right in through nesting habitat. I have never, ever in my whole life seen a local down there
at the loch during nesting time, never, ever. I've seen them with a gun
at the back end of the year, and the rule there is that if you put it down
you bloody well eat it. And if you don't get it that night you make sure
you do next morning. That was how I was brought up. It cuts down on
the layabouts, I assure you. If somebody was coming in here firing off
willy-nilly the locals would deal with them, believe me. It wouldn't be
the law, it would be some locals who would deal with them. I've never
seen a problem until the RSPB came, "protecting" the area.'

'What were they supposed to be protecting it from?'

'People,' Magnie said. 'People. You see when the RSPB came to
Shetland, Shetland had this abundance of wildlife, and they saw something that they could sell. This loch, Loch Hillwell, is the best migrating
loch in Shetland, but that is only because it is low and there is agricultural
land round about, so there's feed and shelter. And the humans respected
it. It's manageable, but it's not managed. Farmers are all supposed to be
bad. We've been criticised by the bodies that be, over and over again.
Why is it that right in the heart of Shetland's agriculture we have the best
migrating and the best breeding loch?'

'Has it always been like that?'

'Bar the few years that those people got in. They rendered the loch
birdless. No young birds fledged one year at all. They would disagree
with me. You can believe who you want. I live here. I love the birds. I see
them every day without going down there. There were no young birds
fledged one year, and we'd be looking for approximately sixty young
birds fledging on the loch. Then you get your shore birds. The next three
years there was a one and a two and a three. You cannot have that. The
population is just four years older. I started addressing people, RSPB
mainly, but also other official bodies. That didn't work, so I addressed
everybody who came down to the loch at nesting time for the four years
it took me to stop the disturbance. Of the people that I talked to I'd say
RSPB members were over 70 per cent. They would blame twitchers, but
I can recognise an RSPB guy a mile away as opposed to a twitcher or a
tourist. Tourists I have no problem with.'

'How do you recognise an RSPB member?'

'Attitude.'

'Of what sort?'

'Arrogance. I even know when I see a car coming down the road what they're going to do, just about. Total arrogance. Damnable arrogance. We belong to something and it's right.'

'Why do you think they're so arrogant?'

'That's an English thing. At least their export model has an arrogance that a lot of other people don't have. I call them the export model. They always take their shit with them to the next place. They say, "I've got an opportunity to start again. I can be anybody I want." Normal people don't have that opportunity. They've left something that, very often, they detested, then they try and reintroduce the shit where they move to. Shetland's a nice place, why the hell change it?'

'So in the end how did you beat them?'

'The way I beat them was they were there in the name of the environment. Their usual thing was, "Do you realise who you're talking to?" I was just a little cave dweller from Shetland. I usually let them say that three times, then I told them how little that meant to me. But they were members of the RSPB. They were paying their subscription, therefore they had a right to go anywhere they want. I can't understand that. It's like a grouse beat. That's how city people go through the countryside. They don't walk in single file, they spread out, so they trample everything. There was quite a bit of verbal abuse, but just before I would leave them I'd come right back down to human terms, and say, "Here we drink whisky; where you come from it'll be cheese and wine. When you're having one of your cheese and wines and the RSPB is telling how much they are doing for the country, especially in Shetland, put a few of the points I have made to you back to them." That's how I beat them, because there's nothing like an Englishman, if you get him on side he'll fight just as hard the other way round. Nobody goes to the loch in the breeding season now.'

'Do they own the ground?'

'No, no, no. The RSPB owns nothing. They're just advertising that which is on somebody else's land. The wildlife shares this place with me. It's not my wildlife. But if I am prepared to lock off fields for the birds to reproduce, I see no good reason for a bird club to come in and sell that. If it's for sale, I want the greenbacks. These people always come at the migrating periods of the year and they always come at nesting time, because the poor little bird is sitting on the ground and they can see it. For that period the bird must be left alone to incubate. Humans are the violator. I've never taken a pound for wildlife; I wouldn't be able to do that because I wasn't brought up like that. The old folk would turn in their graves. I wouldn't be able to live with myself. It's creation, for Christ's sake, and these people tell me it has to be managed. But it has been managed, inasfar that we have respected it. They're like otters. The otter is the next thing to human for causing damage to wildlife. A polecat generally hunts to survive, but an otter hunts for sport. It is the nearest to a human.'

Magnie's concern was wider than just the RSPB. Taking conservationists generally he asked, 'These people that's running the show, would they have a job anywhere else? Could they have a job in industry? They wouldnae survive where I survive. Would they survive doing what you're doing? Very questionable. It's all about their own position rather than protection of wildlife. It's basically political.'

'Talking of politics,' I said, 'what is your view of the right to roam which will soon be enshrined in Scots law?'

'We had a meeting with Jim Wallace, our MSP, at the time of the Tall Ships Race,' Magnie replied.[3] I asked him what I should do about people who leave my gates open and the bull gets out. "Sue them," he said. Ridiculous. I'd have to stand there and watch every one who went through the gate. The next person I meet might be a perfect gentleman. Wallace amazed me for a lawyer and a man in his position. Sometimes you have a dozen people climbing over a fence, and that is like a Charolais bull going over it. A wire gets broken and if a guy comes by tomorrow and that wire is loose and lacerates him, I am responsible. Wallace didn't know that, or at least he acted as if he didn't know that. For that kind of

---

3 Jim Wallace was leader of the Scottish Liberal Democrats from 1992–2005, Deputy First Minister in the coalition government and Minister for Enterprise and Lifelong Learning. As Justice Minister, he piloted the Land Reform Bill through parliament in 2002. Wallace practised as an advocate before succeeding Jo Grimond as MP for Orkney and Shetland in 1983 at the age of twenty-nine. The Scottish parliament split the constituency so that, from 1997, he was the MSP for Orkney only, though he remained MP for both island groups until the general election in 2001. The current MSP for Shetland is Tavish Scott, the Liberal Democrat spokesman on fishing and son of a recent Lord-Lieutenant of the county. The Westminster MP is now Alistair Carmichael, who, incidentally, comes from Islay.

people to start making rules and regulations in the countryside is very worrying. It's not practical to say if any damage is done, sue them. That's an American thing. I don't want to sue anyone. I just want them to have respect.'

Outside, the sun was shining strongly. Magnie suggested a trip round the farm. As we walked across the dusty expanse of his farm-yard, I asked if he ever had corncrakes on his land.

'The last corncrake to breed here was hunted off the ground by bird-watchers,' he said. 'They did a 24-hour video, they camped on site, they played back recordings till eventually we never heard them again. The last one in Cuningsburgh was exactly the same. The local people tried to get them to leave the birds alone, but there was some guy there who knew how to crawl after birds. He had some degree or other and would not take local advice to stay away. Everybody was delighted to hear the bird, but then one spring it never re-appeared. He said. "At least we now know that it was a corncrake," as if local people did not know what a corncrake was.'

Sitting in his substantial 4-wheel drive vehicle, Magnie expanded on the problem of know-alls in small island communities. His basic point was that people were perfectly happy with incomers, indeed in many ways welcomed them, so long as their numbers were small enough that they could be integrated into local society rather than forming a self-contained alternative community of expatriates, such as Clare Scott had described on Mull.

'The thing about the Englishman in Shetland,' he said as we drove out towards the hill behind Fitful Head, 'was that the minute he got here, he'd involve himself. He had to be on a committee. Very often the committee wasn't formed, so they formed a committee. And the next you knew they were taking major local decisions. If I went down to England I'm quite sure I'd sit tight for at least a generation, unless I was very sure that I could help. We dinnae like committees. I know the people up north. They were brought up the same way I was brought up. I know exactly what they're thinking without any committee. We don't need to pass around bits of paper; we know what each other thinks. But that's not to be anti-English,' he added. 'I have to tell you that some of my best friends are English. There are some damn good Englishmen, but they do seem to have an export model. It's something about their teaching when they're kids. They do seem to think they're better than everybody else. But on the other hand that may be an inferiority thing with us, I don't know. I have some very good English friends. Good people. So that's OK as well. People are people.'

He pointed out with pride his Shetland cattle, the traditional house cow because they milk most of the year round. 'But,' he said, 'the *Braer* changed my approach to these cattle.'

'The *Braer*!' I said, mystified. 'How was that?'

'The *Braer* hit just at the south end of Fitful,' Magnie said. 'It contained 85,000 tons of the most toxic crude known to man. If you pour it over your vehicle the paint will lift. Machinery went red with rust within the year. As soon as the sun came out the following spring, three months later, the first thing you saw was little black spots on felt roofs. Next time you passed the black spot was bigger. The felt just fragmented.[4] And the amount of fencing we've had to do following the *Braer* is just unbelievable, high tensile fences more than the mild steel fences. They flaked and rusted to the point where they were needle-thin and breaking.'

'And that was all to do with this toxic oil?'

'If wasn't that, then what the hell was it? The lighter the crude the more toxic it is. I had a friend in BP. We had played around together as boys and he phoned me a couple of days after the *Braer*. He said, "How're you getting on, Mansie?" I said, "It's a hell of a mess at the moment, but they tell me it's all going to evaporate." He said, "I just want you to know that that is the most toxic crude you could have, there's heavy metals in there that'll be in the ground 500 years." It's very worrying. You can't do that to the ground, to the animals. You can't do that to people either. So I started talking about it, but I was scared because there are people who do not want me to talk about it because what does Shetland have? A clean image. Heather died. It took ten years to die completely, but none of the official bodies supposed to be looking after us said a word. It was a complete cover-up. Where was SNH? Where was the RSPB? They went to ground right quick, didn't they? During the first week, every time I turned the TV on, there was

---

4 This point was litigated on in 1999. In the Court of Session, Lord Gill dismissed the claims for compensation on the ground that they were 'unscientific' because the claimants had not monitored the condition of the roofs *before* the accident and therefore could not prove a link between the oil spill and the damage.

another RSPB man making a statement.[5] Never ever heard from them
again. That's needing to be looked at. I buried 102 sheep the first year
of the *Braer*.'

'Why?'

'The main symptom following the *Braer* was the most hellish tiredness, the most unbelievable tiredness beyond anything that anybody
could describe. I went to the doctor ten months after the *Braer*, but
it was a year or so more before I realised what the cattle were feeling.
With animals, because their life-span is shorter, things happen faster.
There was no joint in my body that I did not eventually feel seriously,
ligaments and so on. I've worked with animals all my life, very closely,
and I knew what they were going through. They were scared to move
in case they fell, because they werenae sure that a leg was going to do
what they thought it was going to do. I lost my co-ordination. My best
work when I was young was hanging off that cliff at the back of Fitful.
It's one of the highest in Britain. We had sheep there. I just loved it. The
biggest adrenalin buzz I ever got was hanging off that cliff, no ropes, free
climbing. There were places where you knew it was virtually one finger
between you and death. Stupid maybe, but I was young, I was fit, I was
able, and that's what I liked doing. But I had to stay off that cliff because
my co-ordination had gone. For instance, I was coming out of the shed
one day and pulled an electric drill off the wall and there was a crowbar

---

5 Oil spills are one of the best generators of impulse subscriptions to wildlife compassion organisations and are especially welcomed by those non-
   welfare organsiations which therefore do not have to help any of the affected
   animals. Though they make unpleasant television viewing, oil spills are rarely
   very damaging. In the case of the *Braer*, Professor William Ritchie of the
   University of Aberdeen made a study of the true consequences of the strand-
   ing. The ship grounded on 5 January 1993. By 20 January the official casualty list was 1,285 dead birds and 17 mammals, plus a further 239 live oiled
   birds and 13 live oiled mammals. Prof. Ritchie wrote: 'Some of these oiled
   casualties would survive thanks to well-organised retrieving and cleaning by
   the Wildlife Response Co-ordinating Committee working with the Scottish
   Society for the Prevention of Cruelty to Animals and the Hillswick Animal
   Sanctuary.' (*Scottish Geographical Magazine* vol. 109, 1993, pp. 50–55) By 30
   January, the oil had almost completely dispersed, so these figures are close to
   the final casualty totals. Though regrettable, they should be seen, as an avoid-
   able disaster, in the context of the 100 million-odd birds which are killed
   every year by domestic cats in Britain, of which RSPB members must, due to
   their numerical proportion of the population, be responsible for 2 million.

next to it and the lead pulled the bar away. I saw the thing falling, I knew I had to step back, but I didnae manage to step back. It fractured two of my toes. The heavy metals in the ground must have been getting through to the animals. The first five days I was round that ground virtually every day. When I came in at night I could run my tongue round my gum and the skin would come off. That's what it was doing to your gum. What the hell was it doing to your gut? This has never been admitted.'

'Were there any other symptoms?'

'Landslides.'

'Landslides!'

'Eight years later,' Magnie said, 'I found out that the instructions for use of one of the components used in the dispersal clearly stated that this component was not to be used inshore because it killed flora.[6] After the *Braer*, we got black strips of mud running hundreds of feet down the cliff. If you have mud running down a slope like that it is not long before the stones come away, then the water gets into the cliff and then you have a landslide. Soil erosion was always on an African hillside where the white man took the trees off. On a Shetland cliff, the protection is the grass. There aren't that many trees.'

'What was the official reaction to all this?'

'RSPB didn't help us; SNH didn't help us. No organisation related to the government helped us. The only councillor who spoke up and tried to ask questions was Willie Tait. But he got nowhere. The official line from the council was that there was absolutely no problem at all. There wasn't one press release that related to the truth. We were basically told by officialdom to behave ourselves, definitely don't speak out, we want to protect the clean image of Shetland. I said I was perfectly happy to be deemed to be polluted for fifteen years if need be in order to be able to come out of that and say truthfully I was clean. I dunnae feel we can abuse our client, who is the housewife. If we continue to abuse her, as our industry has tended to do, usually through political pressure, how often is she going to let us off with it? Without our client we don't have an industry.'

'Talking of cover-ups,' I said, 'here's a conspiracy theory for you. It's

---

6 In the article quoted above, Prof. Ritchie wrote: 'Dispersants were used in the sea area close to the *Braer*. Their use aroused some controversy, and it would be unwise to discuss their precise chemical content and possible short- and long-term effects since the matter is presently *sub judice*.'

just a suggestion, not an assertion, but tell me honestly what you think. The reason government involves itself in trivial conservation issues, like pretending the corncrake is a rare species, is so that it can point to actions, like paying for corncrake-friendly cutting of silage fields, which give the public the impression that it cares about the environment, when in fact those campaigns are simply cover for inaction and indifference to what it well knows are the real disasters, like the *Braer*, which for commercial and political reasons it is too frightened to tackle effectively? Things like corncrakes, and the UK Biodiversity Action Plan, are just bread and circuses for the huge, electorally-crucial birdtable-owning class, to divert their attention from toxic oil spills or nuclear power or whatever. Might you agree with that, or am I getting too conspiratorial?'

'I would hate to think that that was the case,' Magnie said, speaking slowly. 'I would hate to be a human being and think that. Perhaps I wouldn't even want to be a human being at all if I thought that could happen. But you and I are both old enough to know that that is *exactly* what happens.'

From Magnie's farm I drove up the west side of the south mainland as I was keen to see St Ninian's Isle, the background to a very controversial court case centring on the discovery of buried treasure there but turning on the status of udal law in the Northern Isles. Though connected to the mainland by a sand spit, the island has been uninhabited since the late eighteenth century. Since the late nineteenth century it has been farmed by the Budge family of Bigton, the village on the hill above it. In 1955 Jim Budge, father of the current owner (who is also called Jim), gave permission for the Aberdeen University Geographical Society, under the direction of Professor Andrew O'Dell, to excavate with a view to unearthing the remains of a medieval Celtic church which was rumoured to have been situated on the island but which, if there, was covered by a layer of wind-blown sand.

The archaeologists found their church, along with a considerable quantity of artifacts. Amidst considerable publicity, they also found a pre-Christian, probably Pictish silver hoard, one of the largest and most elaborate ever discovered in Britain. The Shetland County Archivist, Brian Smith, described it to me as 'one of the great silver hoards, a very rare example of Pictish treasure. There is a lot of it, twenty-three pieces, and the craftsmanship is superb.' Jim Budge was happy to transfer any rights he had in the hoard to Aberdeen University, because he thought it the most likely institution to display it, at least some of the time, in Shetland. But, like vultures descending on a recently-killed wildebeest, the Queen's and Lord Treasurer's Remembrancer swooped on the treasure, claiming it for the Crown. Neither the university nor Mr Budge regarded this as lawful. Two actions in the Court of Session resulted. Though most of the artifacts were obviously very valuable, some were very much less so, for example the porpoise bone which the Crown also claimed under the law of treasure trove.[7]

The essential issue behind the litigation was whether the law of Scotland applies to Shetland in cases such as this, or whether custom derived from pre-existing Norse law – to the extent that that can be known – applies. As far as treasure is concerned it is the feudal-based law of both Scotland and England that ownerless objects, whether abandoned or lost, can be claimed by the Crown, though in Scotland the law of prescription restricts the exercise of that right to the twenty years after discovery. Under udal law, ownerless things belong to the person on whose land they are found. This is the Roman, or Civil, law view and it still obtains under Scots law with regard to wild animals which are considered *res nullius* until killed or captured. Historically, the Crown tended to assert its right to treasure only when very valuable objects were found. With the award of the St Ninian's Isle porpoise bone to the Crown by the Inner House of the Court of Session in 1963, the law in this area was extended significantly. A senior advocate has commented, 'On this view the Crown owns and can claim any derelict thing during the prescriptive period of twenty years. What chance now has the rag picker against the Royal Rummager of Dustbins?'[8]

The Norse tradition on such matters seems a little more equitable. Under the Code of Magnus the Law-mender, promulgated in 1274 and not repealed or superseded by the time of the impignoration in 1469, a person searching for treasure with the permission of the landowner could keep a third of everything found, while another third went to the

---

7 The hoard is now displayed in the National Museum of Scotland in Edinburgh. Only once, in 1966, was it loaned to Shetland, where it was displayed in the Lerwick Public Library under 24-hour guard. There are hopes that when the new Shetland Museum is completed in a few years' time that it will be sent north more frequently than once in forty years.

8 T.B. Smith QC in *St Ninian's Isle and its Treasure*, Alan Small, Charles Thomas and David Wilson, Aberdeen 1973, p. 163.

landowner himself and the final third to the king. Whales driven ashore and killed were divided in this way, except that the hunters who chased them ashore all shared the finder's third.

As late as 1589, the Scottish government laid down that the laws of Shetland – essentially Norse law – should be observed in Shetland. This was in line with the terms of the impignoration just over a century before when the King of Denmark (and therefore Norway) had surrendered to Scotland only the rights that he actually possessed in the islands. Obviously, he could not deliver that which was not his to deliver. Cases were heard at Tingwall, inland from Lerwick, where the Shetland Lawthing sat, and appeals were referred to Bergen.

To a much greater extent than Orkney, and, with much more pitiable results, Shetland was plundered by greedy Scottish adventurers from the late sixteenth century onwards. The most ruthless, arrogant and despotic of these was Earl Patrick Stewart, son of the Earl Robert who had first been given the Crown estates on Orkney and Shetland by his half-sister, Mary, Queen of Scots. Before he was arrested, incarcerated (in Dumbarton Castle) and beheaded (in 1615), the noble earl had reduced Shetland to what Eric Linklater calls 'surly poverty', on the back of which he built the strangely impressive Scalloway Castle, whose ruins still dominate the town. As the advocate quoted above observes in his discussion of the background to the St Ninian's case: 'It may be salutary for Scots irked by anglicisation to remember the beam in their own eye . . . The Scottish – later British – Crown has a particularly infamous record for its exactions and for facilitating the exploitation of the islanders by Crown nominees or donatories.' (p. 153)

An indirect result of Earl Patrick's misrule was the, arguably 'unconstitutional', abolition of Norse law in the Northern Isles by the Scottish Privy Council in 1611 and the mysterious disappearance of the old Shetland Law Book.[9] The fact that the equivalent Orkney Law Book

---

9 Strictly, it was not Norse law which was abolished, but 'foreign law'. But subsequent practice gave the authority of custom to the view that it was Norse, or udal law, that had been abolished. At least one writer has gone so far as to suggest that it might be non-udal law – i.e. law foreign to Shetland – which the Privy Council intended to abolish. At the very least, it should be remembered that all courts in Scotland today accept that udal law survives in relation to fishing and the foreshore, so restrictive judicial interpretations of the 1611 Act seem shakily founded.

disappeared around the same time suggests that they might have been deliberately destroyed to prevent any recrudescence of inconvenient non-feudal notions. The consequence was the destruction of the legal and administrative independence of Orkney and Shetland as part of James VI's attempt, after he became James I of England, to create a homogenised and centralised state in Britain. This is the most important part of the answer to the question posed so clearly by the archivist, Brian Smith:

> When I look at Shetland society a hundred years after 1469 . . . I see a flourishing society with a vigorous local government, with a trilingual population, full of fructifying influences from Scotland, Norway and Germany. If I did not dislike the phrase so intensely I might refer to the late sixteenth century as a Golden Age in Shetland history. In 1700 Shetland did not have a grassroots local government or a vigorous plebeian culture. What had happened?[10]

The village of Bigton looks out across the sand spit which runs a hundred yards or so out to St Ninian's Isle. I had hoped to be able to drive as far as the mainland shore, but found that Jim Budge had recently erected a sign forbidding vehicular traffic on the farm track which leads past his house and down to the beach. Though the wind was still blowing at near gale force, the sun was shining strongly and the sand around the island glowed a lustrous ivory. I was tempted to park in the village and walk the half mile or so down to the island. But I had an appointment on the isle of Trondra and did not have time. My immediate reaction was: mean, bloody farmer. But I soon realised that this was very far from being a simple case of proprietorial selfishness.

The current Jim Budge's son, David, now farms the ground and, not unnaturally, wants a house of his own. In 1999 he applied for planning permission to build one. Though the recommendation of the Council planning officials was against the house, the members of the Council's Planning Committee rejected this advice and unanimously approved

---

10 Shetland, Scandinavia, Scotland 1300–1700, in *Scotland and Scandinavia 800–1800*, ed. Grant Simpson, Edinburgh 1990, p. 32. No scholarly general history of Shetland exists comparable to William Thompson's *History of Orkney*. Thompson wrote to me saying that of the many contemporary scholars of Shetland history, he considers Brian Smith the best: he is presently at work on just such a history.

the application. There were no objections locally and the policy of the Shetland Islands Council (SIC) is to promote the locally traditional practice of isolated rural dwellings (Foula-style). At that point, Scotland intervened, in the shape of SNH, which lodged an objection. That triggered intervention by the Scottish Executive, which exercised its right to take the decision in Edinburgh. The Scottish Executive predictably upheld the SNH view, the main reason being that the site was on the edge of something called a National Scenic Area. This is a landscape designation, based on what was called 'unsurpassed quality' by the Perth-based Countryside Commission twenty years ago.[11] This stopped the Budges in their tracks. Four hundred years after King James VI, the British state is still structured in such a way that three agencies of central government can be involved in so small a matter as the construction of a single farmhouse on a remote group of islands, none of whose inhabitants had any objection to the development.

Judging by the letters in the *Shetland Times*, Shetlanders were outraged. One writer talked of 'environmental colonialism' and said, 'It is intolerable that, despite the multitude of politicians now representing the views of the community, governments are all too easily influenced by the petty officials and unelected quangos who now dominate our lives. In Shetland, the most predatory of all these quangos is Scottish

---

11 The Countryside Commission for Scotland was formed in 1967 by Harold Wilson's Labour government as a reluctant sop to campaigning ramblers and National Parks activists. Wilson gave it few powers so it had very little to do. The arrival of the more interventionist Conservative government in 1979 saved it from slow death by bureaucratic redundancy. The remedy was the creation of the network of National Scenic Areas in 1980. The Chair of the Commission from 1972–82 was Jean Balfour, who told me in an interview in 1996 that the NSA programme was invented because 'we had to have something to designate'. Now SNH is the controlling authority, having absorbed the Countryside Commission in 1992. NSAs cover 1,001,800 hectares (2.5 million acres), which is nearly 15 per cent of rural Scotland. Only one has any positive management associated with it (yet – this is another area SNH is now invading: a Plan for the Wester Ross NSA has recently been mooted by SNH, resisted locally then imposed by Edinburgh; others may follow). As they are, formally, designated under Section 262C of the Town and Country Planning (Scotland) Act (1972), their main administrative utility is as a weapon to defeat the plans of people like David Budge who might want to live in those parts of the country which the group of 'landscape experts' who drew up the NSA boundaries in the late 1970s considered attractive.

Natural Heritage who, despite no local mandate, assume the right to disregard public opinion, including that of our elected Council, when that opinion is contrary to their agenda.' There were numerous others in similar vein. The only letter in favour of SNH's stance came from an ornithologist, resident in Perthshire, who wrote to say that the view of the sand spit 'does not just belong to Shetland, but to the world, and not just for now, but forever'.

Having allowed vehicular access across his farm to the beach for twenty years, Mr Budge decided that his only way of making a protest was to stop it and make everyone walk. Now it was SNH's turn to be furious, resenting the adverse publicity which resulted. Every islander who wrote to the *Shetland Times* approved Budge's stance and blamed SNH for the problem. I had been given a clue to the strength of feeling on my previous visit to Shetland, when I talked to Paul Harvey, who used to run the SNH office in Lerwick but who resigned and went to work for the Shetland Islands Amenity Trust. I asked him why he left a secure job with a good pension. He replied, 'Because I was sick of being the most hated person in Shetland.'

The resentment at SNH's interventions often springs from its over-zealous interpretation of the many bureaucratic designations restricting the freedom of development in rural Scotland.[12] In this case, SNH based its interference on nothing more than the following short passage in the citation for the NSA designation produced by the Countryside Commission in 1980:

> Within the south-west Mainland area, stretching from Fitful Head to the Deeps, there is a variety of contrasting landscapes . . . all combining to make a western oceanic seascape of strong character and atmosphere in which the constantly changing skies play an important part. The area is further diversified and enhanced by the softer features of St Ninian's Isle with its fine tombolo and the adjacent enclosed and humanised landscape around the Loch of Spiggie.

That is all. On the basis of those words, David Budge was told by Edinburgh he could not have a new house on his farm. Yet the Loch of

---

12 So complex is the list that in 1998 the Scottish Office published, over the signature of Lord Sewell, the then Minister, a 24-page booklet entitled *Guide to Natural Heritage Designations in Scotland.*

Spiggie, with its 'enclosed and humanised landscape' is only a mile and a half away.

To my regret I was not able to meet Jim Budge, who was very busy on the farm while the weather was so good. We spoke later on the telephone, after his son had put in a second application for a house three-quarters of a mile from the original site, right in the middle of the NSA.

'This application was approved,' Jim said, 'much to my disgust, because it contravenes every policy that the first application contravenes and more.'

'So why did they disregard the rules that were so important a year before?'

'That's a good question. I asked SNH if they were going to contest this application and they said, no. Yet one of the main objections that the planning officials had to the first application was that it was too far away from the village. This one could not be further away. So to me it doesn't make sense. Another issue was that it was too far from the main sewer and he would need a septic tank. Now there is no chance of getting into the main sewer from this distance. The main factor going for this one is that it is more or less out of the gaze of the public.'

'So what do you think happened in the meantime?'

'They got so much bad PR about that time due to my son's application and also the raingeese thing on Yell' – a controversy stoked by Robert, which will be discussed below – 'that I believe they got a fairly severe ticking off from headquarters about their handling of the situation, about how insensitive they were and how there had been no consultation with the local people at all. Though I'm glad they did nothing, I still think it is morally wrong for SNH not to have objected to the second application. To be quite honest with you, it saddened me that they could do such a turn-about for no real, apparent sensible reason. With them, it's just an entire game of chance.'

My appointment on Trondra, an island now connected to the mainland by a bridge, was with the councillor for this part of the county, Alastair Goodlad. He is Managing Director of Saga Seafood of Scalloway, which guts, grades and packs between 15 and 18,000 tons of Shetland salmon per year. He is the author of the only history of the local fishing industry, *Shetland's Fishing Saga*, which he wrote as a PhD thesis. His brother, Morgan, is Chief Executive of the SIC.

Alastair lives in a large, modern house on the eastern shore, with a jetty at the bottom of the garden, alongside which an expensive-looking power-boat was tied up. I was met by an attractive, dark-skinned girl of college-going age wearing gardening gloves and carrying a secateur. Within minutes, a Mercedes 4x4 swept down the hill and a blond, fit-looking man of about my own age stepped out and greeted me in an accent which struck me as having an element of both North America and northern Europe in it. After administering a bone-crushing handshake, he took me inside and offered me a cup of Earl Grey tea. We talked in a large, sun-filled kitchen-dining room which looked out towards the cliffs of the mainland. One entire wall and part of another were composed of floor-to-ceiling glass.

Explaining the purpose of my trip, I mentioned my own connection with Shetland, through my mother's family, which had ended less than ten years earlier when the last of my relatives had died on her croft near Hillswick.

'I see,' Alastair said, leaning back in his chair and smiling. 'You know they call us North Sea Chinamen?'

'No. Why?'

'We do any work on any ocean. But really I sometimes think there is a touch of Arab in us. I remember in 1975 I was in Oman, very soon after the new sultan came to power, the first roads were just beginning to be built, and we were starting up a fisheries operation for them, myself and a New Zealander. We were taken by the Ministry of Agriculture way back into the desert behind the ridge of mountains on the Omani coast. Every once in a while there is this brilliant splash of green, emerald green. Our guide was an Omani who had been many generations in Zanzibar. We were looking to see if there was any way to distribute fish to the hinterland. We'd been driving two days back through the wadis and we came into this oasis in late afternoon, when the sun had cooled down a little bit. It is a classic picture which sticks in your mind – a green oasis and a little opening round the palm tree. All the men were there, with the Sheik sitting on the ground. Looking at the guide, he said, "Who might this be?" The others replied, "He's Mahommed ben Ahmed, the son of Ahmed, the son of Said, the son of so and so." They went back about thirteen generations, then the old man turned to the guide and said, "Ah, now I know who you are." We're the same in Shetland. We like to know who we're talking to.'

'Me too,' I said. 'So why do you not have a Scottish accent?'

'That's because I'm speaking English to you.' Then he pronounced several incomprehensible syllables which, he explained, were in Norse. When Shetlanders speak to outsiders they are said to be 'knappen' (pronouncing the 'k'), or 'napping', if they are saying the word in English.

'When you are not speaking English, what do you call it?' I asked.

'Just speaking Shetland, our normal, natural way of speaking,' Alastair said.[13] 'The rest of you speak very strangely. If we are speaking about day-to-day things which do not have any particular modern content, then there is a very high proportion of our dialect which is straight from Old Norse, speaking about the sea, the hills, the weather. For things like "ladder" we can use two words, for a small, rough ladder we can say "trapp", that's pure Norwegian, or we can say "leider" [he pronounced it 'lay-der'], which is English for a modern ladder. It also happens that the Norwegians say "leider" too. And all our place names, 95 per cent anyway, have Norse origins. Morgan's house, my brother, is called Sea Grind, "Gateway to the Sea"; "grind" is a gate, as it is in modern Norwegian, and so on and so on.'

'Is it dying out amongst the younger people?'

'Yes, like everywhere. When I was a boy – I speak Norwegian better than I speak English, so I pick up a lot of the connections – my father and our neighbour would speak about things like bulls and sheep and it took me quite a while to catch what they were saying. But not now; it is changing very fast. Most of the teachers are Scottish, and we're under the Scottish education system. Also, 60 per cent of the teachers come in here with what I call urbanised social attitudes. We'd rather grow our own teachers, but that's the way it is.'

I asked about his connection with Norway.

'We have personal and business connections,' he said. 'My sister is married to a Norwegian. I own a company in Norway and run a boat which is registered in Norway.'

'What is it like working in Norway?'

'It has good things and bad things. It is go-ahead, it is modern, things work well, but there's a sharpness in their society which we don't have. We get along better with each other. They get along fine with each other,

---

13 As recently as the middle of the nineteenth century, Shetlanders and Faeroese could converse with each other in their native tongues without difficulty.

but not as well as we do. There is more of the pushy, grabby type of attitude. They also have a better – no, maybe I shouldn't say "better", that's
judgmental – they have a kind of government which is more attuned to
regional aspirations, whereas we have a more centralist type of government, whether it is in London or in Edinburgh. They wouldn't have Jim
Wallace coming from Galloway to represent Shetland; they'd laugh.'

'I didn't realise he came from Galloway, I thought he was an Orcadian.'

'No, no, not at all. He's from Galloway – and a wimp besides. They
just wouldn't have anything like that. Someone representing Shetland
would be from Shetland, and the central government would look upon
it as that is the way it's supposed to be. There wouldn't be a party hack of
some kind, oh you go and take this place and you that.'

'That's the imperial tradition.'

'Absolutely. Norway is different. It gives much more self-respect to
the outlying communities. They stand up and say, we are who we are.
It doesn't do in Britain to have a little group of people who think they
have more rights than other people somewhere else. We tried it with the
salmon farmers and the Crown Estate Commissioners.'

'How?'

'In the early to mid-'80s we started farming salmon and to do that
we got permission from the Shetland Islands Council which, due to the
Zetland County Council Act which set it up in the 1970s, is allowed to
control its own waters. We sat down with them and evolved a pattern
of working which was good for Shetland and the farmers, and away we
went. Then we had a visit from some guys from the Scottish Salmon
Farmers Association with ties and accents slightly better than ours, I
suppose, who said, "Ah! you have to get permission from the Crown."
We said, "Crown? This is the sea. What has it got to do with the Crown?"
"We get permission from the Crown," they said, "so you've also got to
get permission from the Crown." '

'They were worried about competition?'

'They wanted us to be part of their associational system, so we said,
"Bugger off, go away and run your own country and industry and we'll
run ours." But of course the Crown was then on to us and the Crown
said, "Ah, you need permission from us." We said, "Bugger off, what's
this got to do with you? It's ours under the local government Act," and
so on. They said, "No, no. All the seabed is part of the British realm and
is owned by the British Crown and we are your landlord." So we said the

Norwegian king could only give the Scottish king what rights he had
and he didn't have rights to the sea because the rights in the sea go with
the adjacent farm and so on. We never stood a chance. We got to the
Court of Session and they wouldn't accept our pleas, so we finally had to
submit to the Crown. We were represented by James Moncrieff, who is
now the Chief Executive of the Shetland Amenity Trust. Jimmy was at
that time Chief Executive of the Salmon Farmers and he was a lawyer.
We got away for five or six years before they finally made us submit and
pay them rent.'[14]

'Did they ask for back rent?'

'No they didn't,' he said with a grin. 'So we got away with a million
quid, which kept the case going, paid the lawyers. But we didn't want to
give away anything. "Why should the queen get our money?" we said.
They said, "But we're not really the queen." I said, "Then why are you
called the Crown Estate?"'

I mentioned that I had read some of what Gordon Donaldson had
written about udal law and the related question, which some people still
think of as a real one, of whether Shetland is, in international law, really
part of the United Kingdom.

'Gordon Donaldson was of course a resident Scot,' Alastair said. 'His
name was actually Danielson, did you know that?'

'No.'

'His folks came from Yell and they went to Scotland, as Danielson,
before he was born. But of course "Danielson" was taken as "Donaldson"
because when we are not napping we say "*Daan*ilson". So he was
Danielson on Yell and became Donaldson in Edinburgh. That gave him
Scottish cover, of course. But there is no chance of Britain ever letting us

14 *Shetland Salmon Farmers Association and Trustees of the Port and Harbour
of Lerwick v Crown Estate Commissioners* (1990) SCLR 484. The court was
asked three questions: was the seabed around Shetland governed by udal law;
did the Crown have a right of property in the seabed; and could fish farming be carried without a licence from the Crown Estate? In the Inner House
of the Court of Session three judges found, first, that the Crown does not
merely have a duty of public custody of the seabed, but owns it; secondly that
this ownership derives from British sovereignty over the Shetland islands;
thirdly that this ownership, being founded on sovereignty is part of the Royal
prerogative and is therefore not dependent on feudal tenure; fourthly that no
operations like salmon farming may be carried out without a licence from
the Crown; and fifthly that udal law does not apply to the seabed.

go. Why should they? These are the kinds of things which make you see that justice is cloaked in power. You just have to live and make the best of it, and enjoy the fun when you can.'

'Are these issues considered important in Shetland?'

'There is a very strong feeling in Shetland that we are Shetland and that the Scots and the English and all those people are somewhere down there and we get pissed off when they bother us. When they leave us alone it is not so bad. There is a very strong feeling of identity here.'

'Is Foula a reflection of that?' I asked.

'No. Foula just doesn't work as a community,' he said emphatically.

'In what sense?'

'Nobody works together; they're as lazy as they're long; they're messy; and they're all arguing with each other, complaining about each other. It's just a hopelessly put together society.'

'How has that come to be?'

'There's no local people there. There's one local family, the Gear family, but they've only been there 140 years – four generations, if that. Most of the rest are blow-ins, as the Newfoundlanders call them. So there has been nothing to build a community on. Whereas on Fair Isle there are quite a few blow-ins too, but it is a much more stable community. It works very well. The council has put millions into Foula.'

'I must say I was staggered at the sums when they told me. How does the council justify all that expenditure?'

'The council didn't have to justify it,' Alastair said. 'It just did it. The council had lots of money at the time and, give the council their due, they wanted to look after outlying communities. They put a lot of money into Fair Isle and Foula, Skerries and Unst. It is just that you look at Foula and you say, did they really deserve it? You go to Skerries and there is no question but that those people deserve it, a thriving community.'

'But Skerries is a long established community.'

'And Fair Isle the same. But Papa Stour and Foula should be towed out to sea and sunk. We all have our burdens to bear. Ours is Foula. And you wouldn't mind if the people were like the Fair Isle and Skerries, good people doing their best and keeping a good community in place, but Foula's largely a bunch of bloody wasters.'

'Well, I thought Foula interesting,' I said. 'I must agree about Papa Stour, though, which I thought very depressing.'

'In Shetland we feel we have to do the right thing. Incoming hippies make a lot of noise: we're from Papa Stour; we're the local community. And therefore they got lots of money and lots of things were done for them. In Shetland we tend to restrict those who obey the rules. If there isn't a rule we go and make one, or find one. You know what the motto is for Shetland?'

'No.'

'May lowgam scalanda beejer,' he said, or something which sounded like that. 'We build our country on law. By Christ, if we haven't got a law we'll make one.'

'How do you spell that?'

On my notepad he wrote *Meä løgum skal landa byggja*.

'That's Old Norse?'

'Ja. Up until 1712 Lerwick was run by the Hanseatic merchants. We were part of the northern North Sea circuit of the league. The main office for that area was in Bergen but we weren't attached to that office. We were directed by Bremen. But the Salt Tax of 1712 made it no longer possible for the merchants to import salt for fish curing. So the whole industry was destroyed, which is actually quite a topical question at the moment.'

'How's that?' I asked.

'It was a law which was put in place by London to protect British interests which very severely penalised little people like us who had no part of the greater British interest but were struggling to scrape a living from a few salt fish. Whether it really protected British interests, I've no idea. But it sure fucked up things here. That was the end of the Hanseatic system, which hadn't been too bad. It was cash. It allowed people to import consumer products from Germany and pay for them in fish. When that collapsed, the whole place was in desperate straits and the landlords had no choice but to pick up the business. By the 1740s they had got it going again but under their ownership. They had the rent and the income and the trade all under their own fiefdom or tutelage. The landlords then started to push harder and harder. There were no Shetlanders, only Scots. One thing they did do by pushing it harder was that they developed the fishery and brought in the sixareen boat during the 1740s/60s for the deep sea fishery in summer. That only started to be affected when cod fishing from decked boats developed, and that happened as a result of us seeing London ships – London of all places! – on their way to Iceland, fishing cod in Shetland. There was a little money in Shetland, not much, but some invested in these half-deck boats and a new merchant class developed during the early part of the nineteenth century and they began to replace the lairds in a lot of ways. They were not tied to the land. By the middle of the century we were fishing off Faeroe, Iceland and Greenland and had a very big fishery which was totally outside the traditional one where you fished for the landlord. Then the herring fishery started on the back of these big boats; it was easier to fish off your own shore than it was to go to Greenland. Then a commercial economy got going. In the 1880s, at the same time all this was happening, the truck system collapsed and the Crofters Act gave almost everybody security of tenure. Most of the new merchants were Shetlanders. My family was deeply involved in it, with sailing boats and herring drifters.'

'But where is the modern parallel?' I asked.

'The fishing,' he said bluntly. 'It isn't that we should be taking out of the sea more than the sea can stand. Of course not, we shouldn't do that, no matter who we are – and we're as bad as everybody else. But what rankles with us is that we live from the sea, while the people who make the laws don't. We have no choice. There's not much else: oil, but that'll come to an end. We also have to consider, you know, we are Shetland. We're not Britain; we're not Scotland. What's ours should be halfway between us and you. We should have certain preferential rights at least. We take 15 per cent of all the fish that are taken in this area. That's all. It gives us scope for development. We can't build nuclear power plants or car factories on Shetland, but we could develop our fishing. We are not allowed to because there is a centralised power which says that is not yours and you can get a little bit of what Britain has. The Brits take 60–70 per cent of what is caught in Shetland waters and we take 10–15 per cent. The Scots, or Scotties as we call those from the North-east, take most of it, but also the English, and the French are hauling up saithe north-west of Shetland at the moment, whereas the Shetland quotas are finished.'

'Is the Common Fisheries Policy to blame?'

'Not really. If the there were no CFP we would still not have it, the Scotties would have it.'

'Why don't the Shetland people lobby to be independent like the Faeroes?'

'Because we are chicken. We've been held under the boot of the British Crown and government for so long that we think we can't do things for ourselves, better to let the Brits do it for us. We've had Scottish ministers, Scottish teachers drumming it into us all the time, Scotland, Scotland, Scotland, but at the back of our minds we are still Shetland. People keep comparing us to the Faeroese, but the Faeroese had a lot of advantages we don't have. Faeroe is very remote from the controlling authority in Denmark and the Second World War broke the link.[15] We didn't have that opportunity. During the war the Faeroese were released. After the war they said to Denmark, leave us alone, we can do it. And they did. We've never had that opportunity. During the war we had occupation.'

'By the British army, you mean?'

'Absolutely, and most of our people were taken off to go and get shot for the king and queen. I remember my father saying – he was in the navy on defence patrols, in Norway to begin with when the action was there, then the Channel and then back up here shooting mines – I remember him saying when I was a boy, "If that bloody king wants to have a war again, he can shoot me first and then he can take me to his war." That was the attitude of many of them. Many people here were indoctrinated to think they were British soldiers fighting for the king.'[16]

'How would you view it?'

'He can piss off and fight his own war. Maybe it is foolish, but I think that if you say this is ours, we would like to do our best for it, give it to us, people might just say, "Well yeah, you can have some." But if you

15 Faeroe was occupied by Britain immediately after Denmark was invaded by Germany, on 9 April 1940. It was returned to Denmark in 1945. A referendum was held soon afterwards in which the Faeroese voted for independence. But political manoeuvering by Denmark resulted in a compromise Home Rule regime, agreed in 1948, which operates to this day.

16 The irony of the sacrifice of Shetland's local interests in the eighteenth century was that at the crucial battle which secured British political and commercial freedom in the nineteenth – Trafalgar, Shetlanders were much more heavily represented than any other part of the British Isles – 1 in 20, when Shetlanders were 1 in 2,000 of the population of Britain. They were even more disproportionately represented in the war against Napoleon than Highlanders (who tended to be in the army). There is almost no mention of this fact in British histories of the war. Much the same happened in the Second World War, during which 617 Shetlanders lost their lives, equivalent to a UK total of 1.3 million deaths, when total British fatalities were about 360,000.

don't ask, you'll never get. I also look around me and I see the goons who are in the central government controlling our affairs, and I see the goons in our own council controlling our affairs. One's as bad as the other. They're no smarter down there than they are up here. So why can't we do it just as badly as they do? No reason why not. We have fish and we have oil, and a bit of tourism. But fish can quite easily keep us in very good shape if we had what we could sensibly take. This is why I look at the Faeroese. They have no oil; they have fish. They have booms, they have busts. They go broke once in a while. But they just think, "We can do this," and they get on and do it. They don't look at what they do in Denmark, or the European Union. They just get on with things. Maybe that explains why they are the world's worst correspondents. We go by the law and by the book; not them. Our Head of Tourism, Maurice Mullay, has a wry way of putting it. He says if you want to get something from the Faeroese, you write them a letter, a very flowery nice letter, about the weather here and what a good season we've been having and so on. You write it, you think about it, leave it overnight. Then take it out again and have another go at it, get the prose right, print it on very nice paper, put it in an envelope, stamp it, then throw it in the bin. You'll never get a reply from the Faeroese anyway. But if you go there and talk to them, then you can get on with them. But they have their way of doing it and that's that. They're quite different from us.'

'In what sense?'

'They are very independent-minded. We may be a little bit, but they just won't bloody do it.'

'What about Norway? It strikes me as a country of independent-minded people?'

'Very much so. I have a lot of respect for the Norwegians. I also think they are a bunch of bloody pirates, too. They take; they don't give out. They take, and they take, and they take. It's very interesting to deal with them on a company board, for example. They'll be across the table and there'll be some dispute going on and they'll fight and they'll argue, but they sort it. The aim is to sort it, not to argue about it. Very positive. It's not a hundred per cent true but the Scottish–British mentality is that there is a problem out there, and another problem and another one. They never end. The Norwegians want to get them out of the way.'

Just then the woman I had seen outside cast a shadow on the glass door of the room and glided in. This was one of Alastair's daughters.

I was startled to hear that they talked to each other in French. He explained she was just about to go to university in Italy.

'Both of my daughters were born in the Middle East,' he said. 'I was married to a girl from Haiti, who had been brought up in big cities. She was a political refugee, I suppose. Her father had been the president before Papa Doc Duvalier. So they had to leave in 1956, and they lived in Paris and New York. I was working for the United Nations in Rome and we met there. I left the UN and went to the Middle East and the kids were born there. Because my wife was Francophone we spoke French at home, the rationale being, a bit like what you were saying with your children and their Gaelic-medium education, that they'll always have English. Then we came home for twelve years to give the girls at least a grounding in a solid education system, then off they went to college in Canada in the early '90s. Then one went to Aberdeen University and this one, Alexandra, to St Andrews. She finished there, went back to Canada then did an internship at the UN in New York. She's been interested in international relations and was looking around when she was offered a scholarship by the European Union to do this thing in Padova.'

'It's nice to hear such an international orientation,' I said. 'Is that unusual here?'

'Not really. We're the North Sea Chinamen, remember? We'll do any work in any ocean; you'll find us everywhere. There's always been an outlooking and outgoingness in Shetland, the Hanseatic merchants walked the streets of Lerwick for centuries; it was quite a cosmopolitan community. Some of our dialect has Low German in it, Plattdeutch. The merchant navy took Shetlanders all over the world.'

'What happens now that we don't even have much of a merchant navy?'

'Young people just travel anyhow. People like me, for example. I went out when I was seventeen years old. I came back when I was forty-odd.'

'Why did you go?'

'Not much to do here, plus the fact that my parents made me get educated. Otherwise I would have been a millionaire fishing skipper.'

'Like the ones I have been told about on Whalsay?'

'The value of the fleet in Whalsay is probably around £100 million.'

'How many people live on Whalsay?'

'One thousand, one hundred. The fleet is owned by no more than fifty people.'

'All on Whalsay?'

'Oh yes, yes. The average guy working on one of those boats, if he is not an owner, will probably earn between £50,000 and £80,000 a year, a bog standard guy standing on deck. Good for them!'

'Is that still going or is it under threat?'

'No, no. Fishing has never been better. Mackerel and herring stocks are very secure and very good. They could go to hell tomorrow, but the fishing effort on them has now, for twenty years, been very stable. What has changed is the price. The price has gone up. That's why they make so much money.'

'Are you saying that over-fishing's over-played? Presumably it's true that cod stocks have gone down.'

'I don't know,' he said quizzically. 'We've never caught more cod than we caught last year and this year. In fact I got lots last week off Foula. But that's a small sample and anecdotal. But there is something in it. The white fish stocks are very heavily fished. Personally I feel there has to be a reduction in the fishing effort. The fishermen say the French are taking the fish. That's shite too. Fish stocks are reasonable in Faeroe, and Norway, so it's not impossible to manage stocks properly.'

'I thought the Norwegians had quota-busting Russians hoovering up everything.'

'The Norwegians are just as big crooks as anybody else. What they do is they build new boats and they bareboat lease them to Russian companies. Russians can't afford new boats. The Russian company will be an office, a Mercedes car and a plaque on the wall. The Russians then pay for the boat by fishing Russian quota and landing it in Norway. Norwegian boat, Norwegian officers, fishing Russian quota with Russian seamen, landing in Norway to the same guy whose leasing out the boat. It's just a big scam to get Russian quota. The boat is owned by a company in Bermuda, funded by a Norwegian bank and leased to a man with a cigar in Murmansk.'

'For goodness sake!'

'It is terrible. Everyone's at it. It's very difficult to get an honest fisheries policy. Our guys bust the rules, not so much with the white fish, but the pelagic guys, and again not so much now because the prices are good so they don't have to, but for years they did it. The Norwegians don't do it so much in their own waters because they have very strict policing. The Dutchmen are at it too. The Dutch herring and mackerel quota in the

North Sea is not enough to keep one big freezer trawler going and yet they have twenty or thirty of them. So they say, "Oh but we're fishing non-quota species, horse mackerel." They come up here, off Ireland or Scotland and fish mackerel. They'll have a quota of, I don't know, 2,000 tons of mackerel. They put grading bars on deck. They'll catch 10,000 tons of mackerel. They'll grade out the fat two and let the rest go back in the sea, dead. They'll freeze the fat 2,000 tons aboard, then they'll land them in Las Palmas for shipment to Africa and say they caught 3,000 tons, and so on they go.'

'I'm curious about these environmental scares, because as far as I can see many of them are very over-hyped.'

'Absolutely! It is a business in itself, a big business,' Alastair said with a cynical grin, 'It's one business competing with another: the environmentalists competing with those who use the environment.'

'Except that the environmentalists don't make profits.'

'Not necessarily; some of them make very good profits. There is a chap in Canada who ran the very first of the anti-sealing campaigns. He was a Brit who emigrated to New Brunswick in the mid-'60s. I was in Newfoundland in the late '60s, catching herring, and he was trying to get a campaign going against the seal catching in Labrador. He set up a fund, which became very popular in North America. Little old ladies would send him money. There was no real accounting for the thing, it was registered in some odd place. He was the guy who got Brigitte Bardot to speak about seals, so you wonder how well those people are monitored.'

'Is there anything you can do about that?' I asked.

'You can't fight motherhood,' he said emphatically. 'I find it on the council. These Biodiversity Forums: we have to have one. I said, we don't have to have one. It's going to make not a jot of difference. Oh, we have to, the Scottish Office thinks we have to have one. So we have to hire some gink from somewhere. Another job for the boys, another little niche for them in the system, then another department, and round and round it goes. It's very difficult to fight. The marine side is something the same; they're only getting into that now.'

'With Marine National Parks and Integrated Coastal Zone Management?'

'Yah. I keep asking them what are you managing? How are you doing it? What is the plan? Managing something must mean you are stopping somebody doing something. Oh no, no, no. You can always do what you've done before, but in order to change anything you have to go through a management plan process. We've got the Papa Stour Special Area of Conservation, which we fought for quite a while until the Scottish Office just said you've got to have it. Then of course came the one in Sullom Voe, which we fought as hard as we could. BP? They just folded. They want to be seen to be green. They want to look good. They thought this could be an accolade for them. When you can't get people like BP on your side, how do you fight it? I've just had a meeting with the minister, Allan Wilson. He listened to us, but with a jaundiced eye. I could see when we were making our case that he just wasn't interested.'

'What's the council's view of all this designation and interference? Is it beginning to harden against it?'

'I think it is. We have one councillor who lives from all these sort of committees, but apart from him everyone else on the council is pretty well anti all this shite.'

'And the people in Shetland?'

'Generally the same. I should qualify that because we do have young incoming urbanites who are of the soft left-wing variety who come to do all these jobs. Now they've brought in rangers to show us round our own land. They hired two rangers last year to show us Shetland! It makes me want to piss blood. In the Faeroes they just tell them to bugger off. The Faeroese just go and eat whales: that's what we do, don't bother us.'

'International pressure doesn't bother them?'

'No. They still eat whales. So do the Norwegians. They have a much healthier attitude, even though their history of taking things from the sea is not good. The Norwegians did decimate the whales. The Norwegians are great ones for booms and bust. There was a shrimp fishing boom in the early '80s. The Norwegians put millions into it. Their whole financial system swung behind it. Then it was scallops in the Barents Sea, a big shallow sea with all sorts of different types of scallops there. One boat actually made £1 million in the first year. Within a year and a half there were seventy-five massive trawlers fitted out for scallop fishing in the Barents Sea. Seventy-four of them went bust and one was sold to Canada. In the herring fishery they started purse-seining. They are technical masters at sea: good ships, well looked after, expert guys, they stay at sea for months, no problem. But they're really a bunch of sea rovers.'

*   *   *

By the time I left Alastair, it was getting on for six o'clock, the time at which I had agreed to meet some other sea rovers in the bar of the Lerwick Boating Club. Robert's turbo-charged Land Rover pounded up the steep hill out of Scalloway and rattled down into the quiet streets of the old merchant quarter of Lerwick. I found Eddie Knight and Stephen Johnson drinking lager at a table in the huge window of the bar which looks out over the harbour. Though still blowing hard outside, it was a fine, sunny evening and I was charmed to be invited, without Sheriff MacKenzie's 'second touch', to join a boat for the annual race to Out Skerries which would leave in the morning. It being a Saturday, I was assured of a great party on Skerries.

Eddie, a middle-aged Shetlander with a ready laugh, is an ex-merchant navy officer and now skipper of one of the tugs at Sullom Voe. Stephen, a quieter, more cautious-looking man with a beard, is a chartered surveyor who, like so many Shetlanders, does a lot of recreational sailing. They told me about the regattas which are held in most of the more sheltered voes by one or other of the various sailing clubs in the islands. Few summer weekends go by without an evening's, or a day's, racing being held somewhere. Both had sailed to Norway many times, and also entertained Norwegian yacht crews in Lerwick.

'Which boat would you like to go on, Ian?' Eddie said to me. 'There'll probably be crew spaces on most of them.'

'The most luxurious,' I replied, hoping for a change from the chaos of *Foggy Dew*.

'Oh well, that's Archie.'

So it was settled. I drank a second beer than set off up the road to Robert's. The wind was forecast to ease overnight and the chances of a breezy race under blue skies looked good.

Back at the ranch, Robert had, after a certain amount of joshing and cajolery, managed to persuade Brian to help him castrate 150 tups the following day. Brian was looking a little green at the prospect, never having been closer to a lamb than the meat counter in the Thornliebank superstore. But he was manfully determined not to flunk out, so declined my offer to join the race, however much I told him it would be fun.

'No, Ian,' he said firmly. 'You just go to Skerries and have a ball.'

'And you stay here and have 300,' I replied.

Archie's boat, *Sea Delta*, turned out to be a Sparkman and Stephen's 32-footer, very different from *Foggy Dew*: narrower, lighter and a lot less spacious on deck, though more modern above and below. Everything was ship-shape and the engine so quiet that over the sound of slatting halyards and shrouds alongside the quay before departure, I could hardly hear it running.

The wind was still north-east but now an accommodating four rather than the challenging 6 or 7 it had been the previous evening. There was a thin grey overcast, which looked as if it might lift. We tacked up the harbour, past the huge floating dry-dock owned by Malakoff and William Moore, the Lerwick shipbuilding and repair company. Outside the north mouth, the profusion of skerries was obvious. Archie told me about some of the better-known shipwrecks. By lunch-time we were in the open sea, sailing close-hauled under blue skies with a smudge of islands fine on the port bow. The wind slowly died all afternoon, and the day got warmer. At about 5 p.m. we sailed into Da Bod Voe – *bod'* is Norwegian for shed, or shop – under clear blue skies, with hardly a ripple left on the sea and a fierce heat in the sun. The unusual summer weather which Brian and I had experienced from Stornoway to Orkney was still holding up, to such an extent that on Skerries there was a drought. Water was being brought in by tanker from Lerwick.

The Skerries fishing fleet had very obligingly moved off the pier and anchored further up the Voe to allow the visiting boats – about ten of them – to tie up alongside. It was not long before cans were cracked and the first dram splashed out into a waiting glass.

'Du'st waant a cooshn?' a kindly-eyed but statuesque blond woman said to me, in an accent that caused me a moment's hesitation about the exact meaning of her question. Here, amongst Shetlanders and their whisky and rum bottles, there was no 'napping'. Quietly-spoken words were the hardest to understand. Luckily, there were not many of those.

The evening went with a swing, especially later on up at the Skerries hall where Da?, the local equivalent of the Islay Accordion and Fiddle Club, played until long after I left.

Having not had time to fetch a sleeping-bag from *Foggy Dew* that morning before leaving, I squeezed myself into the forepeak and wrapped the spinnaker round me. Being air-tight, sails make very good bedding. I woke at 7.30, climbed out of the fore-hatch and went ashore for a wash and brush-up. The rest of the crew were snoring loudly and I did not want to disturb them by making tea. But I badly needed a huge mug of something liquid. I thought I would try some of the other boats to see if anyone was up. No luck there either. It must have been a very late night.

The morning was absolutely still and there was a thick mist on the sea. Shortly before nine, I heard the noise of a really heavy diesel rumbling somewhere out to sea. Then a large shape emerged: it was the ferry for the mainland. Robert had said that if I were back by early afternoon on the Sunday, I would be welcome to go caaing – gathering – the sheep on the Graveland scattald with him and the rest of the local crofters. I did a quick calculation: it was clearly going to be some time before the boats were ready to leave, and then they would most likely have to motor back all the way back to Lerwick, which would not be much fun. I hurriedly explained the situation to a rather pale-looking Archie, who had by then poked his head through the hatch. He understood and offered me tea – but I had to refuse as I would not have had time to drink it.

An hour later we emerged from the mist into Vidlin Voe, where the ferry docked. With nothing available on the ship, I hoped I might find a cup of something at the terminus. No such luck. Vidlin amounted to little more than a slip and a small-boat harbour, plus a few houses and a large number of sheep bleating somewhere in the mist above the fenced in-bye. Otherwise it was as quiet as the grave. This was the isolated voe from where the Shetland Bus operation was run during the early part of World War II, before it moved to Scalloway.

Not only was there no tea in Vidlin, but no lifts either on the single-track road leading out of the hamlet – the word 'village' would convey far too bustling an impression. I walked three miles before I saw a car that was not either full or turning off somewhere. Eventually I was picked up by an Englishman wearing a red bandanna and driving an off-road vehicle who shot past me, thought about it, turned round and drove back, which is unusual. I was particularly grateful as, due to the overcast, the midges were out in force.

'They're the worst thing about Shetland,' he said in a vigorously 'oop North' accent.

'What's the best?' I asked.

'No class,' he said emphatically. 'When we came 'ere, m'wife got a job in t' school. She's a geography teacher. On t' first day she started, she said to t' headmaster, " 'Allo Mr Johnston." He said, "It's not Mr Johnston, it's Ollie. We're all peasants here." '

They had moved north just before the oil had started to change things, he said, and seen the last of the 'old Shetland', as he called it. 'Loved it. Now it's all gone.' 'So what are you going to do?' I asked. 'Move to France,' he said decisively.

An hour later I was at the Yell ferry, but there was nothing there except a slip and a car park. Likewise on the ferry, no refreshments are supplied on the twenty-minute crossing. Brian drove down in Robert's vehicle to collect me. The result was that it was 2.30 before I had my morning mug of tea. I went straight into my room and made it, before wandering through to the kitchen where, to my amazement and gratitude, Robert already had bacon and eggs frying for me. He obviously knew what cruises to Skerries involve.

After all the effort to get back, the caaing was cancelled due to a lack of dogs. So Robert took Brian and me up to see Lumbister, the large RSPB-owned reserve which lies next to the northern end of Robert's ground. It is 5,000 acres of peat bog on which the main species of interest is the raingoose (known in England and official Scotland as the red-throated diver). I found out about this a year before while preparing Robert's objection to the SNH designation imposed on his ground for the supposed benefit of these birds.

Robert likes his raingeese and has tried to keep the breeding lochs as free from disturbance by visiting bird-watchers as possible. The result has been that the total for the Graveland area alone is more than 1 per cent of the British breeding population of the species, which is why it qualified for the designation. Robert encouraged research by Dr Jim Fowler, an environmental biologist from the David Attenborough Laboratory at De Montford University in Leicester. For a quarter of a century Dr Fowler travelled to Shetland every summer to count the birds and their chicks, eventually producing one of the longest series of observations of raingoose breeding in Britain. Not only were the birds doing well and Robert happy, but the scientific community was getting a piece of the statistical action too.

Then SNH wrecked the whole happy arrangement by designating Graveland as an SSSI and an SPA for the raingoose.[17] This would mean

---

17 SSSI is a Site of Special Scientific Interest, which is designated, at SNH's suggestion, under the UK's Wildlife and Countryside Act (1981). SPA is a Special Protection Area which is designated for birds under the European Union's Birds Directive (1979). It is essentially the same as an SAC (Special Area of Conservation) which is designated for non-avian species and all sorts of habitat under the EU's Habitats Directive (1992).

that Robert would now need to obtain permission from SNH for any change in farming practice on any of this ground. His sensitive steward-ship has been rewarded by having control of his land taken away from him. SNH added insult to injury by telling Robert that he should regard their intrusion as an 'accolade'.[18]

Robert objected to the SNH designation on the ground that it confis-cated rights over his own property without either reasonable compensa-tion or any form of independent appeals procedure such as that which operates in the planning system. Trying to be constructive, he coun-tered by proposing a management agreement with SNH which would bind him to ensure that the birds on his ground were given the breeding conditions he knew they needed but which would not cede ultimate control of farming operations to the staff of the SNH office in Lerwick. As part of this agreement, Robert proposed that SNH take various habi-tat-enhancing measures, including the installation of rafts on some of the lochans so that the birds could feel more secure at nesting time. This has been proven to help black-throated divers and might well help red-throats.

But SNH ignored his offer. In a mood of frustration Robert wrote to the SNH Director of Strategy and Operations in Inverness saying:

> These rafts are precisely the sort of habitat-enhancing management proposal which SNH ought, in my opinion, to be advancing and for which I would be enthusiastic under a freely negotiated agreement, but which it is not because either it does not know or does not care. I am sorry to say I suspect the latter reason since it is so painfully obvi-ous that the proposed designations amount only to political hype. The catch for SNH, of course, is that to install and maintain the rafts would require the co-operation of all concerned which you know you would not get under your current proposal from me or, I believe, many others.

---

18 Robert has sixteen confirmed breeding pairs of the species, *Gavia stellata*, out of a British population of 1200 to 1500 pairs. Numbers are thought to be increasing, while the birds' range is certainly expanding. (See *Birds of the Western Palearctic, op. cit.*, p. 4.) It is a bird of the high latitudes and therefore more at home in Iceland, Norway, Sweden, Finland, Russia, Canada and the United States. The world population is unknown but at least quarter of a million pairs. It is not an endangered species.

With respect, I think the time has come when SNH has to decide if it is in the business of protecting/enhancing wildlife, and educating people to be aware of it, or simply in the business of extending what a recent correspondent in *The Scotsman* called its repressive bureaucratic policies – rightly so, I think.

The director replied saying SNH would not fund any rafts, though it might fund research into rafts. This is its normal response to such suggestions. Money goes to conservationists not land-managers. But that does not necessarily help the birds, as the RSPB has demonstrated on Lumbister.

The RSPB's reserve is as good raingoose ground as Robert's. The Society's magazine declared at the time of purchase: 'The wailing cry of the red-throated diver is evocative of Lumbister's remote wildness and we plan to keep it this way, allowing divers their vital freedom from human disturbance.'[19] Within five years of the RSPB's arrival at Lumbister, the number of raingeese had gone down by 75 per cent, sinking from nearly thirty breeding pairs in the early 1980s to as low as four in the late 1980s. The birds have never recovered, numbers staying below ten pairs. In the last year for which figures are publicly available (2000) the RSPB total was seven pairs. Right next door, Robert has maintained a steady average of around sixteen pairs on a much smaller area of ground.[20]

The people of Yell support Robert. Many of them are involved as there are nearly thirty shareholders in the common grazing which forms part of the designated area. The Yell Community Council took the matter up. When appeals to SNH fell on deaf ears, they petitioned parliament. Dan Thompson, a wealthy retired fish-farm owner, was chairman at the time. He spoke to the press in uncompromising terms: 'In the nineteenth century, the landlords had control of the land, but the Crofters Act put an end to that. Now it feels as though the landlords are back. SNH just seems to want more and more control and I haven't found anyone around here that likes it.'[21]

---

19 *Birds,* Winter 1981, p. 51.
20 See An Examination of Population Levels and Breeding Output of Red-Throated Divers in Shetland during the 1980s and 1990s, by R. Riddington and D. Watson. This report was prepared for SNH by the Shetland Biological Records Centre in 2001.
21 *Scotland on Sunday,* 10 March 2002.

After we had plodded about the bog for a while, Robert took me in to see Laurie Henry, whose family have farmed Lumbister since long before the RSPB arrived. In his cosily chaotic front room, I asked Laurie why he thought the raingeese had declined on the estate so soon after the RSPB took over.

'They should leave the bloody things alone,' he said emphatically.

'What do they do?' I asked.

'They go and check the eggs, check when the young's coming out and so on.'

'What about the visitors? The RSPB advertise this as a reserve. Do visiting birdwatchers also impact on the raingeese?'

'Yes, I think so,' he said. 'I would have thought that they look at the map and say, oh this is where we go.'

'Do you get egg-collectors?'

'Oh yes.'

'And where do they come from?'

'Down south. They're soothmoothers,' he said, laughing nervously, as if the common Shetland term for people who come in through the south entrance to Bressay Sound – that is from outside Shetland – should not be used too freely with strangers.

'Doesn't the warden keep them under control?' I asked.

'I suppose he tries.'

It is perhaps symptomatic of the state of relations between the land-owner and its only tenant on that ground that when I asked Laurie who the reserve warden was, he could not, even after giving the matter a couple of minutes thought, remember the man's name.

More interesting than the barren fastness of the Lumbister peat bog were the pipes and tanks, jetties and flares of Sullom Voe which Brian and I were given a tour of two days later. Being the largest oil terminal in Europe, the whole installation is impressive to look at, though there was a surprising amount of rust visible. From the inside, the plant looked much smaller than aerial photographs make it seem. We were told about the amount of soil that had to be moved to create the present site, espe-cially the infilling of Orka Voe – the voe of the killer whales? – on the Yell Sound side of the little peninsula on which the terminal sits. To me the most impressive aspect of the place was the recital of the marine safety record: not a single significant spillage since 1978, which makes it the cleanest oil terminal in the world. More than 10,000 tankers have loaded over 7 billion barrels of oil without affecting the sea otter population for which Sullom Voe is locally well known and Shetland as a whole is famous.

'We pride ourselves on the quality of our pilotage and our tug fleet,' the rather bored-looking public relations man said, referring to Eddie Knight and his colleagues. Part of the credit should also go to SOTEAG, the Shetland Oil Terminal Environmental Advisory Group. SOTEAG, was set up right at the start by the Shetland Islands Council – or Zetland County Council as it was at the time – which owns the port. It brought in the pipeline operators and hired a diverse but authoritative group of experts whose chairman until recently was Professor William Ritchie, the head of the Scottish government's high-level Advisory Committee on Sites of Special Scientific Interest (ACSSSI).[22]

SOTEAG has collected environmental data about Sullom Voe over the last quarter of a century. More information has been assembled about this site than all others in Shetland put together. The result has been that, as Alastair Goodlad told me, it has been designated as Special Area of Conservation (SAC) by SNH. The rationale was that the Voe is 'a representative of the most northerly geographical range and ecological

22 This body was formed at the same time as SNH, and in response to the politicisation of science by its predecessor body, the Nature Conservancy Council. The initiative to establish formal review of SSSI designations was taken in the House of Lords when the statute which created SNH, the Natural Heritage (Scotland) Bill, was being debated. The main protagonists were Lady Saltoun of Abernethy who said, 'To create a body such as SNH without there being any right of appeal against its diktats is unacceptable, undemocratic and worthy only of such regimes as Saddam Hussein's' (*Hansard,* 22 January 1991, Col. 156), and Lord Pearson of Rannoch who inserted a clause requiring review of all existing SSSIs. His reason was that 'Narrow scientific minds will be applied to the unfathomable mysteries of nature, and it is inconceivable that they will always be right'. (*Ibid.,* Col. 173) Subsequently in Committee in the Commons, Donald Dewar opposed this view, saying, 'The Countryside Commission for Scotland, the World Wide Fund for Nature, the Royal Society for the Protection of Birds [and] the Scottish Wildlife Trust . . . have written to me to implore wholeheartedly that the clause be removed from the Bill.' (*Ibid.,* 11 February 1991, Col. 639.) Brian Wilson called it a 'wrecking amendment [tabled] by the landowning lobby' (*Ibid.,* Col. 631) and said later in the debate, 'The whole breed of landowners, particularly absentee landowners in the highlands and islands, are parasites.' (*Ibid.,* 25 April 1991, Col. 1287)

variation of Large Shallow Inlets and Bays with the UK and as the only example of the physiographic sub-type Voe.'[23] In fact Sullom Voe is not so much shallow as deep, which is why it is a port capable of handling 400,000 ton tankers. At over 30 metres off the jetties and more than 40 metres in mid-channel, it is one of the deepest voes in Shetland. Indeed it is one of the deepest bulk shipping ports in the world, deeper than Galveston, Vancouver, Rio de Janeiro, Teesport, Madras and Fremantle to name just a few.

The supporting information which SNH published says, 'Large Shallow Inlets and Bays are complex systems . . . They are relatively shallow, usually averaging less than 30 metres in depth . . . across at least 75 per cent of the site.'[24] On that definition, almost every voe in Shetland would qualify, but only Sullom Voe was selected. The reason was that it was supposed to be typical. But no other voe in Shetland has a vast oil terminal within it and, crucially, one which has kept scrupulous account of its activities and their effects on wildlife. Like Robert and his raingeese, Sullom Voe has been penalised for being conscientious. John Uttley, the SNH Area Manager for Shetland, said in a letter to the *Shetland Times* that, though he had considered Busta Voe and Olna Firth, he had 'doubts over the age of our data and its reliability'. In other words, it was SOTEAG's comprehensive data which brought designation down upon the port's head.

Had no records been kept, Sullom Voe would probably not have been singled out for control by Edinburgh.

The designation provoked outrage in Shetland, not only because of the way in which good intentions had been exploited, but also because of the devious behaviour of both SNH and the Scottish Executive. When SNH was asked for sight of its advice to the Executive, it refused. John Uttley wrote to the *Shetland Times* saying, rather pompously, that its report was 'the property of the Scottish Executive' and, as it constituted 'Ministerial Advice', it was 'confidential until a Ministerial decision had been taken'. The SIC then asked the Executive for an assurance that the minister would not recommend the site to Brussels until it had had a chance to look at the arguments and comment on them. Since it was the SIC that was the sponsor of SOTEAG, and thereby indirectly the author

23 Sullom Voe SAC Site Description, SNH Edinburgh 2000, p. 1.
24 *Ibid.*, pp. 2–3.

of the information by which the designation was justified, that was not an unreasonable request. The Scottish Executive said it would do so, but did not, by-passing the Council and sending the recommendation straight to Brussels. The result was that the local authority concerned was not allowed to see or comment on the arguments for designation until after the decision had been taken and could no longer be challenged.

The SIC Convenor, Tom Stove, said he was 'absolutely furious' about the whole matter which was extremely important to the future of the Shetland economy. Councillor Gussie Angus went further, saying, 'We now know why SNH wanted an SAC at Sullom Voe. They want influence on the oil industry. The sooner this quango is wound up the better.'[25] Shetland's member of parliament, Tavish Scott MSP, took the Scottish Executive to task for its 'failure to honour its undertaking to the council'.

Such support as SNH received in the local press was less polite. One correspondent called the councillors who objected to the designation 'fools' whose arguments were 'incoherent and lame' and their record on environmental protection 'abysmal'. Individuals who objected were 'worthy of utter contempt'. Shetlanders in general were 'ignorant, self-ish and greedy', while Tavish Scott was told that he should 'remove his cranium from his fundamental for a while'.

Sitting in his wood-panelled office above the terminal the day after we had been shown round, Captain George Sutherland, the Sullom Voe harbour master and Director of Marine Operations for the SIC, told me how angry he was about both the decision and the underhand way it had been taken.

'We had a meeting with the chairman of SNH, John Markland,' George said. 'I was surprised that they did not sack John Uttley just as a piece of business etiquette, out of respect for the people of Shetland.'

I asked what effect the designation would have. He explained that Sullom Voe is, in the longer term, in competition for oil handling busi-ness with ports like Flotta in Orkney, which is not designated, and Florø in Norway. 'It is my belief,' he said, 'that when investment decisions are being made, all else being equal, designations such as this will nega-tively influence the chances of a place like Sullom, even just due to the uncertainty.'

---

25 *Shetland News*, 12 March 2003.

He was annoyed at the bogus claim of typicalness for the SAC area because, quite aside from the presence of the terminal, the site as designated by SNH also included Orka Voe, which was filled in during the initial groundworks on the site. No other voe in Shetland has ever been filled in. How can that be 'typical'?

The fact that SNH has included the whole of Sullom Voe, Orka Voe and Gluss Voe is also a source of complaint. Though SACs are notified under the authority of the European Habitats Directive, their method of implementation is the responsibility of the local government and its agencies. SNH's methods are quite different from those used elsewhere in Europe.

> On the Continent, there is not one single instance where the approach channels to a port, or the port working area, have been included in the designation. The Dutch, for example, specifically make what they call 'exclaves' from a designated site so that designation does not interfere with normal human activity. By contrast, in the UK, a line is drawn across the headlands, and the whole water area is included.[26]

The exclusion of the oil handling areas from the SAC would have carried no wider environmental risk, since any pollution that moved across the voe from the terminal into the protected area would still be the responsibility of the polluter. But it would have left the port free to manage its affairs without SNH supervision.

And SNH intends to supervise. In March 2003, the SIC Harbour Board learned that due to the designation, dispersants must not be used in the event of an oil spill without the express authorisation of SNH. The first line of defence is a system of booms to contain the oil. But bad weather might make deployment impossible, which would trigger the

---

26 Graham Rabbitts, ex-Environment Manager for Associated British Ports, and now the Department of the Environments's Marine Nature Conservation Panel, in *The Evolving Environment: a Personal Appraisal of the Solent Crisis*. Full details were lodged in the House of Commons Library in 2002 by the Bristol Port Authority in a document called: The Application of the Habitats Directive by Other Member States to Estuaries Containing Their Major Ports. The ports studied include Antwerp, Vlissingen, Bremerhaven, Wilhelmshaven, Hamburg, Rotterdam, Bordeaux, Le Havre, St Nazaire and Cork. None adopts the SNH approach, which therefore creates a highly unequal competitive situation.

use of dispersants. They may be used by the port, but only outside the Sullom Voe SAC area. The Chairman of the Harbour Board is Alastair Goodlad, who told the press, 'I can see us phoning SNH in Edinburgh at three o'clock in the morning on a stormy January night to get a decision on how to deal with an oil spill.'

George described the injustice as he saw it. 'The global environment would be better helped by cleaning up the estuarial ports like Liverpool, Glasgow or the Humber rather than interfering with the work here at Sullom Voe,' he said. 'Just stand on Westminster Bridge and look down at the stuff floating past on the Thames. There used to be salmon there, centuries back, but we still have salmon here in Sullom Voe. Which site is in greater need of environmental restrictions? This was pristine when we started and it still is. None of us wants to see that changed.'

'So what is filthy can be free,' I said, 'but that which is well-looked after must be controlled?'

'Yes,' he replied. 'The main reason why Sullom Voe has been so well managed is because it is run by the local council. All the big strategic decisions were taken very early on, in 1971/2. They were along the lines of: we will own the land; we will control the harbour operation; we will license the company running the site. Everything else is really at the operational level, like moving the ships within very tight parameters. None of that would have been possible without the ZCC Act.'

The Zetland County Council (or ZCC) Act was passed in 1974 to give the council in Shetland authority to control oil-related developments in the islands. Under subsequent local government reform, Shetland retained the autonomy conferred so that it is now the most powerful of the three island councils – the others are the Western Isles Council and the Orkney Islands Council – which in turn are more autonomous than mainland local authorities in Scotland. This has nothing to do with the 'penny a barrel' royalty which the council is paid by the oil companies; that was negotiated separately. But between the two of them, it has given Shetland a unique level of independence from central government. But that has not been enough to save it from SNH.

George walked me down to the front door of the harbour administration building. Outside grey clouds scudded by on a chilly wind whipping in from the north-west. I was particularly struck by his obvious enthusiasm for what, to me, was a bleakly industrial environment. 'I grew up on a croft in Shetland,' he said. 'I can do every single job on the croft, and I never want to do any of them ever again. My father grew old before his time with labour on the croft, which is why so many of his generation went away to sea, as I did.'

I must have looked nonplussed at the scene round about because he said to me, smiling confidently in his trim, naval-style uniform, 'This is a place of sunshine.' He spread his hands in front of him, palms upwards. 'The name "Sullom" comes from the Norse *sol heim*. *Sol* is the word for "sun" and *heim* for "homestead". To the Vikings, this was "the voe of the sunlit home".'

It was now time to think of wrapping up our stay in Shetland. Robert had been inordinately kind, but I did not want to trespass on his hospitality for too long. More than that, George Sutherland had given me a sheaf of weather charts depicting the forecast pressure gradients for the whole of the north Atlantic and North Sea areas at twelve-hourly intervals for the next five days.

'It's going be moderate south-west to south-east for a couple of days, then strong from the east,' he said. 'Go now!'

Anything from south-west to south-east would be perfect for us, as we would be heading east-north-east for Måløy, at the entrance to the Nordfjord. A forecast from so authoritative a source as the harbour master at Sullom Voe was not to be disregarded. I decided we would take his advice and leave the day after next.

I would have left sooner, but I still had a bit of unfinished business in the form of some interviews already arranged. As on Orkney, I felt as if I could have stayed a month. After leaving Sullom, I drove into Lerwick to see one of the founders of the Shetland Movement which had, in the early 1970s, been responsible for promoting the climate of opinion from which the ZCC Act emerged.

My directions led me up a tiny paved wynd in the centre of Lerwick to the house of John Graham, retired headmaster of the Anderson Institute, the high school for the whole of Shetland. The school was founded by Arthur Anderson, a native of the islands who was one of the co-founders of the Peninsular and Oriental Steam Navigation Company, now P&O. In later life Anderson founded Shetland's first newspaper and was the first Shetlander to represent the islands in parliament.

John Graham has written several books about the folk tales of Shetland and has compiled *The Shetland Dictionary*. Inside, his house was cosy and full of books. Bare stone walls were decorated with strikingly colourful paintings and a ledge along one wall held sculptures and small musical instruments. The sloping, wood-panelled ceiling was broken by skylights, through which could be seen the branches of sycamores, threshing in the evening wind against a grey sky. Despite the double-glazing, the sound of seagulls was constant in the background. John is a kindly, elderly man, softly spoken and occasionally a little wandered. From time to time, he would apologise saying, 'I'm still with you physically.'

He told me that the original impetus for the Shetland Movement was not the oil but a centralising proposal made by Harold Wilson's Secretary of State for Scotland, Willie Ross, in the late 1960s, which would have transferred all local authority powers to a new council for the Highlands and Islands, including Argyll, to be based in Inverness. This was completely unacceptable to Shetlanders. In 1970, the new Conservative government of Ted Heath, though equally centralist in outlook, abandoned those plans in favour of its wider plans for local government reform throughout the United Kingdom. Soon afterwards, oil was found in the east Shetland basin and the issue of control of the coastline became urgent. From a local point of view, it became more urgent still after a group of Scottish businessmen started buying land rights to possible oil depots in Shetland, hoping to make a killing from the desperation of the oil companies. Shetlanders were determined that it would be islanders who controlled developments, not speculative businessmen from a country which many felt had plundered their resources for centuries.

Shetland was helped in its campaign by the fact that the Scottish Nationalists set up the cry that it was 'Scotland's oil'. The British government, knowing the scepticism with which the islanders viewed their neighbours on the mainland, thought that by conceding more powers to Shetland – in effect making it more Shetland's oil than Scotland's – they could be seen to be answering the devolutionists' critique while actually spiking their guns. But the government would probably not have made the concessions to local autonomy which it did had it not been for the co-incidence of oil discoveries in the North Sea and an energy crisis provoked by OPEC and the British coal miners. It was desperate to get the oil ashore quickly and prepared to pay a considerable price in administrative de-centralisation to do so.

It was Jo Grimond who piloted the ZCC Bill through parliament, but he was helped by the fact that the Heath government owed him a favour. Ted Heath's main pre-occupation as prime minister was securing British entry to the European Economic Community. The crucial vote for second reading of the Accession Bill, in February 1972, was so finely balanced that the majority was just eight. Of those, five were Liberals, one of whom was Grimond himself. Had they voted the other way, the Bill would have fallen and the great European project been, for the time being anyway, abandoned. The following year the ZCC Bill came before parliament and the Conservatives gave it a fair wind. Such are the chances and stratagems by which important political issues are decided.

John paid a price for his involvement. 'I'm a Labour man but I was chucked out of the party for my support of the Shetland Movement,' he told me. 'Members are not supposed to belong to any other party. But we realised that if you want to go into politics you cannot go pussy-footing around.'

'Do Shetlanders think it is right that they have so much more control over their own affairs than the people of Argyll, for instance?' I asked.

'I think they'd say that it's up to Argyll to campaign for what it wants,' he replied.

For a moment he was lost in thought. I looked at the seagulls swooping overhead.

Then he said, 'I don't know the Western Isles very well, but in Shetland today there is a tremendous efflorescence of energy. Young men take on salmon farms, which is a chancy occupation these days: great risk-takers, Shetlanders. It didn't used to be the case in my youth, but the economy determines your social attitude, I imagine, or maybe times change.'

There was another quiet moment in the twilight. Then he said crisply, 'Been to Faeroe?'

'No, but very much I'd like to.'

'That's the place that has dynamism for independence,' John said.

'Why?'

'I think it was a reaction partly to Denmark's imperialism in the nine-teenth century. Very oppressive they were, like the Shetland lairds but a hundred times worse. They had all kinds of embargoes on Faeroese exports. It was the Second World War that got them going, running fish to Britain. They have seven political parties and seven newspapers. You have to get a certificate in order to buy a drink. Once you pay your income tax, you get a chit which says that this person may buy a drink – legally, anyway. They come down here for weekends on the Faeroese ships. They really paint the pavements red; littered around the hotels, some of them semi-comatose, others wholly comatose.'

'In the Hebrides we have more of the ghillie mentality,' I said.

'We have had our submissive members of society too,' John replied. 'But we never had ghillies. We had people who rowed the boat across to some of the islands, maybe. There is a story told about Bigton: there was a horrible laird there, Stewart Bruce, and he came down and he asked an old man to row him off to a small island and the old man said he would, though he was a notorious anti-laird man, this old boy. There was a fair bit of wind and he backfilled the sail, the boat lurched over and in went the laird. He was drowned. That is recorded fact, that he was drowned being rowed out to a small island. It is folk history that the old man did it, but the fact that it is folk history means that folk approve of it. The fact that people can tell that with relish indicates their attitude.'

'Where did these lairds go?'

'That's the incredible thing: they just died out. They didn't produce successors.'

'Why? Too much inbreeding?'

'Possibly. They bred with ministers' daughters – I suppose because they were the other big house in the community, and well educated too. The community cold-shouldered them and they became very isolated. Now they've gone.'

Rain clouds were sweeping across Yell Sound next morning as I trundled Robert's Land Rover onto the ferry at Ulsta. I thought I would start my last day in Britain by treating myself to an early lunch at the only self-consciously serious eatery on the islands. One of the many contrasts with Orkney is that high quality public eating facilities are abundant there, but on Shetland, they are restricted to the Herrislea House Hotel at Tingwall. It was important, I told myself, to research the local lamb. Robert had given generously of his own stock which was delicious, but it would do no harm to corroborate my impression of the product.

So it was that I sat down under the nose of an immense kudu in the hotel lobby with Gordon Williamson, the owner, manager and, clearly from what followed, PR man. Gordon is a lean, fit-looking Shetlander of about my own age who used to run cargo boats out to the fleet of klondykers when Lerwick was a big herring port for the Soviet fleet in the 1970s. When the Russian migration failed, so to speak, Gordon sold his boats and went into the hotel business. Herrislea House is marketed as a 'country house' hotel, by which it is meant that all sorts of outdoor pursuits, from boating to angling are on offer.

'It's the trout fishing that's best in Shetland,' Gordon said with the enthusiasm of a participant. 'The sea-trout fishing is good too, though of course a few of the boys are making a lot of noise about the salmon cages and the huge seal population.'

'Too many of them?' I asked.

'I would be inclined to think there's too many seals,' he said, choosing his words carefully. 'I come from the south end of Yell originally and the area used to be full of sea-trout. You could have a really good day out there. There was a boy who lived down at Burra and he used to shoot seals full time, and consequently you never saw a seal in the voe at all. You were out into the open sea before you got seals. Now you might count 120 from the shore. They are not growing fat on green grass. It takes a lot to feed an animal that size. But the hill lochs are very good.'

'Do you have to get permits, or how does it work?'

'There is one permit for £25 from the angling association to fish the whole of Shetland the whole season.'

'What! £25 for the whole season for every loch in Shetland?'

'Oh, yeah.'

'And if you come for a week it is still £25?'

'Yes, but having said that they don't police it at all. But it's such good fishing and the angling association does that much good it seems a pity not to pay it. It is a very good deal, really. I see that on the Tay you can pay £2,500 for a single week.'

'But that's for salmon?'

'Yes, but I fished on the Test, in Hampshire, with some boys who came up here who liked it so much they invited me down. That is even more expensive, and it's just brown trout, and some rainbows. I suppose it's in the middle of the stockbroker belt and very difficult to get good fishing without coming right to Scotland.'

'The difficulty with Shetland is that it's so expensive to get here,' I said.

'No question. Air fares are an utter scandal.'

'You can practically get to Johannesburg for the same price that you have to pay to get here,' I said.

'I just booked a flight there this morning,' Gordon said, beaming.

'Really! To Johannesburg?'

'Yes. I'm going on safari,' he said, rubbing his hands together.

'Big game hunting?'

'Yes. Buffalo. I was in Zimbabwe eight years ago. I had planned that since I was a boy. We were just at the stage where we were selling up the boats and I thought whatever else we are going to do we are going to have to start from scratch, which is going to take a long time, so this is the time to go. I had a very good time in Zimbabwe, but as things are now I shall not be going back there in a hurry. It's such a shame.'

'So where are you going now?'

'It's not far from the Kruger National Park.'

'So you're going to eat some biltong?'

'Oh, yeah. I actually sneaked some home from Zimbabwe,' he said, pronouncing 'sneaked' in two syllables: sneak-ed. He pointed to the kudu on the wall above us and said, 'We made a lot of biltong out of that. It was about 500 lbs. They showed me how they made the biltong.'

'Delicious stuff. How *did* they make it?'

'Everybody had their own recipe. What I couldn't understand was that there wasnae a huge amount of seasoning in it, then they just hung it up and dried it in the rafters in the house.'

'Did you have any difficulty bringing the head back?'

'It's a performance, but at the same time it's pretty straight forward,' he said. 'The ivory ban was in place. The inside of the horn is solid ivory, so I couldn't bring it back whole, which I was scunnered at. So they cut it off close to the base, just enough to leave a stump, and took out the rest. They stained the stump black so I couldn't use it as ivory.'

He took off one of the horns to show me the stump and the empty inside of the rest of it. 'Every time I do this,' he said, 'I am reminded of the Monty Python sketch of the talking moose.'

Eventually we got round to the subject of food. He said he did not know if there was any lamb on the menu that day, but if not he'd find some somewhere. He did, then joined me in the bar for a few minutes while I had a drink before lunch. After I mentioned that I was staying with Robert, he told me a story about fishing on Burra in a loch that used to provide the island's water supply, before it was piped from Lerwick. Gordon was just setting up his gear when an anonymous heritage person came over and said would he mind not fishing there because there is a red-throated diver nesting on the bank of that loch. He said, yes he would mind, and that he'd carry on fishing there as it wouldn't bother the bird in the slightest. Raingeese and anglers had coexisted from time immemorial without any problem. Why should he stop now? The heritage person said, 'Well I suppose it doesn't matter because you won't be able to fish there in the future.'

'Why not?' Gordon asked.

'We're going to lower the water level.'

'Why?'

'Because it's rising and approaching the nest.'

'But the bird will just raise its nest,' Gordon said.

'No, it can't do that.'

'Of course it can.'

'No it cannot.'

And so on. Having once been a public water supply, the loch has a sluice to control the level. Sure enough, Gordon told me as the delicious-looking lamb arrived, the water level has since been lowered and the fishing ruined.

Extremely well fed, I sank an hour or so later into a deeply upholstered chair in the office of Councillor Sandy Cluness in the well-appointed council building on top of the hill overlooking Lerwick town centre. In the early seventies, as a newly qualified lawyer, he too had been part of the Shetland Movement. Like almost everybody I spoke too, he felt strongly that Shetland should take more control of its own affairs.

'We have been disappointed by the Scottish parliament,' he said. 'With the best will in the world, saying it's new and you can't have miracles overnight, we've been worried by fundamental failures, like the quango situation. Shetland would have been quite happy to have taken over its own water, for example. Instead you have a single Scottish quango for water; it used to be three and now it is just one. The new shipping service is a total shambles from start to finish. We tried to take over Sumburgh Airport last year because we were far from satisfied that Highlands and Islands Airports was making a good job. The Scottish Executive knocked that back.'

'Why?'

'I don't know why. We see it as part of a control culture. The other thing is that in many cases, due to the oil money, we are in a position to do what we want without central government funding. But even in those circumstances, when we would be saving them money, they won't let us do things. That's *really* irritating.'

'Is it control-freakery, or do you see it as an aspect of Central Belt chauvinism?'

'Probably both. We weren't keen on the Scottish parliament. You've probably heard this old story, but there's a politician going around seeking support in Shetland for the Scottish parliament and he comes to a crofter whom he thought might support SNP and asks him how he is going to vote. He says, "I am going to vote against devolution." Chap says, "Why?" Crofter says, "Westminster don't really care about us, but people in Edinburgh actually hate us." '

'To what extent do people look to Norway?' I asked.

'Shetland and Norway have quite a lot of contact,' he said. 'First of all, about 70 per cent of our salmon farms are owned by Norwegians. All our big pelagic fishing boats are built and serviced in Norway. We must have spent over £100 million in Norway in the last ten years on fishing vessels.'

'Why not the Clyde?'

'Better yards, better technology. Think of all the developments in fisheries and aquaculture in the last twenty or thirty years, they have all come from Norway. There isn't anyone in Britain designing and building new fishing boats like that. That is a consequence of the British government not giving the fishing industry the support needed.'

'Why did it not do that?'

'Partly because it is mostly centred in remote areas and, secondly, after Iceland and Faeroe took over their own fishing grounds in the 1970s there was no long-distance fishery from Hull and Grimsby anymore.'

'So when Hull and Grimsby stopped being important fishing ports, the British government lost interest in fisheries?'

'I think so,' he said quietly. He had his elbows resting on the desk and his face partly obscured by his hands as if this was one of those truths which one dare not articulate openly. 'Those companies had very strong lobbies. The cod wars were a direct result of the Icelanders thinking they had to protect their fish stocks from them. Now they do it very well. They have very strict licensing of ships and they have proper fishery protection. They can close fisheries in days, so it's strictly regulated. Consequently they still have a good fishery. But fisheries are worth, what, 1 per cent? to the British economy, so the government doesn't care. The only time they took an interest in fisheries was when England had these big factory trawlers. They couldn't care less about Scotland. That's why we were so disappointed that the Scottish Executive aren't making more of an effort to support fisheries. The industry provides 30 per cent of the employment here in Shetland. The oil industry is only 10 per cent. The Scottish Executive has simply caved in to Westminster pressure.'

Thinking of oil and Sullom Voe, I asked, 'How does SNH play in Shetland?'

'They're just a bloody nuisance,' Sandy said, lowering his hands and speaking firmly. 'The environment's not really my thing, but I am Chairman of the Development Committee. We could do well without them. As far as we're concerned, Shetland's perfectly capable of looking after our environment without outside interference. It's not only Sullom Voe, we've run into them over fish farms, over the raingeese and things like that. Shetlanders very much resent interference by SNH and bodies of that kind – SEPA's another one, and the Crown Commissioners. In the past, when the Council wanted to build a pier, we would pay them a rent, but under protest. But it was only pence so we didn't much mind it, but now the Crown Commission takes £34 million a year out of Shetland, which is a lot of money. The latest thing is the underwater cable which will give us broadband access to the mainland. They want to charge us for using their seabed, and a very substantial rental too. The cable will go from Iceland to Faeroe to here to Orkney, then Caithness. The Crown Commissioners want, I think, £100,000 a year for that.'

I was so shocked by the thought that the Crown will only permit the citizens of Shetland to have access to modern data transmission facilities if they pay, out of their council tax, a large sum of money for the use of a zero-maintenance asset like the seabed that, after leaving Sandy, I nipped along to the converted fish warehouse on the harbour front where the Chairman of the Shetland Amenity Trust, James Moncrieff, works. He had been Chairman of the Salmon Farmers' Association when it fought the Crown over rents for the salmon cages and, as a lawyer, I thought he might be able to throw some light on the motivation of this mysterious, almost faceless body.

Inside the elegantly modernised stone building, I found James dressed in smart slacks and a tennis shirt – not unlike the Norwegian business-men I was shortly to meet on the other side of the North Sea. He sat behind an expensive-looking wooden desk in a large office with all the windows open, letting in both air and the ubiquitous sound of seagulls. The weather was beginning to clear again, but it was muggy and close.

'I don't know what the Crown Estate charges the salmon farmers now, but they don't charge individual boat owners anything for private moorings,' James said, when I asked him how far that organisation's writ ran. 'If they tried that here there'd be complete anarchy.'

'But they charge in our part of the world,' I said. 'No-one may put down a mooring without payment to the Crown. Otherwise, they tell you, you are "in illegal occupation of the seabed".

'I know. They're there to make money.'

'So they charge wherever they can get away with it?'

'Absolutely,' he said. 'That's exactly right. They started in the south of England with the easy targets, marinas and the yachting fraternity down there. Then they started focusing on marinas and anchorages in Scotland. We stopped them in their tracks to some extent. The idea of a Shetlander paying for a mooring is just a complete and utter anathema. It's a basic right here. Clearly in areas of congestion there needs to be regulation, but that's a different matter. I have a property and it includes the foreshore. If I lived in Scotland the Crown would own it. I have three moorings, and they'll never get money out of me.'

Elsewhere in Scotland, the Crown Estate pursues all such opportunities for making money ruthlessly, on the basis of Lord Dunpark's decision in a case concerning yacht moorings in Fairlie bay in the Clyde estuary.[27] But not in Shetland.

---

27 *Crown Estate Commissioners v Fairlie Yacht Slip Ltd* (1977) SLT 19. The basis of the Crown's case was that it owns the seabed (see the St Ninian's Isle case), which the pursuer did not deny. Instead, the objection was based on the admitted right of navigation and the attempt to argue that mooring was an incidence of navigation. Lord Dunpark dismissed this on the ground that 'the law of England is the same as the law of Scotland in this respect, namely that the public right of navigation does not include the right to lay on, or fix to, the seabed of territorial waters or the foreshore semi-permanent moorings without the consent of the owner of the soil.' Many people feel the case was wrongly argued since Scots law and English law are not identical on this point. Here, they say, the seabed, whether owned or not, is held in trust for the people of Scotland. It is, of course, a cardinal principle of the Law of Trusts that trustees may not profit from their trusteeship. See also the Scottish Law Commission Report of the Law of the Foreshore and Sea Bed (SLComm. no. 190, March 2003), which made recommendations for reform of the law of the sea, taking into account the recent programme of land reform.

'There was a period here in the late 1980s when they really were *personae non gratae*,' James said. 'They backed off a bit. But the real scandal of the salmon farm case was that they took rent on a turnover basis. Was it 2½ per cent? I can't remember exactly. But it was irrespective of whether the business was profitable or not. The more business you did, the more you had to pay them.'

'Do they quote any kind of moral justification for this? After all, ownership of the whole seabed of the British Isles puts them in a classic monopoly position.'

'No, they don't. All they say is that they have a duty to make money. People were outraged, both by that and the fact that they put nothing back.'

Outside amongst the seagulls, I wandered back along the quay-side to where I had parked Robert's Land Rover. I keeked inside the huge shed occupied by Malakoff and William Moore, where one of the crew of *Sea Delta* works as a painter. It being close to knocking-off time, I bumped into him as he was leaving the yard. He invited me in and showed me around. The yard is owned by the Lithgow Group which also owns the shipyard in Buckie and used to own one of the largest yards on the Clyde until it was nationalised in 1977. Until recently when he retired, the moving spirit behind these ventures was Sir William Lithgow, who fought a titanic battle in the European Court of Human Rights for what he saw as fair compensation for shareholders of the nationalised companies. Perhaps because he lost on the main point, Sir William takes a rather caustic view of bureaucracy.[28] At that moment, though I did not know it at the time, the yard was under threat of closure due to SEPA's delays in licensing the floating dry-dock which we had passed at the

---

28 *Lithgow and other v United Kingdom* (1986) 8 EHRR 329. The court held that the British government was permitted to take over the companies as their stock market value rather than the value of their assets. Since the market value had long been depressed by the prospects of nationalisation, this was artificially low. There was no duty to pay full compensation, only reasonable compensation. This meant, for example, that John Kincaid, the famous Greenock engine builder, established in the 1830s, was expropriated for less than the money it had in the bank. The firm was making well over £1 million per annum in profits, had net assets of £6 million, including cash reserves of £5 million. The total payment on nationalisation was just £3.8 million. A few years after being taken over by bureaucrats, this 140 year old firm went out of business, as did most of the others.

beginning of the Skerries race. In the event, it took a year for SEPA to deliver its decision that the dock was legal, and always had been legal. However, by then the yard had run out of cash. As, in law, justice delayed is justice denied, so, in business, operating consent delayed is operating consent denied. In February 2003, after 140 years in business, the only shipyard in Lerwick went into liquidation.

'Scotland today is really collapsing,' Sir William told me when I asked him about this soon after returning home. 'The decision-making process has been removed from within the community and passed to people who are really incapable of sensible decision-making – witness our Scottish parliament. There are very few people in the parliament, perhaps 10 per cent, who would be normally employable in a commercial organisation. They come from a soft public-sector background and they just don't understand the wealth-creating process. What sadly has happened is that, through the indolence and incompetence of government, and particularly the Scottish Executive, it has become unpractical for native people to operate by themselves in commercial business in Scotland. The risks of being mucked up through regulatory incompetence are just commercially unacceptable. Only a multinational which can spread the risks can afford to do it. Look at the aquaculture industry, which we're also involved in. Sensibly, the locals have mostly sold out to the Norwegians. But the result of that is commercial absenteeism. I am a great believer in decisions being taken where the action is. When I started work at Lithgow's in the 1950s we reckoned that 90 per cent of people employed in the shipyards in Port Glasgow and Greenock worked within ten minutes' bicycle ride of where the ultimate decision about their work was taken. They could reach a real boss. Now that world has changed.'

Sir William has a definite view on why that world has changed. 'The problem is eunuchry,' he says, 'all these myriads of economic eunuchs that are now churned out and for which society has no other use than to enrol as bureaucrats and experts. The thing is that enterprise is like sex. Enterprise has a sort of libido and you've got to get on with it. If you don't get on with it, it passes. And you can't get on with it if you've got to prepare umpteen business plans and go to see one outfit of eunuchs after another. A century ago, the population of Faeroe was 15,000. Today it is 50,000. It sustains more poets per capita than anywhere else in Europe. It has one of the highest standards of living in Europe. It bubbles with enterprise, enterprise of every kind. But it is a comparatively unregulated environment. They just get on with it. At Malakoff's, we built some boats for them. The prime minister was a ship's engineer. If they can do it, Scotland could, but it never will so long as the country is run by people in either suits or anoraks and bobble hats who don't understand how to manage anything.'

On my way back to Robert's I called in briefly on Dan Thompson, the Chairman of the Yell Community Council. Dan is a classic example of the enterprising local who has decided to take his profit and get out. He started a fish farm in Basta Voe in the early 1980s. From 5,000 fish, he built his stock up to 280,000 until he judged the game no longer worth the candle. Unusually, he resisted selling it to a multinational for a large fortune. Instead, he sold it to the workforce for a smaller one.

Dan is a tall, strong-looking man in late middle age, whose accent, even when speaking to me, is occasionally impenetrable. When not 'napping', his accent is totally impenetrable. I had liked him from the moment I met him a year before. This was more in the nature of a courtesy call because the raingoose designation had now gone to Brussels. Despite its being a social visit, we soon got onto the subject of 'eunuchs'.

'They just don't like anything that makes any money,' Dan said.

'Is there anything you can do about them?' I asked.

'It so infuriates and annoys me,' he replied, 'that I would not like to get involved in anything. They will cull hedgehogs in the Western Isles because they are eating birds' eggs, but they will not cull seals here, though they're eating fish. If you're against culling you should be against culling everything, not selecting what *they* think ought to be culled. But they know damn all anyway. Local people know far more about these things than they do. We have these rangers now, two of them, one for the North and the Islands and the other for the South Mainland and so on. One came to speak to the Community Council. It was just a case of being tolerant. How can a Geordie come up here and tell people what they should be doing? If they're going to have a ranger it should be a bloody local [pronounced "laacl"]. It's all a lot of bullshit.'

'What exactly does a ranger do?'

'I don't really know,' Dan said. 'It's not something I'm tremendously interested in because I am completely opposed to all this interference. I don't know what they do because I've never asked them. And I've never asked them because I wouldn't believe a bloody word they'd say.'

'What does the rest of the Community Council think?'

'Much the same, really.'

Back at the North Haa, Brian and I were to be given a farewell dinner. Sitting round the kitchen table while the smell of cooking filled air, I proposed another Ardbeg Moment.

Sipping the mind-expanding fluid, we talked about the past which the conservation industry seems to consider as a sort of golden age.

'It is a lot of nonsense,' Robert said emphatically. 'It was a really hard life here before the oil came. Now the young can stay and contribute to life in Shetland instead of going away, and some of those who have left can return. Then, anybody who was any good got up and got out, or they joined the merchant navy.'

'I was talking to George Sutherland about this,' I said, 'and we agreed that at least those who got out into the merchant navy saw the world. Don't you think it is a good thing that people went to sea for a while?'

'No, I don't, because the people who went to see the world from a merchant ship actually never saw the world. What they saw was a merchant ship and occasionally it would stop in Bangkok or wherever and all they got to see were the brothels and the pubs in Bangkok and, frankly, a brothel or a pub is the same whether it is in Bangkok, or Sydney, or Lerwick.'

'Do they have those in Lerwick?'

'Pubs, yes,' he said with a half-suppressed grin. 'But there's more to it than that. What happened was that when the men went away the women ran things. Shetland used to be very inward-looking and self-serving. There was no fresh blood. The difference between Orkney and Shetland is that in Orkney the land was rich and closer to the mainland so you got fresh blood coming in. In Shetland you got inbreeding. You got "we're all right, Jack, and the rest of the world can go and hang" attitude. You had no to-ing and fro-ing with the big wide world. Now you do have to-ing and fro-ing and it makes for much better attitude: new blood coming in; hybrid vigour. People now have a sense of their own worth in the context of the outside world, rather than in the narrow context.'

'But some people have said to me that in the olden days people were contented in a way that they are not now.'

'Yes, perhaps,' Robert said, pursing his lips and rocking his head from side to side. 'But they were contented because they didn't know very much beyond what they knew, if you see what I mean. They didn't have any aspirations. I dare say that a battery hen is contented.'

'This was all before the arrival of television?'

'Yes, but it's not just that they had no television. They had no water. If you wanted water you got a bucket and walked a hundred yards and brought it back. You didn't have any Hydro bills, though, or NOSWA bills.'

'And the conservationists would like to take us all back to the past.'

'And that's *exactly* why it is a bad thing. These people regard us as specimens to be observed under a microscope. "We want you back where you were." People here have got enough wit to see that. Dan Thompson will tell you that. We don't want to go back. OK, so it was a lovely golden age, but golden ages are when you want to have a shit you have to pull down your breeks and go behind a peat stack. It's bloody cold. It was not all a golden age, and what the hell did you do in the evenings?'

Though the food looked as if it was nearly ready, I though we might risk another Ardbeg before dinner. Brian did not demur, but Robert refused, saying, 'I'll be drunk.'

'My strongest impression of Shetland on this visit,' I said to Robert, 'has been that strength of feeling for the importance of local autonomy. On Islay, nobody even imagines that the island might run its own affairs.'

'It's all due to the ZCC Act, as I have no doubt you will have been told,' he said. 'I actually went and spoke at the ZCC inquiry in 1972. I went down to Edinburgh for two weeks. It was the first time ever that they had had parliamentary hearings outside Westminster.'

'What did you say?'

'That the fact that a crofter could be deprived of his croft at twenty-eight days' notice, which is what they were going to do, was absolutely scandalous. It was in the Bill. They drew a line round two areas where the oil might come ashore, one in Unst and one in Sullom, and within that line any crofter could be got out on twenty-eight days' notice. This was monstrous.'

'Was that the famous Ian Clark?' I asked. Clark had been Chief Executive of the Zetland County Council at the time. It was he who negotiated so successfully with the oil companies, getting the 'penny a barrel' which finances the Shetland Amenity Trust and other such

things. The moguls of Houston conceived such a respect for his negotiating skills that he ended up leaving the Council and going to work for
one of the oil majors.

'Yes, it was his idea. He was religious, Ian Clark. I liked him actually,
but he was obsessive about it. It was actually Jo Grimond who stepped
in and sorted it out behind the scenes.'

'When we went round Sullom Voe,' I said, 'the PR man told us that it
was an empty area, that there had been nobody there at all.'

'Absolute balls. There was always somebody there, always crofters with
grazing rights. There was always somebody who was going to suffer, and
they were going to ride roughshod over the whole sodding set-up. So I
objected to that.'

'What was so good about Ian Clark?'

'I remember going to see him one day when I was at a loose end in
Lerwick. In those days, the Yell ferry was a retired fishing boat which
went once a day. You were better off on deck because if you went down
below it stank of diesel and God knows what. You then crossed Yell
Sound, and stumbled up a weed-strewn jetty and got into a bus and
you arrived in Lerwick at exactly the time all the shops were closing, 1
o'clock. You had to spend the night in town because there was no way
back, except on Thursdays, when the bus did a double trip. Anyway, I
had time on my hands and went in to see Ian Clark. I can't remember
what it was about. But I remember him saying to me, "It'll be a sad day
when the ordinary chap in the street cannot wander into my office and
say what's on his mind," which is exactly what I'd done. Of course, the
thought of going into the Chief Executive now, just wandering in without an appointment, is ridiculous, laughable. He was a good chap, Ian
Clark, but he had a mission and he wanted to drag Shetland, kicking and
screaming, into the real world. As it eventually turned out, the ZCC Act
was a very good Act, though a lot of the credit should go to Jo Grimond
for making it into something sensible. It was Mrs Thatcher who brought
in this dreadful centralisation thing, actually. It was Mrs Thatcher who
hated local authorities. She set up housing associations because she didn't
like council houses; she rate-capped; she said you've got to sell off your
houses – and you're not getting the money; we're getting it.'

'So it's lucky the oil was not discovered ten years later.'

'Absolutely right,' Robert said, picking up a carving knife and motion-
ing to Brian to pour out the wine.

7
OVER TO NORWAY

As IF WE WERE condemned men, Robert gave Brian and me a huge breakfast before we set off down to *Foggy Dew* to make ready for our departure. The north-going stream in the Sound of Yell, which we wanted to catch, was due to start running (as the tide ebbed) from about half past two. That would carry us round Muckle Flugga as the ebb runs from west to east there. But the tides in Southladie Voe seem to peak well before they turn in the Sound outside, and also to rise and fall at uneven rates. This is not an uncommon situation, but it can become difficult when there is so little water that crossing the bar – in this case the underwater extension of the Urabug – is possible only around the top of the tide.

By the time we had stowed all our gear and made everything ready for sea, it was after 1.30. Though it was raining, there was a moderate easterly breeze blowing, which would have been perfect for a passage down the Voe and up the Sound, especially if it strengthened a little outside. I raised the mainsail and unfurled the headsail while Brian manned the anchor chain. It was so well bedded in that it took the two of us nearly ten minutes to haul it up. By the time we had freed it, the tide had fallen to the point where we grounded very slightly on the sand spit. I started the engine while Brian tried to use one of the spinnaker booms to punt us off. When that did not work, I inflated the dinghy, loaded the anchor and rowed out to deeper water where I dropped the anchor so we could try to kedge off. By the time I was back aboard, ready to run a diagonal rope off the chain to one of the winches (which would give us the maximum force), the boat was already heeling over. We were stuck fast.

The irritation of realising that we had missed the tide was as nothing beside Brian's news from the foredeck.

'Ian, I think you should come and see this,' he said softly, in the sort of tone that you might tell someone that a relative of theirs had been found to have cancer. 'A hole's appeared.'

Sure enough, in the stress of all the anchor work on the foredeck the plywood had disintegrated in a small area just inboard of the portside cleat. THIS IS SERIOUS, I thought to myself: rot – and just when we are about to embark on a North Sea crossing. I thought of the surveyor and the previous owner. Then I thought: this is no time for thinking.

While Brian cleared the forepeak so I could get access to the hole area from underneath, I used a screwdriver to punch and lever away all adjacent rotten ply. The final hole was just over an inch wide and about a foot long. I rowed ashore and found Robert at his paperwork, amazed to see us again so soon. He managed to locate a piece of 8-mm ply which would fit over the hole. I rowed back out to the boat, which was by now heeling at an angle of 30 degrees, and asked Brian to cut the wood to size while I drilled small holes round the rotted area to aid saturation by a temporary anti-rot agent (which in the event worked extremely well). Next it was a layer of mastic, then the ply with grip-fast nails and finally two coats of primer – all applied with the angle of the deck getting ever steeper while Brian held a sheet of polythene to keep the work area at least half protected from the drizzle. During this operation he confided to me one of the most amazing facts I learned in the course of the whole trip. 'That's the first time I've ever sawn a piece of wood,' he said. 'I've always given the dimensions to the shop and they've cut it.'

My repair was a bodge, and a worrying one in the circumstances. But it would certainly be watertight, and careful checks on all the ply else-where on deck seemed to reveal no more rot. There was nothing more we could do. By four o'clock we noticed that the boat was not heeling any further. By five, it was definitely beginning to come upright. The tide came in as fast as it had ebbed and by six o'clock we were afloat again. There was no hurry now as we would have the tide against us until after midnight. The rain had stopped and the wind gone down. It was a calm, though overcast, evening. So we invited Robert aboard – he had only seen the boat from the shore – for a look around and a final Ardbeg Moment.

Just after seven, we fired up the engine and motored in an almost flat calm down Southladie Voe and out into Yell Sound. Brian set about preparing our first 'boat food' dinner for a while, and I made a few last-minute calls before we would be out of mobile phone range. The engine was still surging, which was irritating, but not so much as before. At least now it started reasonably freely.

By nine o'clock it was getting dark, and we could see the Muckle Flugga light a few miles ahead on the starboard bow. Then the mist came down. Visibility dropped to a mile or so. Most of the time the light could not be seen at all. We would get it strongly for perhaps a minute, then darkness for the next ten. Mist is the most unpleasant weather to sail in. A good blow, even with rain, is preferable to not knowing where you are and what other vessels are near at hand. Wealthy yachtsmen have radar. I had just two pairs of eyes, one of which was not accustomed to keeping a lookout at sea. So I decided that we would abandon our normal two-hour watch system when on passage and that I would stay on deck from 10 p.m. to 3 a.m., by which time the sky would be just beginning to lighten.

There was still very little wind so we motor-sailed into the fog, hoping that all the supertankers steaming into Sullom Voe would have their radar plotters properly manned. Only one ship rumbled past us on a reciprocal course, a mile or so to port. It looked huge nonetheless. For the rest of the five hours I simply sat and started into the darkness.

The Muckle Flugga light, completed in 1857, was the most challenging of all the projects which the 'lighthouse' Stevensons undertook. Unlike the Skerryvore, the base on which this one was to sit was not flat-topped. Instead it is a steep-sided rock rising to a peak at 200 feet above sea level where, during construction, it was still occasionally swept by incoming swells. Lifting granite blocks up these steep sides from lighters which were themselves trying to avoid being smashed into the rock by the ever-present swell proved impossible with the technology of the day, so this tower was the first one ever to be built of brick. On occasion, the wind was so fierce that the workmen on the rock could only make their way from their (permanently damp) sleeping and messing quarters to the working platform by crawling along the connecting duckboards on their hands and knees.

Lighthouses have often been used by economists as examples of the limits of private enterprise as they are publicly beneficial goods which can only be supplied as a public service. It is not practical to collect dues from users sailing by and there is no direct 'cost-of-sale' reason for doing so. No extra expense is incurred when one more ship passes in the

night and 'consumes' the light. The situation has parallels with that of
the Crown Commissioners and the seabed. It will cost the Crown no
more to provide space on the ocean floor for the Northern Isles' broadband cable than it cost the Northern Lighthouse Board to supply light
to *Foggy Dew* on the night of 9–10 August 2002. The difference is that
since 1786 the Board has been operated as a public service, rather than a
monopoly enterprise run by the state.

I woke Brian at three o'clock, by which time the wind had backed to
the south-east, which would have been fine had there been any strength
in it, but it was blowing a hesitant 2 at the most. As the mist rose, it
revealed an empty sea. Brian settled down in the cockpit with a mug
of coffee and a sandwich, and I clambered gratefully into my sleeping
bag. Not even the thumping of the engine woke me until Brian did, at
7.30, by which time we were sailing slowly, without the engine, under a
clear, sunlit sky on the route used by many of the people who took the
Shetland Bus to Norway during the war.

Throughout the morning the wind gradually picked up. We were
pulling along at a fine clip by the time we came close to the first of the
oil rigs. Soon after we passed through the first line of rigs, we were hit by
a sudden squall which completely soaked Brian who was on the helm at
the time. *Foggy Dew* was performing beautifully when under sail and I
think he was reassured by the ease with which she rode the gusts. At 5.21
p.m. I calculated we had crossed into Norwegian territorial waters and so
proposed an Ardbeg Moment. The visibility being good now, Brian took
the helm from eight until midnight. I slept soundly and was shouted up
at about a quarter to twelve.

'Everything OK?' I asked, looking at the chart-table and his list of
GPS plots.

'No problem,' he said, 'except that there are some diagonal lights
ahead. Could that be a lighthouse?'

'Certainly not here,' I said, going below to take my own GPS reading and check the chart. I was not sure what he meant by 'diagonal
lights' but I could see a sort of pyramid of red and white lights some
way off, on the starboard bow. I presumed it was an unusually dimly
lit rig. Emerging on deck five minutes later, I saw it was a huge ship,
almost totally unlit apart from its navigation lights, which was crossing
our bow from south to north no more than a quarter of a mile ahead.
Brian had not realised the lights were moving, a mistake easily made as

there were so many others on the rigs round about. He was therefore steering further and further round to port, in effect round the ship's bow. We were going far too slowly to be anywhere near a collision course, but it is always a shock to see danger emerge where you think there is none.

There seemed to be a good deal more activity on and around the Norwegian rigs than we had noticed near the British ones. But we were more or less past them by then. Throughout my four hour watch, their lights sank steadily astern until, when I handed over to Brian at four o'clock, the sea was empty and the sky streaked enticingly with dawnlight. We had both found the four-hour watches to be a bit of a strain and decided to revert to the two-hour system which had suited us so well as far as Shetland. Thus I was back on deck at six o'clock to see a glorious morning, with a little haze over the mountains which were rising above the horizon ahead. Brian said they had been visible for most of the two hours he had been on deck. He must have sighted them about 50 nautical miles off shore, which will give some idea of their height, as we were only a few feet above sea level.

By mid-morning I could feel warm air blowing off the land. It gave the impression of real heat ashore. This was the first time we had had proper 'holiday weather' on the trip. Then the wind dropped to nothing and we started the engine again. As we motored towards the mouth of the Nordfjord, I read, then dozed in the sunshine while watching the enormous numbers of ships of all sizes sailing north or south. Soon the smell of bubble and squeak wafted up from the galley. Well, we've come a long way: this is our first meal in Norway, so to speak, so maybe we ought to celebrate with another Ardbeg. What do you think? – just one, honest! Brian is a tolerant crewman and gave his blessing, without demur, to the skipper's plan. We managed to restrict the one to two, but it really was a great moment. The sky and sea were calm and deep blue, the air was deliciously warm after Scotland, and the rough-toothed profile of the mountains ahead looked completely different to any Highland coast. We really were *abroad*.

Ahead we had an island called Bremanger, which is about the wildest on this part of the coast and was therefore one of the main destinations of the voyagers on the Shetland Bus. The height of its cliffs deceived us as to the distance to shore, as did the scale of the charts – almost all Norwegian ones are 1:50,000. The result was that we thought we were closer inshore than we actually were. It was not until six o'clock that we dog-legged through a narrow gap in the islets close inshore and we saw our first brightly-painted Norwegian house. 'Måløy ahoy!' I shouted.

I was struck by the incredible amount of skerries off the coast. It required considerable care to thread a way through them using the chart and magnifying glass down below, and GPS and binoculars on deck. I would not like to be forced to make such a landfall in the dark. Though the main channels are all well buoyed and lit, to a sailor accustomed to Scottish conditions they are often disconcertingly narrow. What we tend to forget is just how deep the fjords are. Often the land rises nearly vertically from the water. It goes down at much the same angle. Places like Gott Bay on Tiree, where the beach takes half a mile to achieve enough depth to float *Foggy Dew*, are non-existent in western Norway.

Brian's main job while I navigated was to hide the bottles of drink we had bought at the bonded stores in Lerwick. A determined investigator would have found them of course, but we planned to say they were in the ship's bonded store and would not be touched until we were off-shore again. I wasn't sure they would accept this and so was a little nervous about the reception we might get when we tied up.

Måløy is a town of around 4,000 inhabitants, situated on the east side of the island of Vågsøy which protects that part of the waterway running north to south along the coast which is known as the Leads. It is one of Norway's main fishing ports, but bears no resemblance to Lerwick, much less Peterhead. The town rises up a steep hillside above the port. Every house is painted a bright colour, and each one is different from its neighbour. Most are made of wood and have balconies, often full of flowers, which give the whole scene a gay, effusive air.

We passed under a huge bridge which brings the national road network onto the island and went alongside the town's yacht pier. By now it was about 9 p.m. local time (8 p.m. British time). It being a Saturday, there was not a lot going on. Where do we tie up? Whom do we report to? What's the scene?

As I was looking around the deserted dock for an official to inform of our arrival, and thinking how easy it would be if we were simply to take the whisky off the boat and stash it behind a skip for twenty minutes while our papers were inspected, a young man with what looked like his grandfather buzzed up to the dock in a little launch. They had clearly been out fishing because they had two boxes of mackerel, already gutted, lying in the bottom of their boat. As the younger man unloaded these I asked him who was in charge around here.

'You want some?' he said.

'No, I was just asking if you knew where we should go to contact the police to notify them of our arrival.'

'You don't want some fish?' he said, looking a little wounded.

'No, I don't mean that at all. I'd love some fish, if you have some to spare. I just wondered where the harbour master or local policeman operates from.'

'How many? Six?'

While the older man found a bag and selected the fish, the younger man pulled out his mobile and made a phone call. After a half a minute's talk, he handed it to me saying, 'He is the policeman.'

'Where do we report in?' I asked after explaining who and where we were and had come from.

'To me.'

'When can you come down to the boat?'

'How long are you here?'

'In Norway about a month; in Måløy probably a week,' I said.

'Maybe I'll see you on Monday.'

'What shall we do in the meantime?'

'If I were you I'd just be happy I was here in Måløy,' he said and put the phone down.

THE BREMANGER BEDROOM, AND HOME FROM UTSIRA

From Måløy, the Bremanger ferry today snakes quietly south between islands for five miles to the hamlet of Oldeide. There, I was met by Øle Stingbak, a tall, lean man of about my own age, with grey hair and a restless manner. He showed me to a battered Nissan with a cracked windscreen and we set off for a tour of the island. By way of greeting, Øle told me about the close contacts between this area and Shetland. Måløy is twinned with Lerwick to commemorate the close wartime ties created by the Shetland Bus, which used the wild country hereabouts as its major arms and agent smuggling base.

Øle pointed out an incredible, smooth, sheer cliff-face called the Horneleset on the north-east corner of the island. 'This is the highest cliff in northern Europe going direct down to the sea,' he said. The great cliffs on Foula rise 1,220 feet from sea level. This one rises 2,820 feet. All the yachting books about Norway warn of down-draughts from the steep sides of the more precipitous fjords. Øle told me about a bus full of school-children coming out of a nearby tunnel which was overturned by a sudden gust. The children all survived, but the driver was killed by chemical burning after the battery acid spilled over him.

We stopped at a hamlet called Leirgulen where the waters of the fjord lapped right up to the steps of the gaily-painted wooden houses. Many had little jetties outside the door with boats attached. They all looked as if they were regularly used.

Skinnarland's radio transmitter was hidden high in the mountains, far from electricity supplies. Batteries were hard to come by in occupied Norway, so he powered his set by a tiny, home-made hydro generator.

'Who lives in a place like this?' I asked. 'There cannot be much work around.'

'There is the shop, but apart from that it is now summer houses. That is the problem in Norway. We have a joke that says when the roads come the trucks come too and take the people to the town.'

'If somebody wanted to come and live here, would it be easy for them to get permission to build a house?'

'Yes.'

'What about foreigners?'

'The Norwegian government helps them a lot,' he said. 'They help them with the ground and everything to build houses. If a house is not a farm, then everybody can buy it. But if it is a farm, I think over 6 acres, then not everybody, especially foreigners, can buy it. The community must accept the change because they want the neighbours to be able to take over so they can get a bigger farm. For houses, the Norwegian government is interested in people from, for example, Holland. They are not so interested in poor people from Africa because it is so long before they can do something. The people from Holland want to come to a peaceful place like this and do some work. They are doctors, truck drivers, ship builders; they can do something. I think that is a good thing because I have served poor people in Africa and I can see the problem to take them from the bush and put them here. I think it is much better we take some money and put it in Africa to help the people there. Many people say that I am a racist, but they don't know what they are speaking about.'

Øle explained that he used to be a building contractor, employing a dozen people, erecting hotels, apartment blocks, schools and so on. Neither of his university-aged children wanted to take his business over, so in 1997 he sold it.

'I know what it is to have good money,' he said, waving his arms round at his elderly car and laughing. 'But it is not good for your body. Everybody wonders what I am living on but you do not need so much money if you are on your own.'

'So you spend your time in Africa?' I said.

'Some time. Last winter I travelled on an American mercy ship. It is a very Christian religious ship travelling with 400 people. I am not religious myself, but I think it is very interesting to see inside the organisation, so I spent three months in Sierra Leone. It is the poorest country in the world. I like to go a little bit outside of the road, if you understand. That is why I am now working for free in Africa. I think if you do things like this you understand people more. So I am a little bit angry when I come back and they call me a racist. I said, help the people where they are living because if we take one million of African people into Norway I think we destroy them and we destroy Norway too. And what about the other 600 million that we cannot bring into Norway? We can do so much more for the money in Africa. For my fiftieth birthday I sent invitations to 170 people and I said I didn't need anything; anything I want I buy. Don't give me more flowers and don't give me more glasses or things. At that time I had three cars, I have a plane, seven houses, a boat: I don't need anything. So give me money. I promised them if they give me money I would use it for the poor people in Africa. I promised them to work free and use the money to pay to go to Freetown. I learned many things. Next year I am going to Tahiti.'

Beyond the narrow tunnel above Oldeide – an unsophisticated, pre-oil boom structure – the island slopes gently down to the south. We drove past small farms on steep ground, with young spruce forests growing here and there above the dyke line where grazing had ceased. Wooden houses with outbuildings dotted the landscape, colourful in the sharp sunlight. Occasionally we saw people out in the fields raking hay or chivvying cows. Some waved at Øle. Mostly the fields looked fallow and the areas around the houses too tidy for working farms.

'In Bremanger it is only in the last years that the grass grew up,' he said. 'Before that the animals held it down, just like in Shetland, the sheep and cows.'

'What happened to the sheep?'

'It's just like everything else,' he said. 'We are too expensive. We only have the oil. People cannot work. In fifty years' time, what shall we work with? We are so expensive now, every company goes to another country. We don't make anything in Norway any more. That's the biggest problem.'

'Except you make plenty of ships.'

'Yah. But we are beginning to be too expensive for that too. We have a very good quality, that's why we build ships.'

'So the oil under the sea has driven the sheep from the hills?'

'Yes, and now the trees grow up. The problem of Bremanger is very old people, and when the old people die out the small farms are used as summer houses. They have a job in Florø or Måløy and come here on the weekend. Then the trees start to grow up and the landscape is not so nice.'

A few miles further south and we came to the village of Bremanger itself, on a bay looking out west to the North Sea. We passed two small fish factories, as well as numerous harbours with fishing boats in them. The skerry-strewn coast must be ideal for lobsters. Øle stopped the car outside the Bremanger Rockklubb, a clapboard hut emblazoned with primitive pictures of guitars and long-haired guitarists, while he went into the bank next door. Then he took me along to Grotle, a holiday village with beautiful white sand, almost deserted. This was where Bård Grotle, mentioned in the Prologue, came from, as did the unrelated Øle Grotle who performed some equally insouciant acts of defiance at the German occupiers. Like so many Norwegian country-dwellers, they were known by the name of their home. Today Grotle is a favourite holiday resort because of the beach.

'When foreigners are speaking about Norway it is only the fjords,' Øle said, 'but I think that the islands are much more beautiful. The fjords are just the same. When you have been in one you have been in all fjords. No people in Norway are sailing in the fjords. I have had boats for twenty years and when we are thinking about holidays we are never thinking about taking it in a fjord.'

'Why?'

'Because when you come to a fjord there is no place to anchor. It is deep, there is no island, no beach, nothing, only the mountains. The most popular place with us is from Måløy to Stavanger, thousands of islands, where you have beaches and the children can play. It is quiet and nice to go there.'

A café had just opened in Bremanger, the first in the village to sell alcohol. We stopped for coffee and, for me, a glass of akavitt, which comes in all flavours, like vodka in Russia. I had peach. Then we drove on to the town of Kalvåg on the small island of Frøya. Though it cannot be significantly less windy than Castlebay, Kalvåg is full of trees, with softwood and birch intermingled. The houses are spacious, modern-looking and brightly painted. Many have landscape-orientated windows. The town is built round a large, sheltered harbour, with a substantial area for pleasure boats. Øle gave me lunch at the seafood restaurant on the quay.

Amongst Bremanger's attractions are: an all-year out-door art exhibition, including carved trees; World War Two gun batteries; beautiful beaches, some of them accessible only by boat; Stone Age rock carvings; and tunnels in the north-east of the island which have such unusual acoustics that they are included in the summer music academy which is run every year on the island. The contrast with Barra was striking. Kalvåg, for example, has no less than four conference centres.

'I don't want to stay in that Florø,' Øle said. 'They use money so stupidly that I am leaving that kommune.'

'How do you mean?'

'I am going to move my tax paying from Florø to Bremanger. They give me 6000 kr extra tax and they waste 50 million kr per year. Here in Bremanger the Kommune is more sensible. But it is a big problem in Norway.'

'What is?'

'We have 4.5 million people in Norway. Of those 850,000 people work for the state,' he said, exaggerating slightly, I later discovered, but not much. 'One million people do productive work. The rest are children, sick or old. More are getting old all the time. I am so glad I am fifty years old.'

'Presumably a large proportion of those 850,000 are bureaucrats?'

'You have to sign forty papers before you can start building a house in Norway. The problem is that very few people take the decisions, they want somebody else to do that. They ask for more and more paper.'

The owner of the restaurant, Svein Inge Fosse, came and sat down. A quietly spoken, alert-looking man, he told us a story about his dealings with the fire department when the restaurant building was being renovated. He had thirty-six exit routes, but that was not good enough.

'Is this worse than other countries, to your knowledge?' I asked.

'Actually I think we are lucky where we live,' Svein said. 'We can have discussion with these officials. They can come in and we talk with them and sort things out. That's the good thing. Our democracy is very good. The problem with officials is that it is easier for them to say "no" or "maybe" than to say "yes". Very few people take decisions; they want somebody else to do that. So they ask for more and more paper.'

We ate a delicious seafood platter, which Svein kindly said was on the house, including two pints of Norwegian beer for me. Like everyone I met in Norway, Øle would not take a single drop of alcohol if he was going to drive. Then we set off to visit the house he had built for himself on a small, sheltered fjord half-way back to the ferry. The ground originally belonged to his wife's family, and her elderly parents still lived in an adjoining house. At a distance, the landscape looked rocky and bare. But, as we dropped down to the side of the fjord, a thick band of birch wood revealed itself along the shore – so thick that we were little more than 50 yards from Øle's house before I could see it. The grass on the roof helped to camouflage it, and the exterior wood had weathered almost to the colour of the rocks. Scattered clumps of wildflowers broke up the lines still further.

'I built this house in 1980,' Øle said as he started brewing some coffee in the spacious kitchen. 'It took two years of my spare time. I built a summer house by the water in 1985 and the hangar for my plane in 1990 and the sauna house in 1995 and the garage in 2000. So every five years I build a house.'

'What's next?'

'I don't know. I have some plans. I have always plans. I tried to build this house so that when you look at it everything is green. I tried to build it into the nature.'

'What are your new plans?'

'I can give you a very special idea. In Norway today you must put houses at least 100 metres away from the sea. Why? Is it any better if you must cross over the road to get to the sea? Why can't we build down to the sea? Over thousands of years Norwegian people have built there. They live by the sea, but now the government says "hundred metres" and everybody can see the houses. If you put a house down by the sea and put grass on top of it you cannot see it. You must build natural then you can build hundreds of summer houses, no problem. If I had wanted to build a hangar here now, they would say no – "No hangar in Bremanger." So I didn't ask them. But I cannot do anything with the law, so now I build a very nice summer house. I can build it here and I can move it about just like a boat and nobody can say anything. It is not a house and it is not a boat.'

'A floating house?'

'Ja ja,' he said enthusiastically. He went through to the sitting room and came back with a set of architectural drawings of an octagonal struc-ture, 12 metres on each side, built on laminated frames with styrofoam filling to floats underneath. On one side was a cabin-like structure, the other was an open deck, shown with a boat moored alongside.

To give me an idea of what it might look like once built, Øle pointed out some of the features of the existing house. I have written about the glass-walled bathroom and bedroom in the Prologue. For the rest, it looked like a hunting cabin, only on a much larger scale. The walls, floor and ceiling were pine; above the settee a rifle was hung between a boar's head and what looked like a roe doe. Everything was organised, simple and modern.

We walked down to the shore to see his hangar and seaplane. This was a two-winged, fabric-covered machine, with two seats and a small engine – it weighed 54 kilos and produced 110 bhp he said – mounted behind the cockpit, facing aft. This he had also built. The walls of the building were hung with tools, all neatly arranged and marked. The twin doors swung out to let the plane run down a short concrete slip into the water. Øle was all set to take me for a flip, until he decided that the cross-wind was just a little too strong for take-off and landing.

Twenty yards along the shore was his two-bedroomed summer house, which doubles as a boat house. He showed me pictures of the four boats he has built, all of them cabin cruisers around 25 feet overall. It was in these that he has sailed to Lerwick, on one occasion in company with 122 other boats from this part of the coast. In 1997 twenty-eight boats – I presumed not cabin cruisers – sailed from Florø to Shetland, Faeroe and then Iceland.

The last thing Øle wanted to show me was a small structure like a miniature sentry-box which he had attached to a post by his garage. It was marked *'post til Bukta'* ('post for Bukta'; *bukt* is Norwegian for 'creek'). About 18 inches high, it had a door on the front which opened to reveal a whisky bottle and two small glasses. This, he explained, was how he courted his current partner, who after divorcing a local farmer, is now the post-lady.

'She will be here now,' Øle said, looking at his watch. Sure enough, a van rolled up and out stepped a trim, dark-haired woman who walked up to the house with us for another cup of coffee which, after inspecting the amazing bedroom, we took on the sofas outside by the barbecue in the glorious sunshine, the water of the fjord glistening below.

Two weeks later we approached the little island of Utsira in complete darkness. It was not late, so the year was obviously marching on. The sea was calm but there was obviously wind at high altitudes as the last of the light revealed strikingly beautiful wisps of cirrus clouds glowing gold and amber above the dark clouds lower down.

Shortly after nine, we crept into the north harbour and tied up astern of the island ferry. Though there were lights on in the houses round about the harbour, there was not a soul about. We climbed into our sleeping bags early as I wanted to be up at dawn to take some photographs of the famous Utsira light in the first of the sun.

Next morning, I walked up to the squat red-and-white cylinder which is the light tower and had a marvellous view of the island from there. Utsira must be about four square miles, and it has a population of 238. The north harbour is mirrored by the south harbour and between them there is some low lying ground which looks fertile. Apart from that, the island is mainly rock and rough grass, with two small, neglected-looking spruce plantations. The community here came to prominence during the nineteenth-century herring boom, at which time there was a haulway between the two harbours so that if the weather precluded departure from one, boats could be dragged across the low ground for the mile that separates them. Today the two harbours mean that the ferry can land in any weather.

I walked down from the lighthouse and round to the south harbour where there was a very well-equipped supermarket. I spent the last of my Norwegian currency on fruit, bread and a couple of beers then set off in search of the mayor of this the smallest kommune in Norway.

'Where does he live?' I asked the first person I met.

'In the biggest house on the island,' came the laconic reply.

At that house, over on the western side, I met the mayor's son and was directed to the Kommune offices where, it by now being after eight o'clock, he would be at work. The offices house no more than four executives and couple of secretaries. They deal with the full range of functions for the island in what must be the ultimate in local democracy. As with every other kommune office I visited, I was able to walk straight into the Mayor's office and be welcomed, in this case by a lean, tough-looking man of middle height in the jeans and tennis shirt which seem to be standard for senior kommune officers. Speaking excellent, forceful English, he introduced himself as Reidar Klovning.

'That's the same name as the supermarket,' I said, having noticed the sign outside saying Leif Klovning. 'Are you from this island?'

'I was born here. He is a distant cousin.'

'Why aren't you called Utsira? People on Svanøy are called Svanøy and on Lygra the only native I met was called Jakob Lygren.'

'Klovning is part of the island,' he said. 'The south-western corner is called Klovning. On my neighbour's farm there is a huge rock which is split into four. It is standing on flat land, it is 20 metres tall and it is split in four. And that is the Norwegian for "splitting" – *klovn*.'

'Like "cloven" in English?'

'Exactly.'

He told me that Utsira used to be part of the Haugesund kommune until the 1920s, when the two local members found the lack of a regular ferry made it so hard to get to meetings that the island was detached. Then the population was over 300, where it stayed until the herring fishery declined, comparatively recently, reaching a low of just over two hundred fifteen years ago. Part of the reason for that was a government de-commissioning scheme for fishing boats, which deprived the younger people of job opportunities on the island. Reidar said that when he was young there were thirty boats over 60 feet long registered on the island. No longer, but now, with an improved ferry service the population has started increasing again. But, he said, they still want more people.

'If somebody wanted to come here to live would it be possible to get a plot of land?' I asked.

'Yes, very easy. And very reasonable.'

'What sort of price?'

'It is usually a quarter of an acre and I can say something between 10–15,000 kr.' That is about £1,000.

'Will people sell the land for housing?'

'That's not a problem. The kommune itself has land, different areas where we can sell plots for housing. We buy it so we always have something to offer.'

'Do you have any Landscape Protection Areas or other problems that might inhibit development?'

'The whole island is an LPA. There are binds, but only a few. For instance, there are stone walls, you cannot remove them, and you even get money to put them back up. There are certain things you cannot do. The kommune bought a building area and we wanted to give the good farmland to the neighbouring farmer and build houses on the rest. Then the archaeologists came and found flint and bones and they said you have to excavate this. You have to get down with a teaspoon and start digging and map what you found there. That costs money, so we said forget it. We found somewhere else.'

Reidar said he was retired from Phillips Petroleum as a 'sea captain', before which he had been whaling skipper. This experience was useful to the island as it was in the process of buying a new ferry from a yard in Poland.

'Buying a new ferry?' I said, aghast. 'This island owns its own ferry?'

'Yes.'

It was a large one, capable of taking cars and trucks. It is fifteen miles into Haugesund and the journey takes an hour and twenty minutes, pier to pier. It makes three journeys a day, the first leaving the island at 6.30 a.m. and the last leaving Haugesund at 8 p.m. Nobody on Utsira commutes to work on the mainland, but still the service is impressive.

I asked about one of the bugbears in the Hebrides, namely the number of times when the ferries do not sail due to bad weather. The seas around Utsira are much more exposed than those in Hebrides, so I was surprised when Reidar told me that the ferry is never cancelled due to bad weather. The only circumstances are when it is 'blowing gale force 12 and nobody is sailing'.

'So if you had a gale and a single passenger appeared, you would still sail?'

'Yes.'

'What happens if you arrive and the ship is full?' I asked.

'We are not too rigid about the number of passengers we take. It has to do with safety and the decision is always, ultimately, with the skipper. The certificate allows for 130 passengers. There are odd days, especially on Sunday afternoons in the summer, when tourists are returning to the mainland, when there are more than 130. It is up to the skipper. We have to use common sense. We have rafts and life jackets and so on far exceeding the number on the safety certificate. Anyway, touch wood, we've never had a problem.'

The fares also make an interesting comparison. Islay is 20 miles from the mainland, not 15, so one would expect fares to be about 30 per cent higher, not 200 per cent. The return fare for a car and driver from Utsira to Haugesund is £24; from Islay to West Loch Tarbert, it is £70.

I told him about the rigid, application of bureaucratic regulations in Scotland and asked how he justified the flexible Norwegian approach.

'People living in these small communities, they know where the shoes are choking,' he said. 'They are the local government. They know the problems. You have to trust people to look after themselves. Being ruled by people far away, in my opinion that's not right. I was in Switzerland and they have over 1,500 kommunes, the smallest one had 220 people. They have an even better system than ours regarding democracy. If they disagree on something they have a referendum in the kommune. And if it is thrown out, then that is it. They have a lot of self-government, and self-determination. If we are going to be run by people living in town, we can't exist. No way. There have been people living on this island for thousands of years. I always say to central politicians, if they want to depopulate the island, the easiest way to do it would be to say we are run by Haugesund.'

Reidar described the facilities on Utsira which, apart from all the obvious ones like a school, include an internet café, a library, a museum, a swimming pool and sports hall.

'How can you offer all that with only four people working for the Kommune?' I asked. 'We have a swimming pool on Islay and there have to be two lifeguards on duty at all times. How is it that you can avoid all that?'

'To avoid lifeguards we implemented a rule that nobody may use the pool unless there is at least one other person there. And you have to be eighteen or more. Everyone who pays a fee is given a key, and the pool is open from 7 a.m. to 11 p.m. If we had lifeguards it would cost an awful lot of money. Everyone has to take responsibility for themselves and the people with them. It works well. We opened it in 1994 and we haven't had any accidents.'

Chatting more broadly, Reidar said, 'I love Shetland. I was over there when I was young, on the whaling boats. I have many friends on Shetland. I was over there four years ago at a whalers' reunion, a big party at Bray, ex-Salvesen whalers. And the Shetlanders, they know how to party! I spent a whole week over there.'

'What sort of whales were you after?' I asked.

'Minke whales, for their meat and the blubber.'

'Do you think whaling should still go on?'

'In my opinion, yes. It is a resource which you should harvest. It should be controlled, though. I am not talking about what went on down in the Antarctic. But I think minke whaling should go on. I was up on Faeroes three years ago, I led a delegation there. We stayed in a hotel in Tórshavn, and I asked the receptionist there if they could tell us of any *grundadráp*, you know, when they drive whales on the beach. There hadn't been any in the Tórshavn area for three years. But on Sunday morning I was called to come down to this beach next to the entrance to the port, there was a slaughtering going on. They killed 317 whales. They chased them on the beach then slit their throats. Then they brought them on the pier in Tórshavn, then they had an old way of dividing the meat up so everyone got a fair slice of it, an old regulation hundreds of years old. They had a long measuring stick and the first one to have a piece of meat was the man who reported the whales, then they had the people in the boats chasing the whales, then they had the people on the beach slaughtering the whales, then there was an officially elected person in charge, like an umpire of the whole operation, because you are not allowed to sell it. Then you had all the elderly people, then the poor, then the hospitals and all those things, and then came the ordinary people in thousands, and all families got their share of that catch. I was lucky to be there, to see that happening. That was an experience.'

'What about seals?'

'Seals,' Reidar said, plonking his elbows on his desk. 'That's a big problem. Here, when I grew up, we never saw a seal, never. Now on the south-west of the island we have what we call a bird reservoir and it is infested with seals. They eat the fish and scare the fish away. And when you catch the fish you find worms in their liver due to the excrement from the seals. It's no good. In my opinion, they should not kill them all, but they should try to get rid of most of them. The reason they are here is that there is so little fish for them up in the Arctic. They are infesting the fjords now too, way in.'

'Are you allowed to shoot them?'

'Not officially, but people do. That's a bad thing.'

'Why?'

'Because they can't use them. If we could harvest them, then we could utilise the blubber and meat. My opinion is that if the resource is there you should be able to harvest it.'

By now it was nearly lunch-time and the sun outside was shining strongly. I suggested to Reidar that we walk down to the boat for an Ardbeg. This was to be our last day in Norway and, by clever timing, we were on our last bottle. He did not take much persuading. We found

Brian lazing in the sunshine with a book, and soon we had glasses in our hands and smiles on our faces – partly due to continuation of the seal discussion.

'I told you that when I was young we never saw a seal here,' Reidar said. 'Well, I can remember during the war time, the first seal I ever saw came into the south harbour area. The Germans thought it was a drifting mine so they rigged up their machine-guns on the harbour wall and killed the poor thing.'

Reidar went on to tell us about the German radar station and the fact that the whole island was divided into quadrants by barbed wire. There were anti-aircraft guns, and barracks for the Germans soldiers.

'Where did the islanders go?' I asked.

'They had to move in with their grandmothers or daughters. They took the school. There were four or five hundred Germans here. They had a bunker up in the hillside. In August 1944, I was about seven years old, me and my oldest brother, we had set lobster pots in the south harbour. Our mother would not let us go to the lobster pots, and of course we ran off when they were having their dinner and took the rowing boat and rowed along the breakwater. Inside there was a Norwegian vessel unloading ammunition. We had one pot between the wall and the ship. We pulled it up and were rowing away, about 50 or 60 metres from the ship, when the whole thing blew up. It sheared in half amidships and all the crew and the German people on board unloading the ammunition were killed. I was sitting at the back of our rowing boat and my brother was rowing. Everything went completely dark, and it was as if it was raining. It was sand and small pebbles coming down on my back. My brother was bleeding from the head. He was crying, and I was crying, but he was alive and I was alive. Another fellow told me he found two German soldiers in the water. They had been blown off the jetty, or the ship, and flown a hundred metres through the air. One of them just had his arm cut off, and another was hanging from the anchor chain. They were alive. That was the major thing that happened on Utsira during the war.'

'No attacks here?'

'No, except air attacks on the radar station and the lighthouse. But there was a lot of drifting mines which went ashore.'

'How did people think of the Germans? Did you have any contact with them?'

'There were good ones and bad ones. We were kids, you know, and they were our heroes, like the Indians and the whites. When they were marching and exercising, we were just following behind them. They had live ammunition exercises and we played next to them. In the later part of the war, 1944 and '45, they came from the Eastern Front, from Russia, and they were without limbs – they were here on recreation – then it was terrible, but in the first part they were very friendly. We were kids, there was a curfew from sunset to sunrise, and a blackout, you had to have your blinds down; if you were fourteen there was a passport. You would be sound asleep, then a mine would go off and throw you out of bed. They arrested sixteen or seventeen young people who were singing the Internationale. They were sent to a prison in Stavanger and kept there for fourteen days then they came back again. I think that was the only major incident.'

'Was there any fraternisation?' I asked.

'There was, unfortunately. In a small community, the girls would see these German officers with riding horses and so on.'

'They were a good catch?'

'Of course. A young girl of sixteen of seventeen did not know anything and when a handsome officer came and chatted you up, you might go along with him.'

'Was there any Norwegian resistance activity here?'

'Not that I knew of. We were confined to the island. When the fishermen went to sea they had to report back at a certain time, that was in 1943. The Kommandant issued an order that the herring boats entering the harbour should be at least 100 metres apart. There were guards on the breakwater with machine guns, and they didn't know who these people were coming in. They shot the skipper on one of the boats, when he was in the wheelhouse. That was a Polak, I remember.'

'What did you think, as a boy, watching that?'

'I didn't see the fellow being shot, but I saw the vessel going aground and I remember the officer in charge was very upset about the incident. But the Polak had his orders. He'd fired a warning shot and the vessel didn't stop so he followed instructions. On the other side, there was an attack near here on a submarine and it was limping on towards the mainland. It was spotted by some British Motor Torpedo Boats and it tried to dive but it couldn't. They killed several of the Germans in the U-boat so they beached it on a small island. There were many dead and injured and the others were freezing, and they were welcomed by someone who was building a house there on this island and they were offered coffee. They put the best table cloth out and said, sit down and have breakfast. Then maybe ten years ago there was a NATO exercise in this area and one of the German soldiers who had been on that submarine came back. A lot of German Torpedo Boats visited that small island and they found this couple, they were in their eighties, and they were awarded one of the highest German medals. Some of them were bastards, no doubt about it. But mostly they were humans, of course they were.'

Reidar refused a second dram, suggesting instead that we went up to the new café-restaurant which had just opened up as a tourist attraction in one of the old fish warehouses next to the small nineteenth-century inner harbour. There we had a couple of beers and he gave Brian and me lunch. The idea for this enterprise had come from a woman from the island who had married an Englishman and gone to live in Birmingham. She couldn't stand the way of life there so got divorced and returned to Utsira. When I asked him what sort of non-Norwegian tourists they received on the island, he said a few bird-watchers.

'Nobody interesting?'

'It is a popular place for Germans,' Reidar said. 'We have one group who bring in bootleg booze and then fish all day. After they come in at night, they drink their booze while gutting and freezing the fish to take back to Germany. They come every summer for two weeks and work from dawn till dusk.'

When I asked how he justified the money spent on Utsira by the various public authorities, he grinned piratically and said, 'I tell them to think of the money they get from the bulge in the Scottish–Norwegian boundary in the North Sea as a result of us out here taking care of all that oil.'

For a while we discussed the possibility of his sailing over to Inverness with us as he had to go to Aberdeen in a few days' time. But then he thought the better of it. He offered to give me any paperwork I might think would be required by the British for re-entering Scotland. 'If there's any problem, just tell them to ring me,' he said. He also invited me to attend a Kommune meeting that evening in the island hall.

After a lazy afternoon, pottering about in the heat preparing for departure – the Met Office on the internet was giving good weather for the week – I ambled up and watched the meeting which he chaired. Afterwards,

Reidar introduced me to a tall, quietly-spoken, dark-haired man wearing a turquoise shirt and, on his right hand, a large turquoise ring. This was the Chief Executive of the Utsira Kommune, Robin Kirkhus. He seemed keen to talk and I felt in the mood for some sort of party to mark the occasion of our departure from Norway, so I invited him down to the boat.

We walked up to his house, where he collected his wife Leila, an attractive blonde woman in striking, electric-blue slacks. The three of us wandered down to the boat in the warm evening sunshine. The heat of the day had been such that the tarmac on the road was still hot at eight o'clock. The island was quiet but for the occasional youngster passing by in a car with a broken exhaust. Like the Fair Isle, Utsira has neither police nor crime.

We stopped to talk briefly to the German fishermen. There were four of them, all middle-aged men in vests sitting on the verandah of their holiday home, with gutting knives in their hands. In front stood a VW camper van with a large aluminium box-trailer behind.

'Fiske gut?' Robin said chattily to the largest of them. He turned to me and said with a wink, 'He's the Reiseführer.' They looked like the sort of people who, had they been English, might have been wearing knotted handkerchiefs on their heads.

As we walked away Robin said, 'We have a Norwegian politician who criticised anti-EU people as "people who wear track suits and take their holidays in caravans". We get 1,500 Germans visiting this island every year. We must welcome them.'

'What other sort of visitor do you get?' I asked.

'This place is like Heligoland and Fair Isle. We had bird watchers here who broke down all the fences and walked over everybody's gardens. Then we had a kind of peace, which really meant that the fences were destroyed so there is nothing more to argue about. We also have the deep sea fishermen, from Germany and America. They spend thousands on their rods and boats – the only thing is to catch the big fish. They are the opposite of the bird watchers, who spend nothing. But at least they do catch the fish and bring it home, instead of, "Oh that's that bird." '

On board, Brian produced four glasses and we had our last Ardbeg Moment. The air was still. As the darkness slowly enveloped us, I asked Robin if he knew about Shetlands Larsen, the legenday skipper of the wartime 'Shetland Bus', whose statue we had seen on the quayside in Bergen.

'I actually met the guy,' he said.

'For goodness sake! What was he like?'

'A very quiet man. After the war they dismissed him from the navy, they said because of his colour-blindness. He didn't get rewards or anything. And in 1972, I think, the Americans were having a great NATO exercise with all their ships and they invited him to run a torpedo boat. He actually sunk the whole fleet by himself! He really did. He planned where to get spare torpedoes and things and where to hide his boat. That was shocking for the Norwegian navy and the Minister. It was so embarrassing that the whole thing was made a secret. But six years later it leaked out because in America all this information was publicly available. He sank so many ships the Americans were amazed that the Norwegian navy had just let him go.'

'Perhaps you can tell me why the Shetland Bus people did not respect Norwegian naval officers?' This was a point David Howarth had made strongly in his book about the operation, which ran spies and saboteurs into and out of Norway throughout the War.

'I cannot understand that,' Robin said, thoughtfully. 'I don't doubt that it is the real story. I think the Norwegian officers took their ideals from the British. In England you have had these upper-class people always being officers. You have certain concepts of what it is to be an officer. In Norway we have a very equal society; it is different. These officers are pretending to be something they are not. The way they do things is that they want to control and be in charge of everything and run all the details. They're like psychopaths, really.'

I took a gulp of my Ardbeg and thought of the minutely detailed regulation of life in the Scottish islands.

'Shetlands Larsen didn't hate these people,' Robin continued, 'he just didn't want anything to do with them, or the Norwegian government. I think they were really assholes. If you look at the Germans officers, they had a logic which is at least consistent. They can explain in their own theories why they had to chase the Jews. What those German officers did made sense within their own soap bubble. But if you look into a Norwegian officer's soap bubble, it doesn't make sense; there is no logic.'

'What happened when you met the great man?'

'The first time was at a veterans' dinner. The father of a student colleague of mine was invited so we went along, and there were several others coming in directly from the street, so to speak. He was a very intelligent man, and very resourceful and skilled. He didn't want to answer any questions about the Norwegian government or navy. He just said, see for yourself. The other time, when he was invited to an officers' meeting, he came in his night suit, night dress. I am sure he did it on purpose.'

'In his pyjamas!'

'No, that is two things. This was one.'

'Nightshirt?'

'Yes, he came and he was sitting there, relaxed. They were taken by surprise. He said, this is what it is all about. If you expect something you can plan for it. You have to do something that is not expected. I just do the unexpected.'

Having finished the Ardbeg, we had to move on to Drambuie which, to avoid us getting too drunk, Brian mixed with our cheap Shetland bonded whisky to make what he said was called a Rusty Nail. It certainly made the evening go with a swing. Before Robin walked home with Leila, he told us about his brush with the civil equivalent of the Norwegian naval officers: the police. He had once been arrested for nothing more than, as he put it, 'showering flowers over a certain guy'.

'He was an important person?'

'To the Tibetan people he is, yes.'

'The Dalai Lama?'

'Ja.'

'You were arrested for throwing flowers at the Dalai Lama?'

'Yes.'

'Why?'

'It was two years ago. He really gave the impression that he was immortal, not afraid of death and dying, whatever's happening. I put my hand inside my jacket and pulled out the flowers.' Robin demonstrated, showing how he deliberately made it look as if he was pulling out a gun. 'Of course if the police and bodyguards had been alert they would have shot me. I was wearing a black robe that we use in Zen.'

'Are you a Buddhist?'

'You can say that.'

'So what happened?'

'It was on television. It was very scary at the time. Now everybody is laughing at it. They arrested me for four or five hours. Seven or eight people were trying to find out why I did it. One was pretending to be my friend. Another guy said to me, "Do you like watching movies with women being raped, tortured, and children being molested?" I said, "Do you watch these movies here, in your work time?" They said, "No, no, do *you* watch them?" They wanted a motive. I said I don't have a motive; I didn't want anything. Of course, what I really wanted was to check if he is immortal. That's my personal thing.'

'Did you actually think he might have been immortal?'

'No, no. He's a politician. If he'd been immortal he wouldn't have been afraid. But I saw fear in his eyes, and I knew he wasn't a god. The police wanted me to say "His Holiness"; they kept stressing "His Holiness". I said, "You say that, that's your view. You're obviously one of his disciples, but it is not for me." "No, no, they said, when *you* talk about him you have to say 'His Holiness'." For three and a half hours they asked me, "What work do you do?" I said, "I am the Chief Executive of the Utsira Kommune." "You can't be," they said. They phoned the mayor. Then they said, "You will not work as a chief executive anymore." I said, "Is this a threat?" "No, no, it's the way things should be." "What's the problem?" I said. "If the Kommune wants to fire me because I showered some flowers on the Dalai Lama, they can do it." But the police just would not accept it. When I left, they said, "Now you go back to work on Monday, and on Tuesday, and on Wednesday, and you STAY ON YOUR ISLAND!" '

At six o'clock next morning the water in the north harbour was like dark glass. Mist rose almost imperceptibly in the chilly air. Above the roofs of the seahouses and the dark spruces on Utsira's eastern slope, the pre-dawn sky was clear but for a few wisps of golden-coloured cloud indicating wind higher up, and therefore hopefully outside. The shipping forecast general synopsis was a shallow low moving north from Malin and a high developing over the English Channel. The forecast for sea area Viking was south-east 5 to 6, moderating to 4 later, with fair weather and good visibility. It was a perfect morning to sail.

After tea and toast Brian raised the mainsail while I started the engine. At 7.15 we cast off from Norwegian soil for the last time. As soon as we were past the harbour wall we could feel the wind. Once we had half a mile's offing, we unfurled the headsail, cut the motor, turned to port and laid a course direct for the Moray Firth. At ten o'clock the wind seemed to back a little and strengthen, so I raised the spinnaker. For the rest of the morning we bowled along at 6.5 knots in brilliant sunshine. Off watch, I lay in the lee side of the cockpit and read or dozed. On watch, I kept an eye on the smart tankers and fishing boats plying up and down the coast. The further off-shore we sailed the less shipping we saw. At six o'clock we took down both the spinnaker and the Norwegian courtesy flag. I changed the ship's clock to British Summer Time. By then the wind was dropping and going more southerly. From then until we raised the first of the oil rigs, about midnight, the sea around us was completely empty.

Soon after midnight, with our speed down to 3.5 knots, I took in the headsail and started the engine. At 4 a.m. we seemed to have oil rigs all around us, plus the occasional moving set of lights of some tender or supply ship. Though the chart appears to show the opposite, my impression was that there was a greater density of rigs here than there had been 200 miles further north on our way out.

Brian and I spent the next day working on the boat. I repaired a loose stanchion base which I had spotted the previous evening, while he tried to find out why the Navtex, the binnacle light and the Autohelm had all stopped working, along with the for'rd navigation lights (not the stern light) and anything else which ran from the lower of the two banks of switches on the antique control panel. All day we motored in a wind which, I see from my log, dropped to nothing around lunchtime, though it came back later. Brian tried this and that to get the Autohelm going again but nothing worked. Eventually, we decided simply to rig a length of new wire direct from the battery to the plug in the cockpit. This worked straight away, suggesting that the wiring was so old it had either broken in its cable or lost its conductivity. I dug out the spare, paraffin-fuelled navigation lights and rigged them for'rd. We did without the Navtex and resorted to a torch instead of the binnacle light.

At 6.30 we crossed the Greenwich meridian and soon afterwards passed out of the area of the oil rigs. As dusk was coming on we saw our first rust-bucket British fishing boat, closely followed by a spectacular sunset in which the red glow of the sun sank below a layer of mist. By midnight, a fine drizzle had come on and I spent my watches staring anxiously into the darkness, worrying that the navigation lights would not be visible from any passing ship. In the main north–south shipping lane off Rattray Head, we saw three or four clusters of lights moving silently across our bow and disappearing alarmingly quickly into the murk. What else was out there?

Sitting in the main hatch while the engine thumped away – it was the only device on the boat working better now than it had been when we left home – I peered into the night and pondered the contrast between the Scottish and Norwegian islands. The basic difference, it seemed to me, between Barra and Bremanger was that the latter is part of a country which controls its own resources, and those alone. There can be no conflict between the nation and the state since the two are identical. Peripheral areas pose no threat to the centre and can therefore be permitted to take responsibility for themselves. Despite its drastically shrunken area of influence, the British state still has Kitchener's passion for rigid control. The simple fact that no Scottish island can be trusted to run its own ferry service, the most important single aspect of island life, illustrates the point. This is not just an inefficient way of organising a transport system in a geographically complicated country, it is administrative habit, born of authoritarian fearfulness, which has survived devolution. SNH's approach to Sullom Voe is an example of this, as is its plan to seize control of Robert's raingoose lochans. Even at the level of nature conservation this is counter-productive. The only way to retain biodiversity is to encourage human diversity. The only way to promote human diversity is to permit true local autonomy, as bureaucracies inevitably bring homogenisation. But for that, a revolution will need to happen in the state as a whole. Local autonomy cannot work without national autonomy. What applies to Barra applies to Scotland as a whole. Let us therefore hope that, like the Norwegian union with Sweden, the United Kingdom can be quietly and constructively dissolved and that England and Scotland can take a leaf out of the Scandinavian book and live in future as peaceful, mature, co-operative, friendly neighbours, making their own rules for whatever is important to each of them. To paraphrase Rolv Petter Vetvik: every country on its own land; every country with its own idea!

At six the darkness began to ebb. The mist still clung to the sea, sometimes almost becoming drizzle again. By breakfast-time, visibility was still no more than half a mile and we passed two huge shapes just distinguishable as tankers beyond that range. By mid-morning the sun had burnt the mist away. We had a hot, sunny but windless afternoon as we motored past Lossiemouth and Nairn. By the time we rounded into the narrows by Fort George, it was dark. With the tide against us it was slow going up to the Kessock Bridge. The lights of Inverness reflected on the flat surface of the sea making it hard to distinguish some of the navigational marks. We slowed right down until we found the entrance to the sea lock which leads into the Caledonian Canal.

It was by now after eleven o'clock. We tied up outside the lock as quickly as we could and almost ran the hundred yards up to the Clachnaharry Inn. Inside, in the familiar fug of a Scottish country pub, Brian and I talked of the strange sensation of being back home. This was the end of the trip. From now on it was simply a question of getting the boat back to base – and subsequently into the boatyard for a stem-to-stern overhaul.

Two pints of Guinness came up, followed by a couple of toasties. Before last orders, we managed to get in another round. Between the music, the craic across the bar with the owner's dark-haired daughter and the sly, sidelong glances that were swivelling elsewhere round the room like disco lights, this struck me forcibly as a very different place from Norway. Whatever political advantages that beautiful country may have over subservient Scotland, I was glad to be back amongst folk who reminded me of the Lass of Cessnock Banks and her 'twa sparkling, roguish e'en'.